Employment in

some critical issues

International Labour Office Geneva

Employment in Africa

Employment in Africa: some critical issues

with an introduction by
Philip Ndegwa and John P. Powelson

International Labour Office Geneva

ISBN (cloth) 92-2-101026-0
(paper) 92-2-101008-2

First published 1973

PRINTED BY " TRIBUNE DE GENÈVE ", GENEVA, SWITZERLAND

Preface

The present volume contains a set of studies [1] prepared by well-known specialists with a wide experience of the African scene as a contribution to action-oriented research aimed at reducing significantly unemployment and underemployment. This research was undertaken within the framework of the ILO's Jobs and Skills Programme for Africa (JASPA), launched in December 1969 by the third African Regional Conference of the ILO as the African component of the World Employment Programme, which constitutes the ILO's major contribution to the International Development Strategy of the Second Development Decade in the area of employment objectives and policies.

The aim of the World Employment Programme is to provide national policy-makers and planners with practical guidelines that will enable them to accelerate the rate of growth of productive employment. Two major means of action for this purpose are used: (i) direct assistance to individual countries with the elaboration, implementation and evaluation of employment-oriented development strategies, as in the case of the comprehensive employment strategy mission that visited Kenya in the spring of 1972 and whose findings are discussed in one of the studies presented below [2], and (ii) a programme of research designed to explore the action that needs to be taken in such fields as population policy, choice of technology, income distribution, education, labour market policy and international trade and aid in order to promote employment.

All the ILO's activities under JASPA are aimed at improving the knowledge base concerning the many facets of the employment problem, so that policies and programmes can be reconsidered and, if necessary, reoriented in order to enhance their effect on employment or to correct negative trends. The present volume forms part of this over-all effort.

Although the " profile " of unemployment differs from country to country, and although statistical data are patchy and are largely based on the performance of the economy in the 1960s and the evidence is thus too partial to permit a comprehensive analysis, certain common features do emerge from the individual studies. In their Introduction Philip Ndegwa, Permanent Secretary to the Treasury, Ministry of Finance

[1] The studies originally appeared in the *International Labour Review* between September 1971 and August 1973.

[2] Somewhat more modest inter-disciplinary missions have been sent by the ILO to Burundi, Ethiopia, Liberia, Madagascar, Morocco, the Sudan and Zaire.

and Planning of Kenya, and John P. Powelson, Professor of Economics in the University of Colorado and Adviser to the Planning Department of the same ministry, take stock of the findings and suggestions presented and offer their own views regarding diagnosis of the employment problem and approaches to its solution.

It is the ILO's hope that this collection will not only lead to a better understanding of some specific characteristics of the employment problem in Africa, but will also be of interest to policy-makers and others concerned with the formulation of development strategies that take employment as an objective in its own right.

Contents

Introduction

Philip NDEGWA [1]
John P. POWELSON [2]

The definition of " unemployment "

Unemployment was scarcely a problem in traditional Africa. All persons had their assigned duties in tribal cultures, whether tending crops, herding goats, acting as warriors, or sitting in councils of the elders. Wars, cattle raids, famine, disease, and poverty were the major problems, not lack of occupation. The colonial authorities considered ways to alleviate labour *shortages* for the expatriate sector (mainly agriculture and mining); to them, rural areas constituted a " reservoir " of workers to be drawn on for burgeoning urban opportunities and settler farms [Hunter [3]]. At independence, the Ivory Coast for example was providing jobs for immigrants [Songre]; unemployment began to be felt seriously only in 1965 [Roussel].

In the first decade of independence, development planning in Africa was strongly influenced by the theory and experience of the industrialised countries. The major focus was on investment and growth of output. Occasionally it would be debated whether maximum growth was compatible with an equitable distribution of income, but few doubted that anything but maximum growth was essential to full employment. If all efforts were devoted to production, then it was assumed that employment would take care of itself.

The first awareness of unemployment came not from the statistics but from the people seen in cities who obviously had nothing to do. They arrived in increasing numbers, lived in shanty towns, and many received help from relatives who had preceded them. Presumably they had come because their economic (and social) prospects were thereby improved. If life in a shanty town, in that sense, was *better*, then one

[1] Permanent Secretary to the Treasury, Ministry of Finance and Planning, Republic of Kenya.

[2] Professor of Economics, University of Colorado, and Adviser to the Planning Department, Ministry of Finance and Planning, Republic of Kenya.

[3] The names in brackets refer to the authors of the studies collected in the present volume.

might well question the socio-economic conditions and terms of employment in the rural areas from which they had come. Unemployment, it turned out, affects whole nations, not just the people in the city.

Even before African independence, economists wrote of " disguised unemployment " as a situation in which two or more persons might do a task for which one alone would be enough. But " disguised unemployment " is a hybrid, fathered by an industrialised country concept of production as the principal reason for work and bred into the situation of the developing countries in which objectives other than maximising output may determine who does what. If this dichotomy is too severe, then the answer is that " disguised unemployment " is not even an appropriate concept for industrialised countries.

Almost all authors in the present volume (especially Hunter) would agree that unemployment, as defined and measured in industrialised countries, is not an appropriate variable in the economic calculus of the developing countries.[1] The only exception might be the open unemployment of the cities, in which the number of able-bodied persons seeking full-time employment can be counted. In rural areas the description becomes complex. Many African countries possess nomadic tribes (e.g. the Masai in Kenya and Tanzania) who have clung to traditional life despite opportunities for change. As social groups they are producing far less than they might, yet no one can be defined as unemployed, nor can motives or aspirations be adequately assessed. The temptation would be to omit such tribes from the " unemployment problem ". But they are linked to it, partly because they suffer periodic hardships from drought and starvation, partly because they may raid the cattle of neighbouring tribes, and partly because they conflict in other ways with the maximum use of resources (which might be achieved, for example, through land registration).

Even in non-nomadic tribes the distinction between who is and who is not in the labour force is far from clear-cut. (This question also affects industrialised countries, but less so.) In family enterprises everyone does the task for which he is most fit or which the culture assigns to him.[1] It need not be full time, the remaining hours being devoted to family care, education or community obligations.

Two directions suggest themselves for a definition. One is to cling to the individual concept of employment but to broaden it into something like the following: that a person is unemployed who has no opportunity to perform those tasks for which he is culturally adapted. The obvious imprecision of this definition might be overcome by heroic decisions, some arbitrary and some taken in the context of local culture (which would make international comparisons difficult). The advantage would

[1] See also Jean Mouly: " Some remarks on the concepts of employment, underemployment and unemployment ", in *International Labour Review* (Geneva, ILO), Vol. 105, No. 2, Feb. 1972, pp. 155-160.

be to preserve the *general* scope of employment by not confining it to occupations for which financial gain is sought.

The other direction is not to tamper with the definition of employment as such but to broaden the unit to which it is applied. In a recent analysis of the concepts of employment, underemployment and unemployment Mouly [1] defines employment as a situation in which remuneration in cash is received in exchange for direct personal participation in the production process. But he proposes that this fundamental relationship should be formulated on several levels: the individual, the family unit, or any social group constituting a production and a consumption unit (such as a co-operative or a subsistence village) in which decisions are taken to maximise the collective advantage.

This definition has the obvious advantage of close approximation to the social function to which the term " employment " is applied. But it presents some difficulties in both ordinal and cardinal measurement. When is a " social group " employed and when unemployed? When is one " more employed " than another? Nor are such problems trivial. Quantification is essential if policy-makers are to be informed of the gravity of a situation and to make rational decisions on the use of resources to overcome it.

Two inter-Agency missions of experts financed by the United Nations Development Programme (UNDP) and organised by the International Labour Office have circumvented this problem, in their reports on Colombia and Kenya [2], by declaring that the concern should be not one of unemployment but of *low income*. The missions found that the distinction is minimal between a person who is unemployed and one who is employed at a very low income [Singer and Jolly]. There is, of course, much truth in this view, but in reality two questions are involved. One is a person's real income. The other is the extent to which he is employed in a psychologically rewarding activity.

The second question opens a Pandora's box of considerations going beyond the traditional definition of employment. Yet is this not the idea to which we are leading when we reject the terms " disguised unemployment " and " underemployment ", and when we consider further that a person on relief, or supported by relatives, may receive an income but not be satisfied with his condition?

Tiano, the only author in the present volume who comes close to conventional classifications, arbitrarily defines a man as fully employed if he works 250 days per year and a woman if she works 150 days. He also distinguishes between " open unemployment " in urban areas and " disguised unemployment " in rural areas. Not only does this definition

[1] Loc. cit.

[2] ILO: *Towards full employment. A programme for Colombia* (Geneva, 1970); and idem: *Employment, incomes and equality. A strategy for increasing productive employment in Kenya* (Geneva, 1972).

have the limitations mentioned above, but it would not satisfy those concerned with discrimination between the sexes in African countries; for example, the proportion of the labour force in agriculture is higher for women than for men [Denti].

The pathology of unemployment

Walter Galenson has stated emphatically that " of the factors that have contributed to the present crisis, none is more important than the sheer growth of population." [1] Not only is this growth high but the *rate of increase* is itself growing—from 2.18 per cent per year in the decade 1950 to 1960 to an estimated 2.86 per cent between 1970 and 1980 [Denti]. In some countries, such as Kenya, the rate of growth is already substantially above 3 per cent per year. While Galenson is correct, nevertheless his observation offers little solace to those who would take action before 1990, which is roughly the first year in which anyone *not now born* might join the labour force. Family planning is a *sine qua non* of the long-run solution to unemployment, but other measures are also essential over the next 15 years. To know what these must be, one must first understand the pathology of the problem.

Unemployment does not affect all jobs equally. Skilled manpower is acutely short in all fields [Jolly and Colclough]. Furthermore, the lowest-paid, most menial jobs often go begging in both countryside and city. Sometimes the reason for unskilled labour shortages is technological and seasonal. Crops must be brought in within a specified period before the rains, and manpower cannot be mobilised and transported rapidly enough. Thus severe seasonal bottlenecks appear side-by-side with chronic unemployment in many regions of Africa [de Wilde].

But the problem goes deeper than that. Because unskilled work is available while labourers are seeking jobs, it is widely and plausibly inferred that many unemployed are particular about the jobs they will take, feeling themselves above the menial. In the Ivory Coast, even though there is much unemployment in cities, low-level jobs are held mostly by immigrants from Upper Volta [Roussel, Songre]. Furthermore, indigenous labourers hold only 20 per cent of wage-paying farm jobs in the Ivory Coast [Roussel]. In Kenya it has been found that migrants coming from the country to Nairobi may spend several months seeking administrative positions in businesses before they accept work of a lower order. [2] The length of time that job aspirants can wait depends on their ability to find subsistence in the meantime. This is frequently offered by friends

[1] ILO: *Essays on employment*, selected and with an Introduction by Walter Galenson (Geneva, 1971), p. 1.

[2] Peter J. Kinyanjui: " The education, training, and employment of Kenya secondary school leavers " (Institute for Development Studies, University of Nairobi, unpublished).

and relatives who have preceded them to the city. Family solidarity and tribal ties make the possible waiting period longer in Africa than it might be anywhere else [Roussel].

Yet this assertion requires much more investigation than it has received. What is a menial task? What are the aspirations of the job-seekers? Why do they consider themselves qualified for more prestigious work than they can obtain? What qualifications did successful aspirants for higher-level work have, and how long did they wait from arrival in the city until they were employed? How long do the unsuccessful wait until they accept an " inferior " place? Finally, is the problem a serious one? For example, if it should turn out—*and we do not suggest that it will*—that most of the urban unemployed are persons with a distorted view of their own potential who will ultimately be content with available lower-prestige positions, then the unemployment problem of Africa would not be nearly so serious as is currently alleged.

Three " causes " of migration and unemployment are mentioned more frequently than others in the short-run context. These are the educational system, the choice of technology (labour-intensive versus capital-intensive), and inadequate attention to agriculture. We treat these separately below.

The educational system

Several of the authors have mentioned education as in one way or another influencing the pattern of unemployment [Elkan, Hunter, de Wilde, Roussel, Jolly and Colclough]. In many African countries, the educational system has been patterned after institutions in the former colonising countries, with emphasis on a classical liberal arts curriculum. It is also easier and less costly, in financial terms, to expand liberal arts education. Furthermore, recent educational reforms in the industrialised countries have scarcely affected Africa, whose students still learn by rote the words the teacher puts on the blackboard. The certificate is all-important. More often than not the level of future wages, and the opportunity of securing employment in the first place, will depend on the certificate received regardless of whether or not the course content of the candidate's education has anything to do with the type of work.

In the early colonial era formal education was little appreciated by Africans [Hunter]. It received some impetus from missionaries, and then —late in the 1950s—the prospect of independence brought a surge of demand, associated with visions of new rewards for the educated. The ensuing debate on whether limited resources should be dedicated to primary education or to technically qualified high-level manpower was cut short by an overwhelming popular demand for literacy and numeracy, felt in all countries of sub-Saharan Africa. In Kenya, where the Government was unable to afford free education for all, government schools were partly financed by school fees, while self-help *(Harambee)* schools were constructed, financed and administered entirely by local communities. In all these countries only a small portion of students entering primary school achieved secondary. The great mass left after approximately seven years and formed the bulk of jobseeking migrants to the city. Most considered themselves too well qualified for menial positions, yet their training had stopped short of the skills that would have made them valuable in modern industry [Elkan]. This problem is now beginning to affect secondary-school leavers as well in many African countries—due to rapid expansion (as for example in Kenya, Ghana and Nigeria) of liberal-arts-based secondary education.

Choice of technology

If machines and labourers were completely substitutable for one another, in that anything one could (and would) do the other could (and would) do also, there would be no debate on the choice of technology in African countries. So long as labourers are available with no alternative employment, they should be employed instead of machines. That they are not is attributed to the following:

1. Developing countries have been influenced by the growth theory and recent experience of industrialised countries, in which both the supply of and demand for incremental output depends on the amount of capital invested.

2. There is a psychological factor, in which modernity is associated with capital-intensiveness—a problem often made worse by engineers and architects attuned to producing a more modern factory than the last one.

3. Because of the abundance of labour and sometimes of land in developing countries, it was supposed that the reason for failure to develop lay in shortage of capital. Capital was therefore often made available by international institutions and the governments of industrialised countries on terms that tended to make its use cheaper than the use of labour and this favoured the introduction of labour-saving equipment.

4. The developing countries themselves instituted policies to attract investment. Interest rates were kept artificially low for borrowers, tax incentives were accorded to investors, and capital goods were admitted at low rates of duty or with none at all, while the finished goods they produced were heavily protected.

5. Because developing countries were traditionally exporters of primary products, it was at first believed that they could export little else. Big, efficient, highly protected enterprises were thought to monopolise the markets of the industrialised countries for manufactured goods.

Therefore, the hope for industrialisation was seen to lie not in exports (other than traditional goods), but in substituting for imports. By promoting over-valuation of currencies, the high protection on imports of finished goods discriminated against exports, including traditional goods produced by labour-intensive methods.

6. Trade unions, often protected and encouraged by government, raised wages in manufacturing industries to levels much higher than alternative earning possibilities in handicrafts or rural industry. By encouraging employers to substitute machinery for labour, these high wages not only reduced employment possibilities; they also encouraged migration through increasing the attractiveness of urban employment (if it could be got).

Defenders of capital-intensive technology often argue that in its initial stages industrialisation must come from the industrialised countries, which supply both capital and techniques. It is often believed that investors from these countries know only the technology they are accustomed to using at home. This is a matter that has been judged too frequently by intuition and too little by investigation. The ILO Mission discovered in Kenya examples of foreign firms using more labour-intensive techniques than locally owned firms producing the same goods, and of a foreign firm using a higher labour-capital ratio for operations in Kenya than for similar production in its home country.[1] One of the principal reasons why foreign firms establish plants in developing countries is to realise the advantages of employing less expensive labour; it would be unusual if in fact they did not do so.

Capital-intensive technology is also defended on the ground that labour is " unreliable ". Sometimes unreliability means not arriving or leaving on time or not operating machinery carefully or maintaining it well. But it also means the propensity to strike. During pre-independence days, labour unions were vehicles of political pressure on colonial powers, and striking was patriotic. Once workers had learned the power of the strike, they were loath to give it up once their countries had become independent.

Machines may be required instead of labour if they replace menial tasks that unemployed workers are unwilling to do. Roussel reports this to be the situation in the Ivory Coast. Furthermore, in some projects the case can be made that use of capital *increases* the opportunity for employment of labour. This can happen in agriculture, for example when the use of tractors for certain operations makes double-cropping possible. In addition, advanced technologies can sometimes be combined with dispersed, small-scale activity [Hunter]. In Japan large-scale, capital-intensive firms have spawned smaller, labour-intensive satellite suppliers,

[1] *Employment, incomes and equality*, op. cit., p. 141.

a phenomenon observable in virtually all industrialised countries. The problem is not a simple one of replacing labour with capital, but of determining those functions in which they replace and those in which they complement one another, with mutual reinforcement.

Several authors approach the subject in this manner. The work of the Intermediate Technology Group [Schumacher] is to discover labour-intensive technology which may nevertheless require the use of capital. One principle adopted by this Group appears to us, however, questionable: the notion that much of the research must be done in industrialised countries where technical and organisational knowledge and facilities exist. Not only does such a practice deprive the developing countries of an opportunity to develop their own research—a capability that is an important ingredient of growth—but it runs the risk that the wrong technology will be found. Factor endowments and other inputs in developing countries differ from those in industrialised countries, either currently or at comparable stages of development. Economic historians of the United States, for example, have reported that immigrant producers from Europe early in the nineteenth century often sought new methods of production for just that reason. The oft-heard idea that "intermediate technology" requires the rediscovery of techniques long forgotten is not always accurate.

Whether or not farms should be mechanised is a hotly debated point. There are very few agricultural operations that machines can do but labourers with rudimentary tools cannot, *provided the labourers are available in sufficient numbers*. Digging a deep well is perhaps one, and even this depends on circumstances. If one accepts that lack of management expertise or agricultural skills is *not* a reason for substituting machines—people should be trained instead—then one is hard put to find many arguments for mechanised farming at all. Nevertheless, there are some. Seasonal operations (planting and harvesting) might be done either by large numbers of labourers or by machines, but the logistics of moving people in and out when they can be used for only a short period may be insuperable. Some operations, like precision ploughing, can be done better by machines [1], but here a policy question emerges: how much employment should be sacrificed for how great an increase in precision? Two trade-offs are involved, one the possibilities for substitution allowed by the available alternative technologies, and the other the welfare function, or how valuable each result (employment or precision) is to the community. How to maximise community welfare once the two trade-offs are known is a familiar problem to which traditional tools of economic analysis can be applied. The conclusion for farming—as indeed for other sectors—must be that there is no general solution on technology;

[1] See I. Inukai: " Farm mechanisation, output and labour input: a case study in Thailand ", in *Essays on employment*, op. cit., pp. 71-91.

the advantages and disadvantages of alternative technologies must be weighed in individual cases [Hunter].

This general statement should *not*, however, dismiss the technology issue, for it only provides a guideline for the individual case. The evidence is preponderant that *over-all*, developing countries—particularly in Africa—are using a greater proportion of capital and less of labour than the circumstances of their factor availabilities call for. This problem has been studied in some depth for Latin American countries, which are a few years ahead of African countries in the growth of income per head.[1]

According to certain concepts developed by the Economic Commission for Latin America, during the 1950s and 1960s Latin American countries stressed economic growth through import substitution, as opposed to manufactured exports. They protected domestically produced final consumer goods heavily, while permitting capital goods and raw materials to enter freely. Governments also encouraged trade unions, partly for political reasons and partly to extract greater payments to nationals by foreign-owned companies. The result in several countries has been a marked dichotomy between the modern manufacturing sector, comprising plants whose technology and management are little different from those of industrialised countries, and the traditional handicraft and farming sectors. Wages in the modern sector might be up to ten times alternative earnings in the traditional sector, and profits would reach as high as 40 per cent of invested capital per year. But such firms employed little labour, and their competition depressed the markets of the traditional sector. This strategy of economic growth reached its zenith (or nadir, depending on how it is viewed) when the rise in incomes required more imports than traditional exports could pay for. It became necessary to export manufactures, but the manufacturing industries were too high-cost and inefficient to compete in world markets. Several Latin American countries are currently undergoing an agonising reversal of policy under which manufacturing exports must be encouraged. African countries would do well to learn from this example.

Of course the trade policies of the developing countries are not the only culprits. Although their labour-intensive manufactures could be of great advantage to consumers in industrialised countries, unfortunately this opportunity is lessened by the restrictive import practices of the latter. But we do not suppose that these practices will be removed by appeals on ethical grounds. If the African countries are to gain access to industrialised markets for manufactured goods, they must do so through hard negotiation, backed by enterprises of distinctive technology and attractive price. Especially at a time when inflation is serious in

[1] See, for example, R. R. Nelson, T. P. Schultz, and R. L. Slighton: *Colombia's problems and prospects* (Princeton (New Jersey), Princeton University Press, 1971).

the industrialised countries, the opportunities for tough-minded bargaining are increasing.

Greater attention to agriculture

The dichotomy of rural and urban development may appear misguided, since one cannot proceed without the other. The question, rather, is one of proportions. Furthermore, the classical model envisages a rural sector that provides resources, both capital and labour, to urban manufacture. Such transfers contribute to over-all economic growth [Todaro].

Nevertheless, the classical model has limitations in contemporary Africa. It assumes full employment in the countryside and labour shortage in the towns, with migration increasing the marginal output of both those who leave and those who remain. But if there is unemployment in *both* sectors, it is necessary to reconsider the balance and to study how much migration is consistent with maximum national welfare.

Migration takes place because perceived opportunities are greater in the city than in the country. Some have questioned how this can be so when the migrants walk into unemployment. Most likely, the migrant calculates on the basis of *permanent* income; that is, he compares his discounted life time expectancies in the city with those in rural areas, and opts for the higher [Todaro]. For many persons the higher is in the city, despite a delay of perhaps two years. More research needs to be done on this matter. For example how close do perceived opportunities come to the objective probability of their realisation? In the light of Kenyan experience cited earlier, does the migrant initially expect a more prestigious job than he finally accepts, or does he sense that he will ultimately yield but wants to spend some time trying for the better job first? Surely a jobseeker is aware that if he accepts a low-paying and low-prestige job, he has set the pattern, and mobility to a higher job or to better earnings may be difficult. Thus there is more than one variable in the Todaro calculus: the delay period, the level of expected income in the city as compared with the country, and the prestige of the job. There is also the question of how closely the perceived probability approximates the objective probability.

Other variables apply as well. One is the amount of assistance the migrant can expect and for how long. Another is the attraction of " city lights " [Hunter]. " City lights " include not only glamour, but all the social and economic amenities of the city—schools, health services, and opportunities to expand one's personal horizons. In Venezuela a new steel mill in the 1950s opened permanent employment opportunities in Ciudad Guayanas, near the mouth of the Orinoco River (a relatively isolated area). But labour turnover was high. Men would migrate into Ciudad Guayanas from rural areas, stay for about a year, and then drift on to unemployment in the slums of Caracas, where they believed more amenities were available. Another element is separation from family and homeland. In Kenya men migrate to urban jobs, leaving wives to till the home fields and bring up the children. Some allege that this splitting up of the family is accepted because of unwillingness of the family to be separated from its homeland. But more is involved than this. In most cases it would be impossible to house and feed an entire family in the city. The separation is therefore a question of economic survival and is one of the personal tragedies of economic growth.

Berg has pointed out that migration often continues even when urban wages fall quite sharply.[1] This observation, however, does not contradict the Todaro thesis, which is based on lifetime income expectancy rather than wages in the year of migration.

If perceived opportunities are higher than objective probabilities, a case might be made for measures to stem rural-urban migration. To date, however, such errors of perception cannot be demonstrated. Furthermore, with modern communication there is every reason to believe (pending research) that migrants assess their situation well. *If* economic conditions were stable in rural areas, there might even be cause for relaxation. The potential migrant would be no worse off if he stayed at home, and—despite unemployment—he considers himself better off in the city.

Alas, there is no room for relaxation! The sheer weight of population growth is causing rural life to deteriorate. Farms are being subdivided into smaller and smaller sizes. At the same time cultural patterns are changing. Many men no longer undertake warrior training or carry spears. Frequently, menial tasks are no longer acceptable. For the first time in African history a sizeable portion of the rural population finds itself with " nothing to do ". Furthermore, despite rural-urban migration, population in rural areas is *growing rapidly*—in this the African model differs from the classical.

There are two reasons why greater development must occur in rural areas. One is that agriculture is a principal input to economic growth: food supplies must be increased as incomes rise. The other is that deterioration must be prevented. Here it is necessary to consider rural industry. But in some African countries the rural areas consist of villages with no electricity, no roads, and little of the repair services or skilled labour that modern industry needs. Fortunately, however, a few countries have small cities with some infrastructure—such as Nakuru, Kitale, Kisumu, and Eldoret in Kenya. In such countries rural development, based on rural towns as " growth centres ", is likely to be achieved more quickly.

---

[1] Elliot J. Berg: " Wages and employment ", in OECD: *The challenge of unemployment to development and the role of training and research institutes in development* (Paris, 1971).

Conclusions: some policy considerations

Every author in this volume has proposed policies relating to the area of his attention. Todaro has systematically reviewed policy proposals in all subfields of the unemployment problem in Africa and has divided them into short-term, intermediate-term, and long-term. There is no need in this Introduction to duplicate this kind of review. While the authors differ in their fields of special interest, and in relative emphasis, there is no substantial disagreement among them concerning either the diagnosis of the problem or the method of approach.

No author has disagreed that growth of population is the principal spectre, and that unemployment will not be resolved unless rates of population growth are reduced. With varying emphasis, they argue for greater labour intensity in production, a point on which the ILO Mission reports on Colombia and Kenya are also agreed. Even those who argue for modern, capital-using technologies [Hunter] confine their cases to capital *that will in itself increase the employment of labour*, and no one argues that all investment, or even most investment, will do this. The authors also stress the pressing need for rural development as a counterweight to migration. Indeed, this volume turns out to be most uncontroversial.

It is therefore appropriate at this point to mention the controversial nature *in practice* of some of the policies suggested. We do this first in connection with the role of capital, by asking: *can* (not necessarily *do*) policies designed to maximise investment also maximise employment? Next, we question the effectiveness of policies of incentive versus those of coercion. Finally, we add a political dimension to proposals for an incomes policy.

Are maximum investment and maximum employment compatible?

All the discussion on technology in this volume does not resolve this question, which can be restated as follows. Assume two sets of policies. Set A includes tax incentives for investment, low or no duties on the import of capital goods, soft terms for borrowing, and monopoly guarantees for foreign investors. Set B includes none of the above. Instead, it subjects all factors of production equally to competitive principles. Over the long run (say, 15 years), which set will attract more investment?

More casually, the question is put another way. Assume a country that is following set A. Someone points to a foreign investor and asserts: " He has risked *his* capital, which would otherwise have not been available to the nation. Even if he has employed only one or two people, is that not better than zero? " But that is the wrong question. No investor, foreign or other, ever appears out of a vacuum. This one has responded to policy set A. The correct question is: Would other investors have provided greater amounts of investment and/or employment under policy set B?

There is good reason to believe that *over the long run* the answer is yes. Hindsight (in the experience of other countries) has demonstrated that set A (investment concessions) leads to high profit rates, which in turn promote strong trade unions demanding their share. High wage rates choke off further employment as favoured machines are more and more substituted for labour and—especially if the profits are repatriated to foreign countries—incomes are not shared sufficiently to develop a domestic mass market. These protected industries are also priced out of the international market. Whilst early investment in them has been highly profitable, they nevertheless quickly reach a maximum size, where further expansion yields low marginal returns.

By contrast, a country following policy set B provides the foundation on which both investment and employment will continuously grow. The investment will be of that kind (favoured by Hunter, Todaro, and others) which promotes employment rather than diminishes it. Wages in the modern sector will not rise as high as under set A; hence the *marginal efficiency* (or expected return) *of capital* will be kept high, and more investment will be attracted.

There are other advantages. The complaint is often heard that large-scale enterprises do not train adequately. But why should they? A training department requires heavy capital expenditure and high overheads, which are not worth the while unless there is a certain minimum labour force. The propensity to train is probably a positive function of the proportion of labourers to invested capital.

The same principle extends to the school system. Earlier we mentioned that African schools have inherited a colonial tendency towards liberal arts rather than " technical " education in the widest sense of the word, and that qualifications for jobs depend more on the certificate one has obtained than on whether or not one has learned appropriate skills. Obviously this situation must be corrected. But if investment policy has led to a dichotomy between a small corps of skilled workers who can operate modern machines on the one hand, and masses of persons who can aspire to little more than employment in services or handicrafts on the other, what are the incentives to reform the educational system? The requisite changes would be more attractive if a wide range of intermediate skills were demanded, based on an appropriate technology and its conforming capital investment.

This is not an appeal to postpone educational reform until greater demand for technical skills materialises. Reform should be undertaken now. First, it takes a long time to achieve satisfactorily: curricula must be designed, teachers must be prepared, equipment must be obtained, books must be written. Second, a significant source of employment in

Africa must be *self-employment*—a consideration that will deeply affect the kinds of technical education to be introduced.

Incentives versus coercion

Some policies described by authors in this volume are clearly coercive, others less clearly so. Let us distinguish between coercion that is direct, or devolving upon a particular action, and that which is indirect, or limiting a field of action but not an action itself. The Tanzanian policy of forcible return of unemployed migrants to their native areas has been considered by some observers as directly coercive. Indirect coercion includes taxes, and possibly exemptions from them. Indeed, the border between indirect coercion and incentive is not clear.

Now, certain authors propose an incomes policy [Todaro, Hunter, de Wilde] which would favour rural areas and restrain urban wages. Would such a policy be directly coercive? Would trade unions be prevented from negotiating the most advantageous agreements with employers? Would this restraint be consonant with the democratic systems that many African countries want to nurture?

The answer must be taken in broader perspective than the single question. First, we have already pointed to the high rate of industrial profit, consequent on other policies (e.g. set A), which provides unions the opportunity to demand higher wages. If other policies (e.g. set B) are followed, such pressures would not be so strong. Besides, it is hardly fair (even if it is possible) to restrain wages in the face of high profits and uncontrolled prices. Nevertheless, unions represent only the interests of their *members*, and these are only a small portion of the labour force. Some way must be found of reconciling these interests with those of the unemployed.

Finally, whatever direct or indirect controls are used, they will be more palatable if coupled with other policies of a clearly incentive nature. These would include setting up employment exchanges [Roussel], adequate human resources investment [Tiano], and realistic policies to improve the conditions of rural people. These latter open the related, but different, subject of rural development and technical assistance to agriculture, with which we do not deal here.

The political economy of incentives

We have already commented on the consistency in the diagnosis and proposed solutions among the authors in the present volume. Such consistency among academics is not surprising in a subject-matter such as this. What is noteworthy is that the solutions proposed in this volume are a far cry from those currently practised by African countries. In fact, many countries are promoting capital-intensive, unemployment-inducing policies. Why is this so?

We believe the answer is threefold. First, the policies actually applied have short-run advantages. Until the day of reckoning, they may even maximise the inflow of investment (though not employment). They maximise the immediate return to the exchequer and assure the personal success of the policy-makers. The long run is discounted.

Second, despite their academic training in the social sciences, it is often difficult for politicians to conceive of the economy as a system, and to understand that policy measures have more than immediate effects. We have already referred to the belief that investment incentives maximise investment, which over the long run is probably not true. Other illustrations abound: the belief that import controls slow down imports (which again may be true in the short run but not the long), that higher wages improve the welfare of the labourer, and that price controls always stop inflation. (This comment is not confined to policy-makers in developing countries; it applies to industrialised countries as well.) Chains of events are not easy to map, nor is there often understanding that the best way to affect one variable is to start a reaction that begins at some distance from it.

The third part of the answer follows from the other two. In the long run, the economic welfare of rural areas and that of urban areas are so intertwined that a relative setback for one adversely affects the other. But limited foresight or heavy discounting of the long run prevents many policy-makers from understanding this, or from becoming aware of the extent to which the solution to privileged problems (e.g. industrial expansion, level of foreign exchange reserves) depends on policies leading to strong rural development. Further, the urban communities are better organised, articulate, and more vociferous. They therefore tend to get more than their share in the allocation of resources.

* * *

The solution to unemployment in Africa calls for action on three levels. First, the international, with more capital and technical assistance and the opening of markets not now accessible to African exporters. Such markets are restricted by tariffs, fiscal charges, quantitative restrictions, and similar devices. Second, economic co-operation among African countries is essential on a wide front. Such co-operation must go beyond tariffs and movement of factors of production, to include research, curriculum development, infrastructure, and other areas where mutual advantage can be gained. Third, there are some actions that only the country in question can undertake. These include fighting " tribalism ", corruption and nepotism, introduction of realistic family-planning programmes, new structures of land use and distribution, and greater involvement of the masses of people in rural areas.

The first category is not dealt with here or in the studies that follow. Industrialised countries are not going to make concessions to the developing countries unless it is to their own political and economic advantage to do so. Appeals on moral or ethical grounds fall on deaf ears. Either the African countries must accept the international *status quo* as a constraint, or they must make themselves sufficiently strong, both economically and politically, to confront the industrialised countries and force changes in their policies. This strength will come largely through action on the second and third levels—both political and economic.

The present volume deals mainly with action on the third level, for this involves policies that individual African countries can undertake. Because they can be applied now, they have become the most urgent—for without them, not much is likely to be achieved on the other levels.

I. Dimensions

Africa's Labour Force, 1960-80

Ettore DENTI [1]

As part of its research work for the World Employment Programme, the International Labour Office has made estimates and projections of the economically active population, by sex and by age group, for the majority of countries and territories for the period 1950-85; the results are due to be published shortly.[2] The purpose of this article is to provide a brief analysis of the main data relating to Africa for the period 1960-80.

The first part examines the characteristics of the demographic and manpower situation in Africa in 1960, while the second deals with possible changes between 1960 and 1980. The classification of countries by region (see the Appendix tables) follows United Nations practice [3], and the estimates and projections of total population are also those of the United Nations.

Only countries and territories which had a population of at least 250,000 in 1960 have been featured. The remainder have been the subject of an over-all estimate and a projection for each region, which have been incorporated in the corresponding regional total shown in the tables.

I. Total population and economically active population of Africa in 1960

Total population

The United Nations estimates quoted here relating to the population of Africa, by sex and by age [4], are based on censuses or similar population surveys carried out towards the end of the 1950s or the beginning of the 1960s. For some countries, where information on the population and its distribution by sex and age was inadequate quantitatively and qualitatively, the estimates have been derived by using models based on assumed fertility and mortality rates.

---

[1] International Labour Office.

[2] ILO: *Labour force projections* (1971 edition), Part II: *Africa* (Geneva, 1971).

[3] See United Nations: *Demographic yearbook, 1969* (New York, 1970), p. 17.

[4] Idem, Population Division: *Population estimates by regions and countries, 1950-1960* (Working Paper No. 31, May 1970).

In mid-1960 Africa had about 270 million inhabitants, or some 9 per cent of the world's population; a little over four-fifths of the African population were concentrated in the Western (30 per cent), Eastern (29 per cent) and Northern (24 per cent) regions.

The figures in table A in the Appendix show that, in Africa as a whole, the female population predominates slightly (50.2 per cent). Women are proportionately more numerous in Middle Africa (51.4 per cent) and the Eastern region (50.7 per cent) whereas the male population is rather higher in Northern Africa (50.4 per cent) and Western Africa (50.2 per cent). In Southern Africa the two sexes are about balanced. In about two-thirds of the individual countries women are more numerous. Men are more numerous throughout Northern Africa, in four countries of Western Africa (Nigeria, Ghana, Ivory Coast and Gambia), in two of Eastern Africa (Southern Rhodesia and Mauritius) and also in Angola, Equatorial Guinea, the Republic of South Africa and Namibia. With a few exceptions, these are countries of immigration.

Analysis of the distribution by age group shows that the population is young, since 43 per cent of Africans are under the age of 15; 54 per cent are between 15 and 64 and a bare 3 per cent are over that age. Thus, from the point of view of present manpower potential, Africa's age pattern is unfavourable.

Economically active population

The economically active population has been calculated on the basis of ILO estimates of activity rates by sex and age group, which have been used conjointly with the United Nations estimates of total population in 1960.

The main statistical sources used to determine these activity rates have been population censuses and demographic or similar sample surveys. In addition, the ILO has worked out models from which estimates can be made, chiefly on the basis of data from the same sources.

Figures for a date close to 1960 (between 1956 and 1966) have been obtained from censuses undertaken in Northern and Southern African countries and in Ghana, Nigeria, Sierra Leone, Liberia, Mauritius, Mozambique and Angola. For the great majority of French-speaking countries in Western and Middle Africa, the results of population surveys were available. As the criteria used by African countries to define the labour force varied considerably [1], the original statistics of the economically active population had first to be adjusted in some cases in order to

[1] For example, the minimum age limit ranges from 6 to 15; sometimes certain categories of economically active persons are included in the inactive population, e.g. unemployed persons seeking a job for the first time, and family workers. The labour force (or economically active population) is defined to comprise all employed and unemployed persons, including those seeking work for the first time. This definition covers employers, persons working on their own account, salaried employees, wage earners, unpaid family workers, members of producer co-operatives and those serving in the armed forces.

bring them into conformity with standard concepts. These adjustments have been made using empirical estimates based on observations.

The data relating to age distribution also posed a number of problems. For some countries estimates have had to be made to fit the data into the standard age groups adopted.

In addition, the activity rates derived from population censuses or surveys carried out before or after 1960 have been adjusted to obtain estimates for the middle of 1960. This has been done by linear interpolation in all cases where at least two series of comparable activity rates derived from population censuses or surveys held before or after 1960 were available. In other cases, the adjustment has been made empirically in accordance with the " models " specially constructed by the ILO and described below.

For those countries lacking labour force statistics, as in Eastern Africa, empirical estimates have been made using these models. The models, which have been worked out separately for each sex, are based mainly on the functional relationship between the pattern and level of activity rates by age and by sex in a given country and the structure and level of economic and social development. In other words, they reflect the influence of different social and cultural structures on activity rates, especially on those of women, in countries and regions with fairly similar types of economic structure.

Within each model, the relationship between activity rates by sex and by age and the economic structure (the latter being indicated by the proportion of the male labour force in agriculture) [1] has been calculated by means of a regression function which has been worked out graphically. These functions have been derived from the statistics of countries or territories at different stages of economic development, which makes it possible to calculate typical activity rates for each age group and sex at different degrees of development.

On the basis of the available data (in point of fact, a number of African countries and territories had good statistics on the labour force and its composition by economic sector), three models were constructed for each sex—

(1) According to the statistics for Ghana, Upper Volta, Chad, Sierra Leone (women only), Togo and Guinea. These models have been used for Western and Middle Africa (*excluding* the territories under Portuguese and Spanish administration) and for Madagascar, Rwanda and Burundi. Women in Niger and Mauritania constituted an exceptional case in that the model used was based on the activity rates observed in 1964 in the parts of Chad with a predominant Arab population.

[1] The economic structure and more particularly the proportion of the labour force in agriculture is taken as an indicator of the degree of economic development. The close relationship between this proportion and certain indicators of economic and social progress (infant mortality, reproduction, literacy, urbanisation, school attendance rates, etc.) is well known.

(2) According to the statistics taken from the 1960 Angola census. These particular models were used to make estimates for the territories in Western, Eastern and Middle Africa under Portuguese or Spanish administration.

(3) According to the statistical data on the Bantu populations of the Republic of South Africa and Namibia taken from the population censuses held between 1946 and 1960. For women, however, the model employed is a compromise between the Bantu model and model (1). It has, in fact, the same profile as the latter and only differs from it in its lower activity rates for all ages. Models of this third type have also been used for the English-speaking countries and for Ethiopia and Somalia.

CRUDE AND SPECIFIC ACTIVITY RATES

The 1960 economically active population of Africa was estimated at 108,826,000, which in proportion to the total population gives a crude activity rate [1] of 40.4 per cent.

Estimates for each country are given in table B in the Appendix. In the Western, Eastern and Middle regions crude activity rates are of the order of 44-45 per cent, i.e. markedly above the continental average. In Northern Africa the crude rate is particularly low (29 per cent), but this is accounted for by the very limited economic activity of women in Moslem countries. In Southern Africa the rate does not differ greatly from the continental average.

TABLE I. REGIONAL DISTRIBUTION OF TOTAL POPULATION AND ECONOMICALLY ACTIVE POPULATION, 1960
(%)

Region	Total population			Economically active population		
	Both sexes	Men	Women	Both sexes	Men	Women
Africa	**100.0**	**100.0**	**100.0**	**100.0**	**100.0**	**100.0**
Western	29.5	29.7	29.3	32.9	29.1	41.0
Eastern	28.6	28.3	28.9	31.5	29.7	35.3
Middle	10.9	10.7	11.1	12.0	10.8	14.8
Northern	24.3	24.5	24.0	17.3	23.6	3.7
Southern	6.7	6.8	6.7	6.3	6.8	5.2

Table I shows the regional distribution, in percentage terms, of the total population and the economically active population. The contribu-

[1] By " crude participation rate " or " crude activity rate " is meant the proportion of economically active persons to the total population.

tion of each region to the total labour force of the continent depends on three factors, viz. the proportion of the total population, the sex and age [1] structure of the population, and the sex and age structure of activity rates.

The crude activity rates for African countries and territories range from 26.7 per cent in Algeria to 57.8 per cent in Mali. Broadly speaking, the highest rates are encountered in the less developed non-Moslem French-speaking States, while the lowest are in the Moslem countries, which have a tendency to underestimate the participation of women in economic activity, as do the African territories under Spanish or Portuguese administration.

MALE ACTIVITY RATES

For the whole of Africa, the crude activity rate for men is estimated at 55.5 per cent. The figures for the five regions do not depart very much from this average, but nevertheless reflect differences in degrees of development.

Table II shows the crude and adjusted [2] activity rates for the five regions, which have been classified in increasing order of economic development. The negative correlation between the degree of economic

TABLE II. CRUDE ACTIVITY RATES OF MALES BY REGION AND ADJUSTED RATES, ACCORDING TO DEGREE OF DEVELOPMENT, 1960

(%)

Region	Degree of development [1]	Crude activity rate	Adjusted activity rate [2]
Eastern Africa	15.9	58.2	58.5
Middle ,,	24.1	56.0	55.2
Western ,,	24.1	54.3	54.8
Northern ,,	32.7	53.5	53.9
Southern ,,	57.5	55.5	52.2

[1] Proportion of total male labour force in non-agricultural activities in 1960. [2] Calculated on the basis of the male activity rates for the relevant age groups in the region and the standard age distribution (that of the male population in Africa).

development and the crude male activity rate is clear, especially if the adjusted regional rates are taken into consideration.

The crude activity rates for individual countries vary fairly substantially—from 68 per cent in Equatorial Guinea to 44.4 per cent for Réunion.

[1] Regional age structures do not differ substantially (see table A in the Appendix).

[2] Rates that have been refined to allow for differences in the age structure of the population.

These variations have two causes: differences in the degree of economic development and differences in the age pattern. Nevertheless, variations in crude activity rates are less considerable in the case of men than in that of women.

The common profile of male activity rates by age shows a peak between the ages of 25 and 44, when virtually all men (98 per cent) belong to the active population. Before and after these ages, the rates tend to fall off progressively (see table III).

TABLE III. REGIONAL MALE ACTIVITY RATES BY AGE GROUP, 1960
(%)

Age group	Africa	Region				
		Western	Eastern	Middle	Northern	Southern
10-14 years	32.8	33.4	42.2	32.1	26.9	12.0
15-19 ,,	74.9	69.3	85.2	72.7	72.4	68.4
20-24 ,,	92.7	89.8	96.6	93.6	90.9	94.6
25-44 ,,	97.8	97.5	98.6	97.5	97.4	98.1
45-54 ,,	97.2	97.5	98.2	95.4	96.4	97.6
55-64 ,,	92.8	93.0	95.1	92.2	90.8	91.7
65+ ,,	71.1	75.2	77.0	75.7	64.3	56.2

Taking Africa as a whole, therefore, the rates are approximately 33, 75 and 93 per cent for the 10-14, 15-19 and 20-24 age groups respectively. After the age of 45, they decline very slowly at first (97 per cent for the 45-54 age group) and then more sharply (93 and 71 per cent for the 55-64 and 65-and-over age groups respectively). Nevertheless, table III also shows that there are major differences in the regional rates, especially for the 10-14, 15-19 and 65-and-over age groups.

The comparatively advanced regions usually have lower rates, especially for the first and last age groups. This is due to the fact that they normally have longer schooling and sometimes operate social security schemes providing old-age pensions.

FEMALE ACTIVITY RATES

A quarter of the women in Africa are economically active. Activity rates vary considerably between regions and also between individual countries and territories (see table B in the Appendix) because of social and cultural factors, the degree of economic development and the use of different criteria to define and calculate the female labour force. Since the curves of female activity rates by age group vary substantially from one country and region to another, the curve for the continent as a whole is without significance.

FIGURE 1. FEMALE ACTIVITY RATES BY AGE GROUP

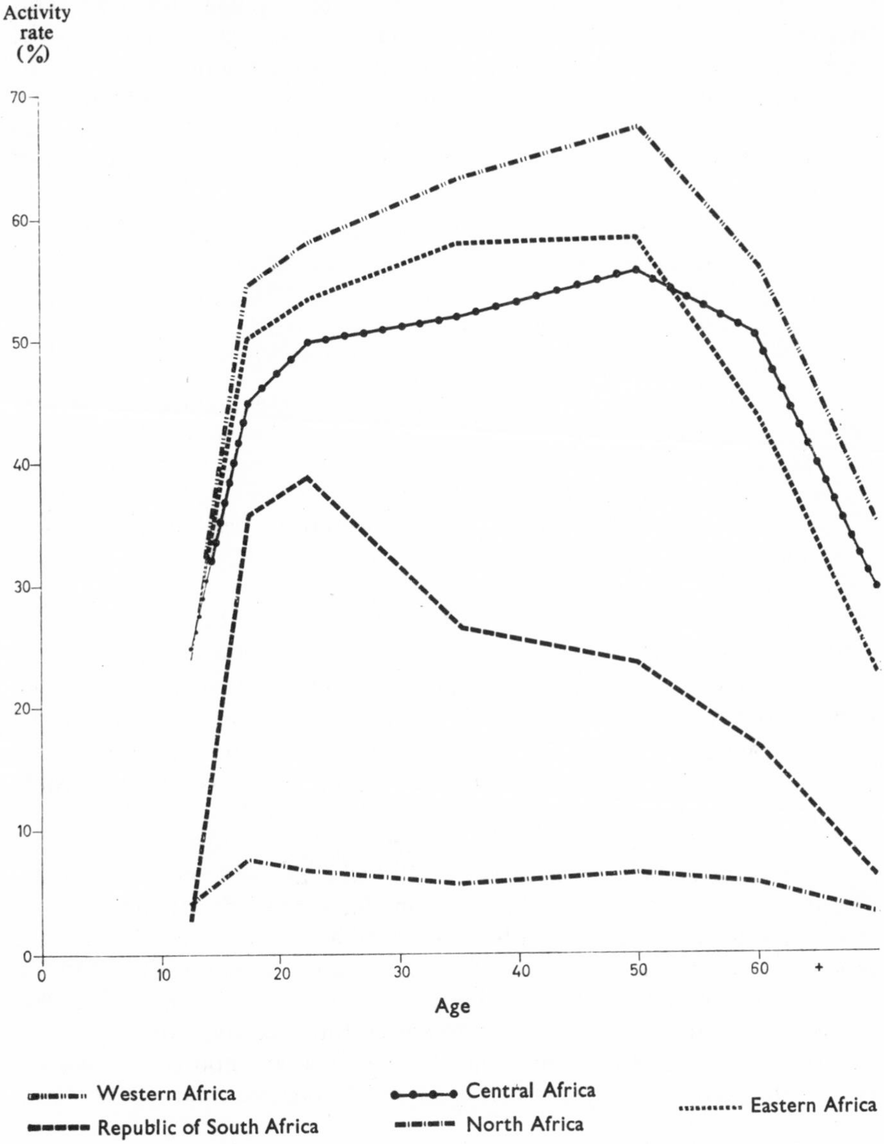

An analysis of the curves for each country and region reveals three typical profiles. The *first*, which is represented in figure 1 by the curves for the Western, Eastern and Middle regions, shows steadily increasing rates between the ages of 10 and 54; subsequently, the curve declines moderately between the ages of 55 and 64 and sharply after 65. This profile is encountered in most of the countries, although sometimes the peak is reached a little earlier, as in the Ivory Coast and Mali.

Differences in activity rates between the countries in this first group are largely due to economic factors, since in each age group the less advanced countries have higher rates than the relatively developed countries.

The *second* profile—which in figure 1 represents Northern Africa—is characterised by very low activity rates for all age groups. These curves are typical of the Moslem countries and of the African territories under Spanish or Portuguese administration. It goes without saying that, in these cases, differences between activity rates are also very slight.

The *third* profile represents the Republic of South Africa and applies to only one other African country—Namibia. It is characterised by a peak at the 20-24 age group and (with or without a variant in the shape of a second peak between 45 and 54) is much the same as in the majority of European countries, the two Americas, certain Asian countries and Australia and New Zealand.[1]

DISTRIBUTION OF THE ECONOMICALLY ACTIVE POPULATION BY ECONOMIC SECTOR

In an earlier study [2] the ILO gave an initial series of estimates of the sectoral and regional distribution of the African labour force based on the statistics available up to 1967. The revised estimates given here are derived from fuller, more detailed information which makes it possible to improve the degree of accuracy of the regional figures and to make tentative estimates by sex and by country.

For some countries the available statistics are still very inadequate, and in certain cases only approximations have been given; these are no more than general indications because there are virtually no data on the labour force and therefore on its distribution by sector. In addition, estimates are often less reliable in the case of women than of men. Furthermore, the distribution of the non-agricultural labour force between industry and services has sometimes been estimated empirically—figure 2 shows the proportionate distribution of the African labour force in

[1] This type of curve is also characteristic of urban areas of the countries under consideration. See Ettore Denti: " Sex-age patterns of labour force participation by urban and rural populations ", in *International Labour Review*, Vol. 98, No. 6, Dec. 1968, pp. 525-550.

[2] See Samuel Baum: " The world's labour force and its industrial distribution, 1950 and 1960 ", in ibid., Vol. 95, Nos. 1-2, Jan-Feb. 1967, pp. 96-112.

FIGURE 2. DISTRIBUTION OF ECONOMICALLY ACTIVE POPULATION BY ECONOMIC SECTOR, 1960

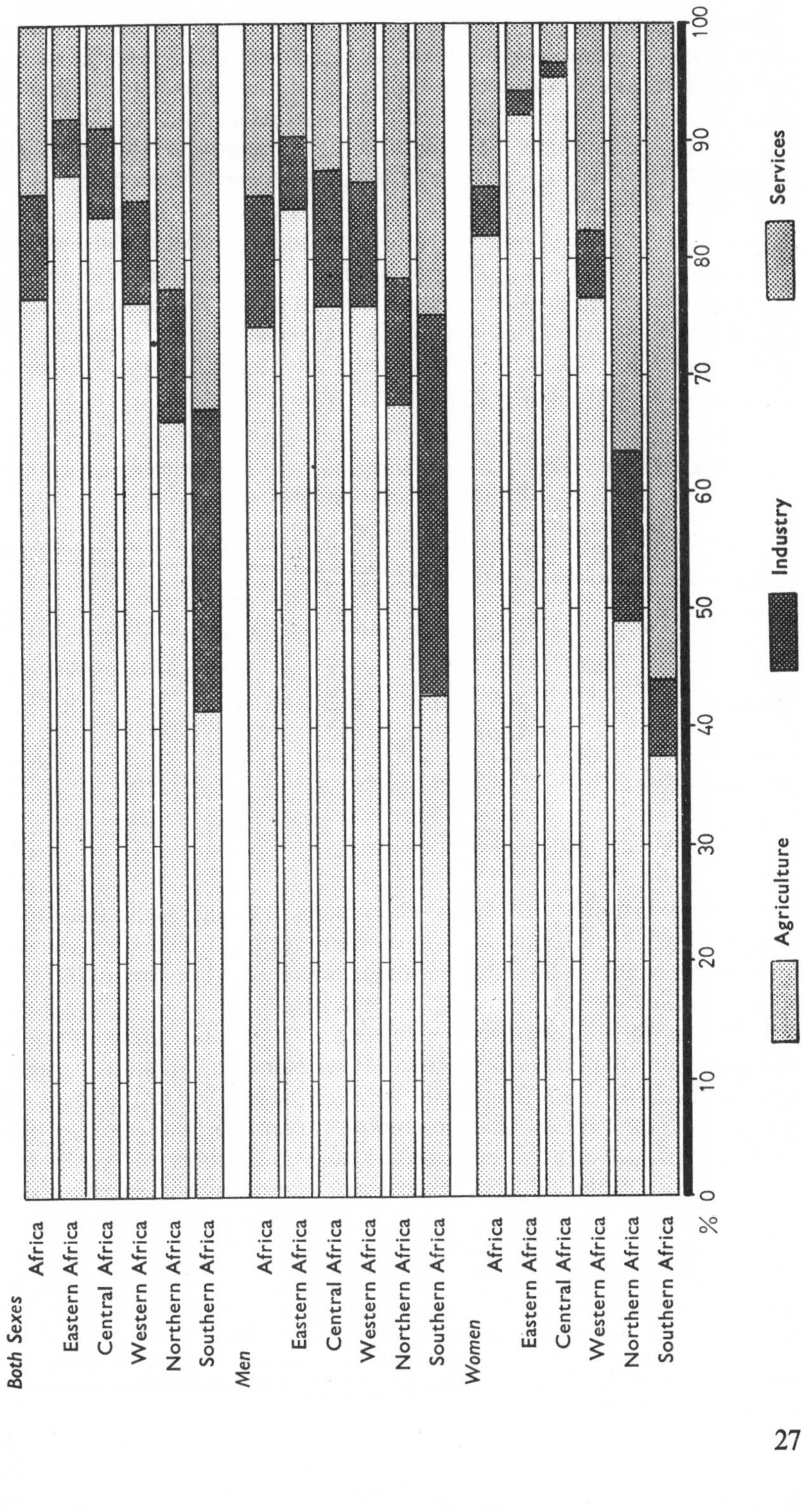

agriculture, industry and services.[1] In 1960 a little over three-quarters of these workers were in agriculture, which accounted for some 84 million. Industry accounted for a little under 10 million persons (8.8 per cent of the total labour force) while services absorbed 16 million (14.5 per cent).

Economic patterns vary considerably from one region to another (see figure 2). The proportion of the labour force in agriculture is highest in Eastern Africa (a little over 85 per cent) and is lowest in Southern Africa (41.3 per cent), which is the most highly industrialised region and also the one with the highest proportion of the labour force in services. The differences in the economic structure of the labour force are illustrated by the figures in table IV. The regional distribution of the African labour force by sector is uneven and demonstrates the differences in degrees of development in 1960.

TABLE IV. DISTRIBUTION OF ECONOMICALLY ACTIVE POPULATION BY REGION AND SECTOR, 1960

(%)

Region	Men				Women			
	Total	Agri-culture	Industry	Services	Total	Agri-culture	Industry	Services
Africa	**100.0**	**100.0**	**100.0**	**100.0**	**100.0**	**100.0**	**100.0**	**100.0**
Western	29.1	29.6	28.2	26.1	41.0	38.7	56.6	51.8
Eastern	29.7	33.9	16.2	19.5	35.3	39.0	18.3	14.2
Middle	10.8	11.0	11.1	9.0	14.8	17.5	3.3	3.5
Northern	23.6	21.6	24.3	34.0	3.7	2.4	13.4	10.1
Southern	6.8	3.9	20.2	11.4	5.2	2.4	8.4	20.4

The distribution of the economically active population by main sector ranges from Niger at one extreme (95, 1.5 and 13.5 per cent in agriculture, industry and services respectively) to the Republic of South Africa at the other (32, 30 and 38 per cent).

Taking the continent as a whole, the proportion of the labour force in agriculture is higher in the case of women than in that of men. This applies to all the countries of the Western region (except Ghana, Upper Volta and Togo), of the Eastern region (except Réunion) and to those of Middle Africa (except Angola and Equatorial Guinea) as well as to three countries in Southern Africa (Botswana, Lesotho and Swaziland).

[1] Under the United Nations *International Standard Industrial Classification of All Economic Activities* (Statistical Papers, Series M, No. 2, Rev. 2 (New York, 1968)), the different activities are divided into ten major divisions that may be grouped under three main sectors: (i) " agriculture ", comprising agriculture, hunting, forestry, and fishing; (ii) " industry ", comprising mining and quarrying, manufacturing, construction and utilities, i.e. electricity, gas and water; and (iii) " services ", comprising commerce, banking, insurance, real estate, transport, storage and communication, as well as public and private services.

In Northern Africa the low proportion of women working in agriculture is due to underestimation of the number of women occupied as family workers in agriculture. This distorts the distribution of female labour by sector, i.e. the proportion of women employed in industry and services is overestimated.

In services women are proportionately more numerous than men in all the countries of Northern Africa and in the territories under Spanish or Portuguese administration (except Mozambique), as well as in the following States or territories: Nigeria, Ghana, Dahomey, Togo, Southern Rhodesia, Réunion, Mauritius, Congo (Brazzaville), Republic of South Africa and Namibia.

For the majority of the regions, and for the continent as a whole, the proportion of women employed in industry is fairly low (with the noteworthy exception of Western Africa). On the other hand it is on the high side for the other two sectors in most regions (see table V).

TABLE V. PROPORTION OF WOMEN IN THE TOTAL LABOUR FORCE BY ECONOMIC SECTOR AND BY REGION, 1960

(%)

Economic sector	Africa	Region					
		Western	Eastern	Middle	Northern	Southern
All sectors	**32**	**39**	**35**	**39**	**7**	**26**
Agriculture	34	40	37	44	5	24
Industry	15	25	16	5	9	7
Services	30	46	24	14	11	44

II. Possible evolution of the total population and the economically active population of Africa between 1960 and 1980

Total population

The projections of the total population given here have, as was stated at the outset, been made by the responsible division of the United Nations.[1] The variant employed is the average based on a fairly marked fall in mortality rates at all ages, combined with a rise in gross reproduction rates in Middle Africa, stability of these rates in Eastern and Southern Africa, a moderate fall in Western Africa and a sharp fall in Northern Africa. These projections do not take account of migratory movements.

[1] For further details of the projection methods used see United Nations, Population Division: *Population prospects 1965-1985 as assessed in 1968* (Working Paper No. 30, Dec. 1969).

On this basis the United Nations has estimated the population of Africa to be 344,484,000 in 1970 and to rise to 456,721,000 in 1980 (see table C in the Appendix). Between 1960 and 1980, it is estimated that there will be an increase of 187 million—a figure not much lower than the total population of Africa in 1950. The annual rate of increase, estimated at 2.18 per cent for the decade 1950-60, should rise during the next twenty years to 2.48 per cent between 1960 and 1970 and to 2.86 per cent between 1970 and 1980.[1] This phenomenon, which is characteristic of virtually all the African countries, would appear to be mainly due to the general decline in mortality. The rates of increase of the five regions are estimated to range from 2 to 2.9 per cent between 1960 and 1970 and from 2.5 to 3.3 per cent between 1970 and 1980. The gaps between individual countries and territories are even wider.

The slight predominance of women will probably extend to two new regions (Western and Southern Africa) and to four new countries (Uganda, Nigeria, Angola and Namibia). Some countries have in the past suffered from a marked imbalance between the sexes caused by migratory movements. The migration factor, however, has not been taken into account in these projections, which would explain to some extent the lessening of the imbalance shown in the figures for these countries between 1960 and 1980.

The evolution in the age structure of the population of the African Continent, regions and countries does not point to any major changes, although with only a few exceptions it is expected that the population will become slightly younger. It should not have any major effect on total manpower supply and crude activity rates.

Economically active population

As stated earlier, the ILO arrived at its assessment of the probable evolution of the economically active population by applying its estimate of activity rates by sex and age group to the United Nations population projections. The method of projecting activity rates by sex and age group devised by the Office is based mainly on the close relationship between the level and trend of these rates on the one hand and the degree and trend of economic development on the other. The sixth part of the study that the ILO is about to publish on labour force projections will in fact describe this method.[2]

The percentage of the total male labour force in agriculture has been used as a measure of the degree of economic development, and thus the difference between the percentages of the agricultural male labour force

[1] With an annual rate of increase of 2.2 per cent, the population would double in thirty-two years; with a rate of 2.9 per cent, this result would be achieved after only twenty-four years.

[2] *Labour force projections*, op. cit., Part VI: *Methodological supplement*.

in 1950 and 1960 measures the progress of economic development. In addition, the trend of activity rates by sex and age has been estimated on the basis of an index (base 1950) of the variation in these rates between 1950 and 1960.

It should be explained that the ILO estimates for 1950 and 1960 were derived from series for 143 countries and territories throughout the world for which data are available on activity rates by sex and age and on the distribution of labour force by sex and economic sector. Using these basic data, a series of very detailed comparative analyses was made with the help of a computer (calculation of various ratios, standard deviations, moving averages, etc.).

For the purpose of projections, these data were used to establish an average scale of variations in activity rates by sex and age group that took into account the average change that normally occurs in the economically active population of a country as it develops. The model used in this case was an eleven-term moving average of the 143 series utilised, which were classified in decreasing order of the proportion of the total male labour force in agriculture in 1960.

In the case of women, it was necessary—in order to allow for the social and cultural factor—to work out two models according to whether their participation in economic activity was slight or considerable.

PROJECTION OF MALE ACTIVITY RATES

The projection models established presuppose a general decline of male activity rates in all age groups during the two decades 1960-70 and 1970-80. This decline should be slight between the ages of 25 and 44, becoming progressively sharper for younger and older males. In general, the higher the country's degree of economic development, the more marked the decline.

The relatively marked fall anticipated in the case of young and old males should reflect a roughly corresponding increase in school attendance and in the proportion of older workers receiving retirement pensions.

PROJECTION OF FEMALE ACTIVITY RATES

The first model was used for all the countries of Northern Africa as well as Niger, Mauritania, Namibia and the territories under Spanish or Portuguese administration. It assumes that in the less developed countries and territories in this group there will be a general rise in activity rates at all ages, and in the more advanced countries an increase between the ages of 20 and 44 (or 54), but a fall before and after these two ages.

The second model has been used for all the other African countries with the exception of the Republic of South Africa. It presupposes a continued decline in activity rates at all ages as development progresses.

This type of evolution reflects the fall in the proportion of women employed in agriculture, the growth of urbanisation and the expansion of non-agricultural activities.

SOME RESULTS OF THE PROJECTIONS

The ILO projections show a total economically active population of 132 million in 1970 and 165 million in 1980. This assumes an increase of some 24 million (22 per cent) between 1960 and 1970 and 33 million (25 per cent) between 1970 and 1980. Estimates by country are given in table D of the Appendix.

For Africa as a whole, the projections show that crude activity rates will fall from 40.4 per cent in 1960 to 38.5 per cent in 1970 and 36.2 per cent in 1980, i.e. more than a tenth in twenty years. In other words, the active population will increase more slowly than the total population.

The fall in crude activity rates appears to be due, firstly, to changes in activity rates by sex and age and, secondly, to changes in the age structure of the population. Using the appropriate statistical technique (standardisation of the population) it is possible to separate the effect of various factors on the increase in the labour force between 1960 and 1980. The results are given in table VI.

If activity rates by sex and age group on the one hand and the population structure by sex and age on the other were the same in 1980 as in 1960, the active population in 1980 would be an estimated 19 million greater, of which 16 million would be accounted for by the continuance of activity rates at 1960 levels and 3 million by the maintenance of the same

TABLE VI. INFLUENCE OF DEMOGRAPHIC FACTORS AND ECONOMIC, SOCIAL AND CULTURAL FACTORS ON GROWTH OF ECONOMICALLY ACTIVE POPULATION, 1960-80

(Million persons)

Factors of change	Africa	Region					Residue [2]
		Western	Eastern	Middle	Northern	Southern	
Changes due to demographic factors (net)	72.1	23.2	21.7	6.8	14.5	3.9	2.0
Total population	75.5	24.2	22.9	7.3	15.6	4.2	1.3
Age structure	−3.4	−1.0	−1.2	−0.5	−1.1	−0.3	0.7
Changes due to ESCO factors [1] (net)	−15.5	−5.4	−3.3	−1.8	−2.4	−0.6	−2.0
Increase 1960-80 (net)	56.6	17.8	18.4	5.0	12.1	3.3	–

[1] Economic, social, cultural and other non-demographic factors. [2] Regional interaction of demographic and ESCO factors.

age structure of the population. In other words, if the economic, social and cultural situation of the African countries and territories were to remain the same as in 1960, the African labour force would expand between 1960 and 1980 by 72 million instead of the 57 million suggested by the ILO's projections.

Similarly, the active male population of Africa is expected to rise over these two decades at a lower rate than that of the total male population. Between 1960 and 1970 the estimated annual rates are 2.05 and 2.48 per cent respectively and for the period 1970-80, 2.31 and 2.86 per cent. Mauritius is the only country to show the opposite trend. The gap between the rates of increase of the economically active population and of the total population is likely to be even wider in the case of women, the corresponding rates being 1.85 and 2.48 per cent per year between 1960 and 1970, and 2.10 and 2.86 between 1970 and 1980. Nevertheless, some countries—especially Niger, Mauritania, Mozambique, Sudan and Réunion—should have a higher rate of growth of their economically active populations between 1970 and 1980 than in the 1960s.

The results of these projections are of course governed by the initial hypotheses. Especially in the case of activity rates by sex and by age, future changes will depend considerably on the progress—economic, social and cultural—that has been or is made by these countries or territories during the decades 1960 to 1970 and 1970 to 1980, having regard to their general level of development.

Conclusions

A distinctive feature of the African countries is the youthfulness of their population. In 1960 the proportion of inhabitants under the age of 15 was far higher than in economically advanced countries while in nearly all cases the proportion of people of working age (between 15 and 64) was relatively lower. In other words, from the point of view of present potential labour supply, the age structure of the population is unfavourable. The same is true of its evolution between 1960 and 1980 which is most likely to result in a further increase in the proportion of young people and a corresponding decline in the fraction of the population of working age.

Activity rates vary considerably from one country to another. Differences are particularly great in the case of women, partly because of cultural and social patterns and partly because standards of economic development are not uniform. In the case of men, on the other hand, the differences are predominantly due to variations in economic development. Differences in the age structure of the population have less effect.

The probable evolution of the economic, social and cultural situation in Africa and of the population's age structure should lead to a general decline between 1960 and 1980 in male activity rates and in over-all activity rates in virtually all countries. In the case of women, crude activity rates are likely to increase slightly in these less developed countries where activity rates are now low while elsewhere the trend should be the same as for men.

It is anticipated that the rate of increase of the total population and of the active population will vary considerably from one country to another and that these variations will tend to accentuate between 1970 and 1980.

The main purpose of the projections discussed above is to give some idea of the structure of African manpower in 1960 and its probable evolution up to 1980. Every effort has been made to assemble basic statistical data on the manpower and activity rates of all African countries. However, in some instances where information on the economic and social situation was lacking, estimates have had to be made empirically using models and these are of course, only approximations. The projections, too, are subject to qualification. Those concerning the labour force are dependent firstly on population trends and secondly on economic, social and cultural progress. Of these two sources of possible error, the latter may not have been gauged sufficiently well to avoid introducing some error in the estimates even in the short term. This makes it essential to carry out periodical reviews of the projections to take account of any new trends suggested by the latest information. When the results of the censuses taken in the 1970s become available the ILO will have an opportunity of checking and where necessary improving the estimates and projections of labour force patterns in general and of activity rates in particular.

APPENDIX

Statistics of population and economically active population

The figures for each country given in the four following tables have been derived or calculated from the statistics published by the ILO in *Labour force projections*, Part II: *Africa*, tables 2, 3 and 5.

The regional totals also cover countries or territories which are not mentioned separately, viz. the Cape Verde Islands and St. Helena and dependencies in Western Africa; the Comoro and Seychelles Islands, the French Territory of the Afars and the Issas, and the British Indian Ocean Territory in Eastern Africa; São Tomé and Prince Island in Middle Africa; Spanish North Africa, Ifni and Spanish Sahara in Northern Africa; and the French Southern and Antarctic Territories in Southern Africa.

The figures have been rounded off for each age group, sex and country, so that the sum of the components may sometimes differ from the corresponding totals given in the tables.

TABLE A. POPULATION IN 1960

Region and country	Total ('000)	Distribution by age group (%) 0-14 years	15-64 years	65+ years	Annual rate of growth 1950-60 (%)	% of females
Africa	**269 577**	**43.2**	**53.9**	**2.9**	**2.18**	**50.2**
Western	*79 530*	*44.2*	*53.4*	*2.4*	*2.16*	*49.8*
Nigeria	42 947	44.8	53.0	2.2	2.26	49.5
Ghana	6 777	46.9	51.2	1.9	3.04	49.5
Upper Volta	4 400	42.4	54.8	2.8	1.56	50.1
Mali	4 089	43.6	53.7	2.7	1.78	50.2
Ivory Coast	3 433	41.9	55.3	2.8	1.98	49.3
Senegal	3 110	42.4	54.7	2.9	1.81	50.4
Guinea	3 183	42.0	55.1	2.9	1.71	50.2
Niger	2 913	46.2	51.5	2.3	2.43	50.5
Sierra Leone	2 136	42.4	54.4	3.2	1.85	50.4
Dahomey	2 113	44.3	53.1	2.6	2.01	50.8
Togo	1 465	44.6	52.7	2.7	2.01	51.5
Liberia	995	38.2	57.7	4.1	1.26	50.5
Mauritania	950	41.7	55.1	3.2	1.78	50.4
Portuguese Guinea	506	35.8	60.2	4.0	0.63	50.0
Gambia	301	39.9	56.8	3.3	1.63	49.2
Eastern	*77 089*	*43.3*	*53.8*	*2.9*	*2.12*	*50.7*
Ethiopia	20 700	41.1	55.7	3.2	1.59	51.0
Tanzania	10 328	44.4	52.8	2.8	2.19	50.6
Kenya	8 115	46.7	50.8	2.5	3.03	50.7
Uganda	6 684	42.6	54.2	3.2	2.27	49.9
Mozambique	6 392	39.4	57.1	3.5	1.40	52.2
Madagascar	5 370	44.6	52.8	2.6	2.18	50.8
Southern Rhodesia	3 640	45.5	52.3	2.2	3.34	48.5
Malawi	3 447	45.1	52.5	2.4	2.41	50.5
Zambia	3 219	47.1	50.5	2.4	2.67	50.3
Rwanda	2 740	45.1	52.4	2.5	2.27	50.7
Burundi	2 908	42.5	54.6	2.9	1.79	50.6
Somalia	2 226	43.8	53.5	2.7	2.00	50.5
Mauritius	662	44.1	52.9	3.0	3.29	49.6
Réunion	338	44.4	52.3	3.3	3.31	51.2
Middle	*29 402*	*41.7*	*55.2*	*3.1*	*1.70*	*51.4*
Congo (Kinshasa)	14 139	41.7	55.2	3.1	1.76	51.6
Angola	4 723	42.6	54.8	2.6	1.75	49.4
Cameroon	4 786	40.2	56.1	3.7	1.56	51.6
Chad	2 975	44.7	52.6	2.7	1.91	52.6
Central African Republic	1 252	41.9	55.0	3.1	1.57	52.1
Congo (Brazzaville)	764	41.6	54.9	3.5	1.68	52.1
Gabon	452	33.6	60.9	5.5	0.41	53.3
Equatorial Guinea	251	32.7	63.3	4.0	1.01	46.6
Northern	*65 392*	*43.4*	*53.5*	*3.1*	*2.44*	*49.6*
UAR (Egypt)	25 832	42.2	54.7	3.1	2.36	49.7
Sudan	11 770	44.3	53.0	2.7	2.64	49.4
Morocco	11 640	44.8	52.6	2.6	2.66	50.0
Algeria	10 800	43.8	52.3	3.9	2.12	49.7
Tunisia	3 778	44.2	52.2	3.6	2.54	48.7
Libya	1 349	43.3	52.7	4.0	2.74	48.7
Southern	*18 164*	*39.8*	*56.2*	*4.0*	*2.38*	*50.0*
South Africa (Rep. of)	15 925	39.7	56.2	4.1	2.49	49.8
Lesotho	885	38.3	57.3	4.4	1.45	52.0
Namibia	528	38.6	58.4	3.0	1.48	49.6
Botswana	506	41.7	55.5	2.8	1.86	51.4
Swaziland	320	46.9	50.3	2.8	2.38	52.2

TABLE B. ECONOMICALLY ACTIVE POPULATION IN 1960

Region and country	Total ('000)	Distribution by age group (%)			Crude activity rate (%)			% of females
		10-14 years	15-64 years	65+ years	Both sexes	Males	Females	
Africa	**108 826**	**7.5**	**89.3**	**3.2**	**40.4**	**55.5**	**25.4**	**31.5**
Western	*35 790*	*7.5*	*89.6*	*2.9*	*45.0*	*54.3*	*35.6*	*39.4*
Nigeria	18 523	6.5	90.6	2.9	43.1	51.9	34.2	39.3
Ghana	2 732	4.4	93.0	2.6	40.3	49.5	31.0	38.0
Upper Volta	2 537	10.1	87.0	2.9	57.7	60.9	54.5	47.3
Mali	2 364	10.5	87.0	2.5	57.8	60.3	55.3	48.0
Ivory Coast	1 904	9.2	88.2	2.6	55.5	61.1	49.7	44.2
Senegal	1 451	8.0	89.3	2.7	46.6	56.7	36.8	39.7
Guinea	1 580	9.2	88.0	2.8	49.6	59.5	39.9	40.4
Niger	937	11.8	85.4	2.8	32.2	58.9	5.9	9.2
Sierra Leone	899	7.9	88.7	3.4	42.1	54.6	29.8	35.7
Dahomey	1 082	8.9	87.9	3.2	51.2	57.1	45.5	45.1
Togo	654	11.3	85.4	3.3	44.6	56.0	33.9	39.1
Liberia	432	6.7	89.2	4.1	43.4	58.1	29.0	33.6
Mauritania	303	10.1	86.3	3.6	31.9	61.8	2.5	4.0
Portuguese Guinea	168	5.6	89.9	4.5	33.2	64.1	2.3	3.6
Gambia	164	6.9	89.7	3.4	54.5	60.0	48.9	43.9
Eastern	*34 246*	*8.9*	*87.8*	*3.3*	*44.4*	*58.2*	*31.0*	*35.4*
Ethiopia	9 659	8.8	87.6	3.6	46.7	61.3	32.6	35.6
Tanzania	4 679	9.5	87.3	3.2	45.3	57.7	33.2	37.1
Kenya	3 340	9.2	87.8	3.0	41.2	54.5	28.2	34.8
Uganda	3 045	9.0	87.3	3.7	45.6	60.0	31.1	34.1
Mozambique	1 930	4.2	92.0	3.8	30.2	57.6	5.1	8.8
Madagascar	2 883	10.7	86.1	3.2	53.7	58.7	48.9	46.2

Southern Rhodesia	1 419	7.5	89.9	2.6	39.0	54.9	22.1	27.5
Malawi	1 603	10.4	86.7	2.9	46.5	58.1	35.1	38.1
Zambia	1 281	8.3	88.8	2.9	39.8	53.3	26.5	33.5
Rwanda	1 547	11.0	86.6	2.4	56.5	58.6	54.4	48.8
Burundi	1 533	9.2	88.0	2.8	52.7	58.5	47.0	45.1
Somalia	925	9.2	87.7	3.1	41.5	58.7	24.7	30.0
Mauritius	200	1.3	96.9	1.8	30.2	49.5	10.6	17.5
Réunion	92	0.8	97.3	1.9	27.1	44.4	10.7	19.6
Middle	*13 085*	*7.4*	*89.4*	*3.2*	*44.5*	*56.0*	*33.6*	*38.7*
Congo (Kinshasa)	6 839	7.3	89.6	3.1	48.4	55.2	41.9	44.7
Angola	1 414	4.0	92.7	3.3	29.9	54.5	4.7	7.8
Cameroon	2 423	7.9	88.5	3.6	50.6	59.0	42.8	43.6
Chad	1 060	11.4	85.4	3.2	35.6	56.3	17.0	25.2
Central African Rep.	723	9.4	87.8	2.8	57.7	59.6	56.0	50.5
Congo (Brazzaville)	286	3.5	93.1	3.4	37.5	48.5	27.3	38.1
Gabon	228	5.9	89.4	4.7	50.5	61.4	41.0	43.4
Equatorial Guinea	94	3.9	91.8	4.3	37.5	68.0	2.6	3.2
Northern	*18 882*	*6.5*	*90.1*	*3.4*	*28.9*	*53.5*	*3.9*	*6.7*
UAR (Egypt)	7 379	5.4	91.4	3.2	28.6	53.1	3.7	6.5
Sudan	3 888	10.4	86.3	3.3	33.0	59.1	6.4	9.6
Morocco	3 278	6.3	90.6	3.1	28.2	52.1	4.2	7.5
Algeria	2 881	4.7	91.4	3.9	26.7	51.3	1.7	3.2
Tunisia	1 026	4.7	90.8	4.5	27.1	49.7	3.4	6.0
Libya	370	6.0	88.9	5.1	27.5	51.0	2.7	4.9
Southern	*6 822*	*2.5*	*94.1*	*3.4*	*37.6*	*55.5*	*19.6*	*26.1*
South Africa (Rep. of)	5 692	1.7	95.2	3.1	35.7	55.0	16.3	22.8
Lesotho	500	5.8	87.9	6.3	56.5	62.4	50.9	46.8
Namibia	208	7.4	89.2	3.4	39.5	61.3	17.4	22.1
Botswana	268	7.6	88.1	4.3	53.0	57.3	49.0	47.4
Swaziland	153	7.9	87.4	4.7	47.8	51.0	44.9	49.0

TABLE C. POPULATION IN 1970 AND 1980

Region and country	1970				1980			
	Total ('000)	Population aged 15-64 (%)	Annual rate of growth 1960-70 (%)	% of females	Total ('000)	Population aged 15-64 (%)	Annual rate of growth 1970-80 (%)	% of females
Africa	**344 484**	**53.4**	**2.48**	**50.2**	**456 721**	**52.4**	**2.86**	**50.2**
Western	*101 271*	*53.2*	*2.45*	*49.9*	*133 406*	*52.3*	*2.79*	*50.1*
Nigeria	55 073	52.9	2.52	49.7	72 784	52.0	2.83	50.0
Ghana	9 026	52.0	2.91	49.5	12 577	52.6	3.37	49.7
Upper Volta	5 376	54.4	2.02	50.1	6 770	53.2	2.33	50.2
Mali	5 088	53.4	2.21	50.1	6 580	52.2	2.60	50.2
Ivory Coast	4 310	54.8	2.30	49.5	5 578	53.1	2.61	49.8
Senegal	3 925	54.3	2.35	50.5	5 083	53.0	2.62	50.5
Guinea	3 921	54.6	2.11	50.4	5 016	53.2	2.49	50.5
Niger	3 848	51.1	2.82	50.5	5 266	49.9	3.19	50.5
Sierra Leone	2 644	54.5	2.16	50.5	3 389	53.8	2.51	50.5
Dahomey	2 686	52.6	2.43	50.8	3 550	51.3	2.83	50.7
Togo	1 861	52.4	2.42	51.4	2 457	51.4	2.82	51.0
Liberia	1 171	57.3	1.64	50.6	1 446	55.2	2.13	50.6
Mauritania	1 170	55.0	2.10	50.5	1 507	53.4	2.56	50.5
Portuguese Guinea	557	59.6	0.96	50.3	646	57.0	1.49	50.5
Gambia	364	56.0	1.92	49.5	454	54.2	2.23	50.0
Eastern	*97 882*	*53.4*	*2.42*	*50.6*	*128 757*	*52.5*	*2.78*	*50.6*
Ethiopia	25 046	55.3	1.92	51.0	31 516	54.1	2.32	50.8
Tanzania	13 235	53.0	2.51	50.6	17 475	52.4	2.82	50.6
Kenya	10 898	51.0	2.99	50.6	15 110	50.7	3.32	50.4
Uganda	8 584	54.1	2.53	50.0	11 336	53.1	2.82	50.1
Mozambique	7 704	56.0	1.88	51.9	9 721	53.9	2.35	51.4
Madagascar	6 933	52.4	2.59	50.8	9 276	51.1	2.95	50.8

Southern Rhodesia	5 049	51.4	3.33	48.9	7 184	49.7	3.59	49.4
Malawi	4 443	52.6	2.57	50.5	5 834	52.2	2.76	50.5
Zambia	4 295	50.8	2.93	50.4	5 911	50.5	3.25	50.4
Ruanda	3 587	51.6	2.73	50.6	4 869	50.1	3.10	50.5
Burundi	3 600	54.1	2.16	50.7	4 634	52.7	2.56	50.6
Somalia	2 789	51.5	2.28	50.6	3 653	54.0	2.74	50.6
Mauritius	862	54.5	2.68	49.8	1 107	57.8	2.53	49.8
Réunion	464	52.2	3.22	51.1	634	52.2	3.17	50.8
Middle	*35 892*	*55.1*	*2.01*	*51.3*	*45 785*	*53.6*	*2.46*	*51.0*
Congo (Kinshasa)	17 424	54.9	2.11	51.4	22 439	53.4	2.56	51.1
Angola	5 693	55.5	1.89	49.7	7 138	53.6	2.29	50.1
Cameroon	5 786	55.9	1.92	51.4	7 343	54.0	2.41	51.1
Chad	3 706	53.1	2.22	52.3	4 785	53.1	2.59	51.6
Central African Rep.	1 522	54.8	1.97	51.8	1 948	53.2	2.50	51.3
Congo (Brazzaville)	935	54.9	2.04	51.8	1 201	53.4	2.54	51.3
Gabon	481	61.1	0.62	53.0	535	60.4	1.07	52.3
Equatorial Guinea	285	61.1	1.28	47.0	335	59.4	1.63	48.1
Northern	*86 606*	*52.3*	*2.85*	*49.6*	*119 385*	*51.6*	*3.26*	*49.5*
UAR (Egypt)	33 872	54.1	2.75	49.6	45 431	53.4	2.98	49.5
Sudan	15 779	52.2	2.97	49.5	21 946	51.0	3.35	49.5
Morocco	15 722	51.4	3.05	49.9	22 202	50.3	3.51	49.7
Algeria	14 012	49.8	2.64	49.8	19 869	49.9	3.55	49.7
Tunisia	5 075	51.2	3.00	49.1	7 041	51.3	3.33	49.2
Libya	1 881	52.4	3.38	48.5	2 602	51.5	3.30	48.9
Southern	*22 832*	*54.7*	*2.31*	*50.0*	*29 386*	*54.3*	*2.56*	*50.1*
South Africa (Rep. of)	20 112	56.1	2.36	49.9	25 952	54.3	2.58	50.0
Lesotho	1 043	57.1	1.66	51.8	1 283	55.9	2.09	51.4
Namibia	633	56.9	1.83	49.8	785	54.5	2.18	50.1
Botswana	622	55.0	2.09	51.3	792	54.2	2.45	51.0
Swaziland	420	50.5	2.76	51.9	574	49.8	3.17	51.4

TABLE D. ECONOMICALLY ACTIVE POPULATION IN 1970 AND 1980

Region and country	1970				1980			
	Total ('000)	Crude activity rate (%)	Annual rate of growth 1960-70 (%)	% of females	Total ('000)	Crude activity rate (%)	Annual rate of growth 1970-80 (%)	% of females
Africa	**132 479**	**38.5**	**1.99**	**31.1**	**165 379**	**36.2**	**2.24**	**30.7**
Western	*43 450*	*42.9*	*1.96*	*38.9*	*53 613*	*40.2*	*2.12*	*38.7*
Nigeria	22 534	40.9	1.98	38.8	27 607	37.9	2.05	38.8
Ghana	3 492	38.7	2.48	37.7	4 695	37.3	3.00	38.0
Upper Volta	2 997	55.7	1.68	46.7	3 600	53.2	1.85	46.1
Mali	2 848	56.0	1.88	47.4	3 517	53.4	2.13	46.7
Ivory Coast	2 302	53.4	1.92	43.8	2 813	50.4	2.02	44.1
Senegal	1 739	44.3	1.83	39.1	2 097	41.3	1.89	38.1
Guinea	1 870	47.7	1.70	40.3	2 260	45.1	1.91	40.0
Niger	1 217	31.6	2.65	9.8	1 620	30.8	2.90	10.6
Sierra Leone	1 054	39.9	1.60	35.0	1 258	37.1	1.78	34.0
Dahomey	1 318	49.1	1.99	44.9	1 638	46.2	2.20	44.4
Togo	800	43.0	2.04	38.6	1 005	40.9	2.31	37.7
Liberia	478	40.8	1.02	32.4	546	37.8	1.34	31.7
Mauritania	366	31.3	1.91	4.1	452	30.0	2.13	4.4
Portuguese Guinea	178	32.0	0.58	3.9	200	30.9	1.17	4.0
Gambia	190	52.2	1.48	44.2	219	48.1	1.43	43.8
Eastern	*41 975*	*42.9*	*2.06*	*35.1*	*52 688*	*40.9*	*2.30*	*34.8*
Ethiopia	11 307	45.1	1.59	35.1	13 575	43.1	1.84	34.7
Tanzania	5 841	44.1	2.24	36.7	7 391	42.3	2.38	36.4
Kenya	4 354	39.9	2.69	34.3	5 783	38.3	2.88	33.7
Uganda	3 796	44.2	2.23	33.7	4 788	42.2	2.35	33.6
Mozambique	2 248	29.2	1.54	9.1	2 692	27.7	1.82	9.4
Madagascar	3 583	51.7	2.20	45.7	4 565	49.2	2.45	45.1

Southern Rhodesia	1 830	36.2	2.58	27.8	2 379	33.1	2.66	28.5
Malawi	2 014	45.3	2.31	37.6	2 554	43.8	2.40	37.0
Zambia	1 649	38.4	2.56	32.8	2 153	36.4	2.70	31.6
Rwanda	1 943	54.2	2.31	48.3	2 510	51.5	2.59	47.7
Burundi	1 828	50.8	1.78	44.8	2 229	48.1	2.00	44.6
Somalia	1 084	38.9	1.60	29.7	1 415	38.7	2.70	29.5
Mauritius	250	29.0	2.26	17.6	336	30.4	3.00	17.9
Réunion	118	25.5	2.52	20.3	162	25.6	3.22	21.6
Middle	*15 257*	*42.5*	*1.55*	*37.9*	*18 114*	*39.6*	*1.73*	*36.9*
Congo (Kinshasa)	7 934	45.5	1.50	43.6	9 384	41.8	1.69	42.5
Angola	1 660	29.2	1.62	8.0	1 939	27.2	1.57	8.7
Cameroon	2 816	48.7	1.51	43.2	3 320	45.2	1.66	42.1
Chad	1 310	35.3	2.14	24.6	1 666	34.8	2.43	23.5
Central African Republic	850	55.8	1.63	49.5	1 031	52.9	1.95	48.2
Congo (Brazzaville)	336	36.0	1.62	36.9	404	33.6	1.86	35.6
Gabon	235	48.8	0.30	42.1	246	46.0	0.46	39.4
Equatorial Guinea	103	36.2	0.92	3.9	112	33.3	0.84	3.6
Northern	*23 601*	*27.3*	*2.26*	*7.1*	*30 969*	*25.9*	*2.75*	*7.4*
UAR (Egypt)	9 174	27.1	2.20	6.6	11 741	25.8	2.50	6.6
Sudan	5 065	32.1	2.68	10.3	6 760	30.8	2.93	11.1
Morocco	4 161	26.5	2.41	7.8	5 543	25.0	2.91	8.2
Algeria	3 369	24.0	1.58	3.4	4 545	22.9	3.04	3.5
Tunisia	1 273	25.1	2.18	6.4	1 685	23.9	2.84	6.4
Libya	488	25.9	2.81	4.7	625	24.0	2.51	4.6
Southern	*8 197*	*35.9*	*1.85*	*26.5*	*9 994*	*34.0*	*2.00*	*27.4*
South Africa (Rep. of)	6 877	34.2	1.91	23.5	8 411	32.4	2.03	24.7
Lesotho	571	54.7	1.34	46.1	671	52.3	1.63	45.2
Namibia	234	37.0	1.18	22.2	266	33.9	1.29	22.9
Botswana	322	51.8	1.85	46.9	391	49.4	1.96	46.3
Swaziland	193	45.9	2.35	48.2	254	44.3	2.78	46.9

Income Expectations, Rural-Urban Migration and Employment in Africa

Michael P. TODARO [1]

IN THE FEW SHORT YEARS since independence, the nations of tropical Africa have experienced an unprecedented increase in the size of their urban populations. From Abidjan to Brazzaville to Nairobi, recorded urban population growth rates of 7 to 10 per cent per annum are a common phenomenon (see table I). Part of this growth is due to the rather rapid rates of over-all population increase in Africa, rates typically around 3 per cent per annum.[2] However, by far the most important contributing factor has been the massive increase in the number of migrants arriving from surrounding rural areas. Numerous factors, both economic and non-economic, underlie the decision of peasant farmers and educated youths to seek the " better life " in the rapidly growing urban centres. In this article I shall examine the relationship between migration, expected income differentials, and urban employment in tropical Africa. I shall begin by briefly presenting a theoretical model of rural-urban migration which places primary emphasis on the economic motivations for migration. This analytical framework, where appropriate, will then be used in the main body of the article, which is devoted to an examination and evaluation of alternative short- and long-run policies designed to curtail the massive influx of rural migrants and to alleviate the concomitant growing unemployment problem in urban Africa.

---

[1] Assistant Director for Social Sciences, Rockefeller Foundation. The views and opinions expressed in this article are the author's own and should not be interpreted as reflecting the views of the Rockefeller Foundation.

[2] For a useful review of African demographic data, see R. K. Som: " Some demographic indicators for Africa ", in John C. Caldwell and Chukuka Okonjo (eds.): *The population of tropical Africa* (London, Longmans, Green & Co., 1968), pp. 187-189.

TABLE I. SUB-SAHARAN AFRICA: URBAN POPULATION GROWTH

City	Year	Population ('000)	Year	Population ('000)		Annual growth (%)	
				City proper	Urban agglom-eration	City proper	Urban agglom-eration
Salisbury	1946	69	1966		330		8.1
Dar es Salaam	1948	69	1967	273		7.5	
Brazzaville	1955	76	1961-62		136		8.7
Dakar	1945	132	1961		375		6.7
Accra	1948	136	1963	616	758	7.8	8.1
Nairobi	1948	119	1968		479		7.2
Abidjan	1955	127	1964		282		9.3
Monrovia	1956	41	1962	81		11.9	
Fort Lamy	1955	29	1964		99		13.6
Cotonou	1945	26	1965	111		7.5	
Mombasa	1948	85	1968		234		5.2
Bamako	1945	37	1965		165		7.8
Bulawayo	1946	53	1966		240		7.8
Lusaka	1950	26	1966		152		11.7
Yaoundé	1955	38	1965	101		10.3	
Douala	1954	118	1965		200		4.9
Addis Ababa	1951	400	1967	644		3.0	
Khartoum-Omdurman	1948	210	1967	390		3.3	
Luanda	1950	150	1960		225		4.1
Léopoldville (Kinshasa)	1946	110	1966	508		8.0	
Elisabethville (Lubumbashi)	1950	103	1966	233		5.2	
Kumasi	1955	75	1968	282	340	10.7	12.3
Lourenço-Marques	1950	94	1960		179		6.7

Sources: United Nations: *Demographic yearbook* (New York), various issues; and William A. Hance: *The geography of modern Africa* (New York, Columbia University Press, 1964), p. 54.

Urban unemployment: a major dilemma

Before turning to a theoretical examination of the economics of rural-urban migration, it should be pointed out that rural-urban migration is by no means an undesirable phenomenon. In fact most of the theories of economic development, which are based largely on the historical experience of Western industrialised nations, emphasise the transformation of an economy from a rural agrarian base to one with an industrial, urban-oriented focus. This process is made possible by the gradual but continuous absorption of " redundant " or " surplus " rural labourers into the growing industrial economy. Under ideal circumstances, the rate of growth of modern sector industries then provides a sufficient number

TABLE II. NON-AGRICULTURAL EMPLOYMENT INDICES IN SELECTED AFRICAN COUNTRIES, 1955-64
(1958 = 100)

Year	Cameroon	Ghana[1]	Kenya	Malawi	Nigeria
1955	102	82	107	88	n.a.
1956	104	91	105	95	95
1957	100	95	105	98	100
1958	**100**	**100**	**100**	**100**	**100**
1959	95	106	100	99	99
1960	91	111	102	96	106
1961	94	122	98	93	89
1962	72	128	97	87	113
1963	91	132	91	87	94
1964	92	n.a.	101	n.a.	n.a.
Rate of growth (%)	−1.0	6.3	−0.5	−0.7	0.1

Year	Sierra Leone	Southern Rhodesia	Tanzania	Uganda	Zambia
1955	87	86	97	94	92
1956	87	92	104	93	100
1957	92	98	101	99	100
1958	**100**	**100**	**100**	**100**	**100**
1959	98	100	96	99	95
1960	101	101	98	99	93
1961	108	98	104	98	90
1962	112	95	101	93	88
1963	119	91	91	89	86
1964	125	90	95	89	91
Rate of growth (%)	0.2	3.0	−0.4	−0.1	−0.9

[1] Note that the relatively high rate of Ghanaian employment growth in the late 1950s and early 1960s was due primarily to the rapid increase in public employment as a result of Nkrumah's " make-work " policy. In the years since 1964, employment growth in Ghana has been negligible since the " make-work " policy could not be sustained for long without undue fiscal strain.

Source: Charles R. Frank, Jr.: *Urban unemployment and economic growth in Africa*, Economic Growth Center Paper No. 120 (New Haven (Connecticut), 1968), p. 254.

of newly created employment opportunities to bring about a more productive and efficient allocation of human resources in the economy as a whole. Unfortunately, real world conditions do not always conform to the hypothetical framework of the economist's development scenario.

In tropical Africa the magnitude of rural-urban migration has greatly exceeded the capacity of the modern industrial sector to absorb the persons concerned, so that it can only employ productively a small proportion of them. Part of the problem relates to the nature of the African industrialisation process itself, a process which has typically failed

TABLE III. URBAN UNEMPLOYMENT RATES IN AFRICA
(%)

Country (urban centres)	Unemployment rate	Country (urban centres)	Unemployment rate
Algeria (1966)	26.6	Kenya (1969)	
Cameroon (1966)		Eight urban areas	17.4
Douala	13.0	Morocco (1960)	20.5
Yaoundé	17.0	Nigeria (1963)	
Congo (1958)		Lagos	15.5
Léopoldville (Kinshasa)	15.0	Ife	19.7
Ghana (1960)		Onitsha	26.3
Large towns	11.6	Kaduna	30.8
Ivory Coast (1963)		Abeokuta	34.6
Abidjan	20.0	Tanzania (1965)	12.6

Sources: *Algeria*, *Ghana*, *Morocco* and *Tanzania*—D. Turnham: *The employment problem in less developed countries : a review of evidence* (Paris, OECD Development Centre, 1970), pp. 193-195. *Cameroon* and *Ivory Coast*—Remi Clignet: " Preliminary notes of a study of unemployment in modern African urban centers ", in *Manpower and unemployment research in Africa*, Vol. 2, Apr. 1969. *Nigeria*—Peter C. W. Gutkind: " The energy of despair: social organisation of the unemployed in two African cities: Lagos and Nairobi ", in *Civilisations* (Brussels), Vol. XVII, 1967, No. 3, pp. 186-211, and No. 4, pp. 380-402. *Congo*—P. Raymachers: *Etude par sondage de la main-d'œuvre à Léopoldville* (Ministère du Plan et de la coopération économique, 1958). *Kenya*—H. Rempel and M. P. Todaro: " Rural-urban labour migration in Kenya: some preliminary findings of a large-scale survey ", in S. Ominde (ed.): *Population growth and economic development* (to be published).

to produce a growth of job opportunities at anything near the rate of output growth. If one uses the standard criterion of output growth as the measuring rod for the success of the industrial development effort, many African economies with output growth rates of 5 to 8 per cent per annum have not done that poorly under the circumstances. However, as table II reveals, the growth rate of non-agricultural employment has typically been negligible and, in many cases, negative.

It is in this context of slowly growing urban employment opportunities accompanied by a disproportionately high rate of rural-urban migration that the chronic urban unemployment and underemployment problem has emerged in tropical Africa. Although there are few hard data on the magnitude of African urban unemployment, owing both to conceptual difficulties in defining unemployment and, more importantly, to the fact that very few studies have been directed to the problem, the limited evidence available provides ample empirical confirmation of what any informed observer already knows—namely that urban unemployment is an extremely serious problem (see table III for a summary of available data on urban unemployment rates in African cities). However, in spite of these rising levels of overt unemployment and even higher levels of underemployment, the rate of rural-urban migration shows no sign of deceleration. To the extent that many newly arrived migrants are likely to join the growing pools of unemployed and highly underemployed workers, and to the extent that an increasingly large proportion of these migrants represent the more educated segments of society whose productive potential is largely being dissipated, the process of continued rural-urban migration at present levels can no longer be said to represent a desirable economic phenomenon. Until something positive is done to relieve this problem, the African development effort will be only partially successful.

A theoretical framework for analysing the economics of rural-urban migration in Africa

In this section I would like to set forth briefly a theoretical framework which yields some important insights into the causes and mechanisms of rural-urban migration in tropical Africa. No attempt will be made to describe this model in any great detail since that has been done elsewhere.[1] I believe that the model can usefully serve two purposes: first, to demonstrate why the continued existence of rural-urban migration in the face of rising levels of urban unemployment often represents a rational economic decision from the point of view of the private individual; and second, to demonstrate how such a theoretical framework can be used in an analysis and evaluation of alternative public policies to alleviate the growing urban unemployment problem.

The individual decision to migrate: some behavioural assumptions

The basic behavioural assumption of the model is that each potential migrant decides whether or not to move to the city on the basis of an implicit, " expected " income maximisation objective. There are two principal economic factors involved in this decision to migrate. The first relates to the existing urban-rural real wage differential that prevails for different skill and educational categories of workers. The existence of large disparities between wages paid to urban workers and those paid to comparably skilled rural labourers has long been recognised as a crucial factor in the decision to migrate.[2] The increasing divergence between

[1] A more detailed description and development of the over-all features of the model can be found in Michael P. Todaro: " The urban employment problem in less developed countries: an analysis of demand and supply ", in *Yale Economic Essays*, Vol. VIII, Fall 1968, pp. 331-402; idem: " A model of labor migration and urban unemployment in less developed countries ", in *American Economic Review* (Menasha (Wisconsin)), Vol. LIX, No. 1, Mar. 1969, pp. 138-148; and John R. Harris and Michael P. Todaro: " Migration, unemployment and development: a two-sector analysis ", ibid., Vol. LX, No. 1, Mar. 1970, pp. 126-142.

[2] Some of the more recent studies identifying economic forces as principal factors affecting the decision to migrate include Ralph E. Beals, Mildred B. Levy and Leon N. Moses: " Rationality and migration in Ghana ", in *Review of Economics and Statistics* (Cambridge (Massachusetts)), Vol. XLIX, No. 4, Nov. 1967, pp. 480-486; John C. Caldwell: *African*

(footnote continued overleaf)

urban and rural incomes has arisen both as a result of the relative stagnation of agricultural earnings (partly as a direct outgrowth of post-war bias toward industrialisation at the expense of agricultural expansion) and the concomitant phenomenon of rapidly rising urban wage rates for unskilled workers. For example, in Nigeria Arthur Lewis noted that " urban wages " are typically at levels twice as high as average farm incomes. Between 1950 and 1963 prices received by farmers through marketing boards in southern Nigeria fell by 25 per cent while at the same time the minimum wage scales of the Federal Government increased by 200 per cent.[1]

In Kenya average earnings of African employees in the non-agricultural sector rose from £97 in 1960 to £180 in 1966, a growth rate of nearly 11 per cent per annum. During the same period the small farm sector of Kenya experienced a growth of estimated family income of only 5 per cent per annum, rising from £57 in 1960 to £77 in 1966. Consequently, urban wages rose more than twice as fast as agricultural incomes in Kenya so that in 1966 average wages in the urban sector were approximately two-and-a-half times as high as average farm family incomes.[2] Moreover, the urban-rural income differential in Kenya in 1968 varied considerably by level of educational attainment. For example, whereas farm income was approximately K£85 in 1968, individuals with zero to four years of primary education in urban areas earned on the average K£102, those with five to eight years of primary education earned K£156, while migrants who had completed from one to six years of secondary education earned on the average K£290 per annum in 1968.[3]

A final example of the growing disparity between urban and rural incomes can be gleaned from Uganda data. During the period 1954 to

rural-urban migration. The movement to Ghana's towns (New York, Columbia University Press, 1969); Lowell E. Gallaway: " Industry variations in geographic labor mobility patterns ", in *Journal of Human Resources* (Madison (Wisconsin)), Vol. II, No. 4, Fall 1967, pp. 461-474; J. Gugler: " On the theory of rural-urban migration: the case of sub-Saharan Africa ", in J. A. Jackson (ed.): *Sociological studies Two : migration* (Cambridge, University Press, 1969), pp. 134-155; John R. Harris and Michael P. Todaro: " Urban unemployment in East Africa: an economic analysis of policy alternatives ", in *East African Economic Review* (Nairobi), Vol. 4 (New Series), No. 2, Dec. 1968, pp. 17-36; and H. Rempel: " Labor migration into urban centers and urban unemployment in Kenya " (unpublished PhD dissertation, University of Wisconsin, 1970). See also C. R. Frank, Jr.: " The problem of urban unemployment in Africa ", Research Program in Economic Development, Discussion Paper No. 16, Princeton University, Nov. 1970, for a useful review of the literature on urban unemployment in Africa.

[1] W. Arthur Lewis: *Reflections on Nigeria's economic growth* (Paris, OECD Development Centre, 1967), p. 42.

[2] Dharam P. Ghai: " Incomes policy in Kenya: need, criteria and machinery ", in *East African Economic Review*, op. cit., Vol. 4 (New Series), June 1968, p. 20.

[3] For an analysis of the relationship between education and migration in Africa, see Michael P. Todaro: " Education and rural-urban migration: theoretical constructs and empirical evidence from Kenya ", paper prepared for the Conference on Urban Unemployment in Africa, Institute for Development Studies, University of Sussex, Sep. 1971, especially pp. 16-30.

1964 agricultural incomes remained essentially unchanged while minimum wages in government employment in Kampala rose by almost 200 per cent from £31 to £90 per annum.[1] It should be noted that in Uganda as in most other African nations the minimum wage often acts as the effective rate which determines the level at which more than 50 per cent of urban unskilled workers are paid. It is also the key weight in the overall wage structure since when the minimum wage changes, the entire wage structure tends to move with it.[2]

The second crucial element, which for the most part has not been formally included in other models of rural-urban migration, relates to the degree of probability that a migrant will be successful in securing an urban job. Without introducing the probability variable it would be extremely difficult to explain the continued and often accelerated rate of migration in the face of sizeable and growing pools of urban unemployed. Arguments about the irrationality of rural peasants who unwittingly migrate to urban areas permeated by widespread unemployment are as ill-conceived and culture-bound as earlier assertions that peasant subsistence farmers were unresponsive to price incentives. The key, in my opinion, to an understanding of the seemingly paradoxical phenomenon of continued migration to centres of high unemployment lies in viewing the migration process from an " expected " or permanent income approach where expected income relates not only to the actual wage paid to an urban worker, but also to the probability that he will be successful in securing wage employment in any given period of time. It is the combination and interaction of these two variables—the urban-rural real income differential and the probability of securing an urban job—which I believe determine the rate and magnitude of rural-urban migration in tropical Africa.

Consider the following illustration. Suppose the average unskilled or semi-skilled rural worker has a choice between being a farm labourer (or working his own land) for an annual average real income of, say, 50 units, or migrating to the city where a worker with his skill or educational background can obtain wage employment yielding an annual real income of 100 units. The more commonly used economic models of migration, which place exclusive emphasis on the income differential factor as the determinant of the decision to migrate, would indicate a clear choice in this situation. The worker should seek the higher-paying urban job. It is important to recognise, however, that these migration

[1] J. B. Knight: " The determination of wages and salaries in Uganda ", in *Bulletin of the Oxford University Institute of Economics and Statistics*, Vol. 29, No. 3, Aug. 1967, pp. 233-264.

[2] For a useful discussion of the relationship between wages and employment in Africa, see Elliot J. Berg: " Wage policy and employment in less developed countries ", paper prepared for the Overseas Study Committee Conference " Prospects for Employment Opportunities in the Nineteen-Seventies ", University of Cambridge, 1970.

models were developed largely in the context of advanced industrial economies and, as such, implicitly assume the existence of full employment or near-full employment. In a full employment environment the decision to migrate can in fact be predicated solely on securing the highest-paying job wherever it becomes available. Simple economic theory would then indicate that such migration should lead to a reduction in wage differentials through the interaction of the forces of supply and demand, both in areas of out-migration and in points of in-migration.

Unfortunately, such an analysis is not very realistic in the context of the institutional and economic framework of most of the nations of tropical Africa. First of all, these countries are beset by a chronic and serious unemployment problem with the result that a typical migrant cannot expect to secure a high-paying urban job immediately. In fact, it is much more likely that upon entering the urban labour market the migrant will either become totally unemployed or will seek casual and part-time employment in the urban traditional sector. Consequently, in his decision to migrate the individual in effect must balance the probabilities and risks of being unemployed or underemployed for a considerable period of time against the positive urban-rural real income differential. The fact that a typical migrant can expect to earn twice the annual real income in an urban area that he can in a rural environment may be of little consequence if his actual probability of securing the higher-paying job within, say, a one-year period is one chance in five. In such a situation we could say that his actual probability of being successful in securing the higher-paying urban job is 20 per cent, so that his " expected " urban income for the one-year period is in fact 20 units and not the 100 units that the fully employed urban worker receives. Thus, with a one-period time horizon and a probability of success of 20 per cent it would be irrational for this migrant to seek an urban job even though the differential between urban and rural earnings capacity is 100 per cent. On the other hand, if the probability of success were, say, 60 per cent, so that the expected urban income is 60 units, then it would be entirely rational for our migrant with his one-period time horizon to try his luck in the urban area even though urban unemployment may be extremely high.

If we now approach the situation more realistically by assuming a considerably longer time horizon, especially in view of the fact that the vast majority of migrants are between the ages of 15 and 23 years, then the decision to migrate should be represented on the basis of a longer-term, more permanent income calculation. If the migrant anticipates a relatively low probability of finding regular wage employment in the initial period but expects this probability to increase over time as he is able to broaden his urban contacts, then it would still be rational for him to migrate even though expected urban income during the initial period or periods might be lower than expected rural income. As long as the present value of the net stream of expected urban income over the migrant's planning horizon exceeds that of the expected rural income, the decision to migrate is justified.

The mathematical details of our model of rural-urban migration are set forth in the Appendix to this article. For our present purposes, suffice it to say that the model attempts to demonstrate the conditions under which the urban-rural " expected " income differential can act to exacerbate the urban *unemployment* situation even though urban *employment* might expand as a direct result of government policy. It all depends on the relationship between migration flows and the expected income differential as expressed in an " elasticity of migration response " term developed in the Appendix.

Since the elasticity of response will itself be directly related to the probability of finding a job and the size of the urban-rural real income differential, the model illustrates the paradox of a completely urban solution to the urban unemployment problem. Policies which operate solely on urban labour demand are not likely to be of much assistance in reducing urban unemployment since, in accordance with our expected income hypothesis, the growth of urban employment *ceteris paribus* also increases the rate of rural-urban migration. If the increase in the growth of the urban labour force caused by migration exceeds the increase in the growth of employment, the level of unemployment in absolute numbers will increase and the unemployment rate itself might also increase. This result will be accentuated if, for any increase in job creation, the urban real wage is permitted to expand at a greater rate than rural real income. A reduction or at least a slow growth in urban wages, therefore, has a dual beneficial effect in that it tends to reduce the rate of rural-urban migration and increase the demand for labour.

A second implication of the above model is that traditional methods of estimating the " shadow " price of rural labour to the urban sector will tend to have a downward bias if the migration response parameter is not taken into account. Typically, this shadow price has been expressed in terms of the marginal product of the rural worker who migrates to the city to secure the additional urban job. However, if for every additional urban job that is created more than one rural worker is induced to migrate, then the opportunity cost will reflect the combined loss of agricultural production of all those induced to migrate, not just the one who is fortunate enough to secure the urban position. It also follows that whenever there are sizeable pools of urban unemployed, traditional estimates of the shadow price of urban labour will reflect an upward bias.

Policies to alleviate urban unemployment and regulate the flow of rural-urban migration

Let us turn now to an examination of alternative policies which might be adopted to relieve the serious urban unemployment problem in tropical African nations. Throughout this examination I shall attempt wherever possible to utilise the analytical framework mentioned in the previous section and developed in the Appendix. Since the urban unemployment problem has short, intermediate and long-range dimensions and since there is a wide range of policies available, some of which can have a more immediate impact than others, I shall attempt to distinguish policies that are likely to have quicker results from those whose effects may be more of an intermediate or long-term nature.

Short-run policies

There are a whole series of possible policy options that can have a relatively short-run impact on both employment and unemployment. Of these, the most significant include (1) the elimination of present factor-price distortions, (2) the establishment of a " dual " wage structure through the use of wage subsidies in some combination with a policy of wage restraint, (3) the immediate creation of new types of employment opportunities through various voluntary agreements, and (4) the restriction of excess migration through the use of moral exhortation to return to the land, the adoption of forced controls on the movement of people, or the establishment of urban labour exchanges to regulate and control the process of job placement. Let us briefly examine each of these policies in turn.

1. ELIMINATING FACTOR-PRICE DISTORTIONS

With the benefit of hindsight, it is now becoming painfully apparent how the conventional wisdom of economic development theory which placed top priority on the rapid accumulation of capital as the key to successful economic progress in the 1950s and early 1960s has led to the serious employment predicament of the 1970s. Typically, a spectrum of policy devices ranging from overvalued exchange rates to accelerated capital depreciation allowances, tax rebates, licensing agreements, and negative effective rates of protection for imported capital goods was instituted, which effectively pushed the price of capital well below its real opportunity cost. On the other hand, in their natural and understandable desire to raise the standard of living of their working populations, African governments acquiesced to pressure both from trade unions and from civil servants in setting urban wage rates at levels considerably in excess of rural average incomes and the over-all opportunity cost of urban labour.

This combination of underpriced capital and overpriced labour has no doubt been a factor in retarding the expansion of urban employment opportunities by encouraging capital-labour substitution in the production process. Moreover, this implicit bias towards relatively capital-intensive methods of production has been aided and abetted by the policies of national aid agencies which continue to insist on tying considerable proportions of their aid to the importation of their own nation's capital equipment. The impact of this distorted factor-price structure is felt not only in urban areas where sophisticated modern equipment is being installed in almost all newly established industries, but also in rural agricultural areas where premature tractor mechanisation is being encouraged by similar policies relating to the importation of farm machinery.

The widespread existence of undervalued capital prices and wages in excess of labour's opportunity cost has also contributed to the influx of rural migrants in spite of the relatively slow growth of urban job openings. By mechanising their production efforts, employers in the modern sector are able to offer relatively high wages for their limited number of employees and unions are able to justify these high wages on the basis of rising levels of labour productivity even though this higher productivity is due not so much to the skills of the workers as to the equipment they are using.

It follows that one of the most immediate and pressing short-run policies that needs to be given serious consideration by governments in tropical Africa is one which attempts to " clear the decks " by eliminating factor-price distortions that inhibit increased labour absorption. In fact, given the pressing need for more employment creation from a political as well as from an economic standpoint, one might even argue that governments should consider the advisability of even distorting factor prices in the opposite direction. This could be achieved by discouraging the further importation of highly capital-intensive equipment by forcing the price of capital above its real opportunity cost, and reducing the effective labour price to producers through, for example, some system of wage subsidies. In any case, governments should at least think seriously about eliminating the current factor-price distortions.

2. WAGE SUBSIDIES AND WAGE RESTRAINT

One of the principal mechanisms for the partial elimination of factor-price distortions and the encouragement of more labour-intensive practices is the establishment of some form of " dual " wage structure that incorporates wage subsidies as part of an over-all employment-generating strategy. The establishment of a dual price structure has long been advocated and practised in other areas of economic activity like trade and agriculture through the use of multiple exchange rates and farm price supports. On *a priori* grounds there is no reason to assume that such a dual price structure would be less suitable for employment generation. Subsidies which lower the effective level of compensation that employers must pay their employees should have a stimulating employment effect so long as the wage elasticity of demand for labour is reasonably positive. A number of recent studies have confirmed the existence of such a positive elasticity.[1] For example, in a study of wages, employment and productivity in Kenya it was estimated that in the manufacturing sector of Kenyan industry the wage elasticity of demand for labour was approximately 0.76.[2] This would indicate that a 10 per cent reduction in wage costs for employers will stimulate a 7½ per cent increase in employment opportunities. Since a good proportion of the subsidy payments will be returned to the government in the form of higher taxation, both corporate and personal, it is reasonable to expect that a system of wage subsidies can operate somewhat in the manner of the traditional wages fund.

Unfortunately, one of the problems associated with any system of wage subsidies, especially when such subsidies are not part of a larger policy package, is that the actual wage paid to the employee will still be in excess of labour's opportunity cost. The result is that the higher wage is now being paid to a larger proportion of the urban workforce, a fact which in turn increases the probability that a typical migrant will be successful in securing a job. Using the model of rural-urban migration, I demonstrated earlier how such a situation could then lead to a worsening of the urban *unemployment* problem through increased migration even though more urban *employment* might be created.

It is essential, therefore, that any wage subsidy programme be accompanied by a general policy of wage restraint. Otherwise, the total effect of the subsidy might be negated by rising levels of over-all wages. From a strictly economic viewpoint, what is probably needed is a general reduction in over-all wages, but the political realities of developing nations usually preclude such a possibility. Nevertheless, as pointed out earlier, a policy of wage restraint can have a dual beneficial effect on the urban labour situation. A restraint on urban wage increases will tend to reduce the rate of rural-urban migration *and* increase the demand for employment. Without wage restraint, efforts to stimulate employment by reducing the capital-labour ratio through the elimination of some of the factor-price distortions referred to above can only have a limited success in reducing urban unemployment.

3. EMPLOYMENT CREATION BY VOLUNTARY AGREEMENT

Another policy of a short-term nature which has attracted considerable interest was the effort on the part of the Government of Kenya in 1964 to stimulate immediate employment creation through the establishment of a Tripartite Agreement between itself, employers, and the trade

[1] See, for example, Lloyd G. Reynolds: " Wages and employment in a labor-surplus economy ", in *American Economic Review*, op. cit., Vol. LV, No. 1, Mar. 1965, pp. 19-39; and John R. Harris and Michael P. Todaro: " Wages, industrial employment and labour productivity: the Kenyan experience ", in *Eastern Africa Economic Review* (Nairobi), June 1969, pp. 29-46.

[2] Harris and Todaro: " Wages, industrial employment...", op. cit., p. 36.

unions. Under this Agreement, the Government and the employers were to increase their total employment by 15 per cent and 10 per cent respectively, while the trade unions, for their part, agreed to hold the line on all wage demands for a twelve-month period. Upon expiry the Agreement was extended for an additional three months. While no detailed study of this most interesting experiment has been undertaken, it is widely believed that the Tripartite Agreement did not have any lasting long-term effect on employment generation. For example, Professor Dharam Ghai of the Institute for Development Studies in Nairobi made the following observations on the 1964 Tripartite Agreement:

> Owing to financial stringency, the Government found itself unable to carry out its pledge. In all, 34,000 jobs were found for persons who were either landless or previously unemployed. But it is doubtful whether these represented a net increase in employment; for while many of the private firms adhered to the letter of the agreement by taking on more employees, they violated its intent by not hiring new employees to make good the loss caused by normal attrition of the labour force. Furthermore, even if the agreement was successful in creating some new jobs, it did not make any particular impact on the level of urban unemployment, for prospects of wage employment stimulated an additional flow of migrants from the rural areas. It is clear that policies of this nature can create additional employment only in the very short-run period.[1]

Once again, our model of rural-urban migration can shed some interesting light on policies such as the Tripartite Agreement which are intended to eliminate or alleviate urban unemployment through a mechanism which attempts essentially to circumvent economic forces. The Tripartite Agreement provides an excellent example of the crucial importance of the probability factor in the decision to migrate. By requiring employers to increase the number of job openings by a certain percentage and blocking any increases in urban wage rates for a fifteen-month period, the Agreement effectively increased the probability that a migrant would successfully secure a job while ensuring that the wage differential would be held constant. Our model tells us that in such a situation there should be an accelerated flow of rural-urban migration resulting from the widening of the " expected " income differential even though the actual differential remains unchanged. This is in fact what actually happened in Kenya immediately following the announcement of the Agreement, when there was a massive influx from the rural areas of job seekers who had learned of the move to increase employment opportunities. The result of the entire process as pointed out by Ghai [2], Harbison [3] and others was that actual levels of urban *unemployment*

[1] Dharam P. Ghai: " Employment performance, prospects and policies in Kenya ", paper prepared for the Overseas Study Committee Conference " Prospects for Employment Opportunities in the Nineteen-Seventies ", University of Cambridge, 1970, p. 11.

[2] Ibid.

[3] Frederick H. Harbison: " The generation of employment in newly developing countries ", in James R. Sheffield (ed.): *Education, employment and rural development* (Nairobi, East African Publishing House, 1967), pp. 173-193.

probably increased whereas the over-all level of *employment* did not change substantially.

It is interesting to note that in June 1970 the Government of Kenya announced another Tripartite Agreement under which both it and private firms were required to increase their employment rolls by 10 per cent. Early reports indicated once again that the net impact of this second attempt at instant employment creation was a further increase in the level of urban unemployment.

The above observations are not meant to belittle the potential importance of voluntary agreements such as those initiated by the Kenyan Government but rather to emphasise the point that when short-run policies are not accompanied by more basic long-run structural changes in the economic system they can have very limited lasting effects.

4. RESTRICTIONS ON MIGRATION

Short-run attempts to ease the urban unemployment problem can also take the form of efforts to restrict the accelerated influx of rural migrants whose chances of securing an urban job are minimal. These policies can range from simple " moral exhortations " to return to the land, as has been intermittently practised by the Kenyan Government, to enforced back-to-the-land movements such as that practised for some time in Tanzania, and the establishment of labour exchanges to control the flow of migration in accordance with job openings, a policy which has been suggested recently by a number of observers.

Exhortations that individuals should return to the land to seek opportunities in agriculture rather than migrating to the cities in a vain search for jobs have been heard repeatedly in speeches by political leaders in East Africa. While these pleas are admirable and economically sound, their ultimate success is highly doubtful. If our model correctly describes the economics of migration it is in the self-interest of individuals to seek urban employment even though the probability of actually finding it is low. Throughout history, policies of moral suasion have met with limited success in persuading individuals to abandon their self-interest. When the social and the private interest do not coincide it is rare that private calculations do not prevail.

A more direct effort to regulate the flow of rural-urban migration, one which forces the urban unemployed to return to their rural areas, has been instituted by the Government of Tanzania, though the policy has not been carried out with exceptional vigour. Individuals in urban areas of Tanzania are required to hold cards stamped to show that they are presently employed. If they cannot produce one they are liable to be returned either to their home area in the countryside or to some other rural location if they are landless. Clearly, if the urban unemployed are individuals who have productive opportunities available to them in rural areas, as most do in the case of Tanzania, the successful repatriation of the unemployed can result in a net increase in national output and thus be socially productive. But, as in the case of moral suasion, it is extremely difficult to convince individuals acting in their own private interests that both the net national interest and the social benefit would be best served by their returning to the rural areas. Along these lines, it is interesting to note that Tanzania is already experiencing difficulties in keeping the repatriated urban unemployed on farm settlements. This is not too surprising given the substantial expected real earnings differential, even though Tanzania has attempted to hold the line on urban wage increases. Moreover, there has been no real attempt to compensate the repatriated workers. In summary, while Tanzania's policy of enforced repatriation represents a promising approach to the problem of urban unemployment, its probable success is at best very limited.

Gugler has recently suggested an interesting alternative short-run approach to restrict migration in countries that have rural opportunities for their urban unemployed.[1] Recognising the importance of the probability variable in the decision to migrate and the fact that most migrants are prepared to risk being unemployed for a considerable period of time, Gugler suggests that, instead of letting individual migrants gamble in the hope of being selected, the government should play the lottery for them through the institution of urban labour exchanges. His idea is that if all employment openings were to be channelled through government labour exchanges, these exchanges would be able to give definitive answers to new migrants on whether or not they will be successful in obtaining a job. Those unsuccessful, having been told that there is no employment for them at that time and that they will not be reconsidered at a later time could thus be persuaded, in Gugler's opinion, to return to their rural homes after a short stay in town. To be successful such a programme would need the full co-operation of employers and a high standard of record keeping at the labour exchanges so that it would be possible to recognise and refuse the man who applied for a second time even though he might change his name.

While I agree that this is an intriguing idea and probably a better approach than simple moral suasion, I am extremely doubtful of its feasibility as an actual policy. In addition to the severe resource and book-keeping problems that would be involved, especially since one would need to have much more than the mere names of rejected migrants, there is the additional and obvious problem of bureaucratic corruption, tribal preferences, and the relinquishment of the individual employer's right to decide who he will hire and who he will not hire. Consequently, of the three short-run approaches to migration restriction, the Tanzanian

[1] Gugler, op. cit.

plan of forced repatriation is probably the most feasible though it too can give rise to serious administrative and political difficulties.

Intermediate-term policies

In addition to the four policy options outlined above, all of which are intended to have more immediate effects on employment generation, there are a number of policies whose impact on job creation can be more lasting and significant although perhaps not as immediately visible as the short-run measures. Three of the most important intermediate term strategies include (1) the establishment of a comprehensive incomes policy, (2) the acceleration of rates of industrial and urban output growth, and (3) the intensification of efforts to stimulate agricultural and rural development.

1. A COMPREHENSIVE INCOMES POLICY

Any serious attempt to tackle the dual problem of massive rural-urban migration and rising unemployment must have as its primary objective the gradual elimination of the substantial and economically unwarranted differential between urban and rural real earnings capacity. In the absence of effective migration control, any policy which attempts to stimulate job creation in the urban areas without at the same time attempting to redress the serious imbalance between urban and rural income levels can only result in ultimate frustration, since any increase in jobs created is likely to be offset by a more rapid increase in new job seekers. Consequently, there is an important need gradually to align urban wage incomes more closely with average incomes in the agricultural sector.

The need for a comprehensive national income and wages policy in efforts to generate more employment opportunities, as well as to remove some of the inequities in the distribution of income, has been a subject of considerable recent discussion. As was pointed out earlier, wages affect the employment problem in two ways. First, rapidly rising urban wage rates tend to reduce the level of employment or to limit its expansion in a growing economy by exerting financial pressure on employers to economise on the use of labour. In the case of Kenya, recent empirical studies have indicated that a decline in annual increases in urban wage rates from, say, 6 per cent to 2 per cent would generate approximately 15,000 additional jobs per year. Second, by increasing the gap which already exists between rural and urban real incomes, rising wages may accentuate the urban unemployment problem by stimulating additional rural-urban migration. It is because of this doubly deleterious effect of rapidly rising wage rates that a programme of wage restraint has to be part of an over-all incomes policy.

Since the vast majority of the population of tropical Africa is agrarian-based, it makes considerable economic sense, as well as being more equitable, to attempt to relate minimum wage rates of unskilled workers in paid employment to the average level of agricultural incomes. This is because the minimum wage rate tends to be the most strategic single rate in most African wage structures.[1] The moral case for equity in income distribution is obvious. The economic rationality of such a wage policy is also clear. By eliminating the artificial incentive for disproportionate migration (which may be privately rational but is also socially costly), an effective policy of urban wage realignment can have an important and positive intermediate-term impact on the national output by improving the distribution of income arising from that national output and generating employment opportunities in both rural and urban areas.

A second aspect of a comprehensive incomes policy directed at the creation of more job opportunities might focus on the use of the tax structure to complement policies of wage restraint in reducing the rural-urban real income differential. Tax concessions can be used to provide incentives to employers to accelerate the marginal rate of labour absorption within their firms as output expands. It is well known that many of the tax structures in contemporary African nations are both regressive in their over-all structure and biased against the agricultural sector in particular. In the absence of a policy of wage restraint or in combination with a policy of gradual wage increases, governments can use their tax powers to reduce the level of effective income differentials. A disproportionately high tax on urban wages, for example, can act as a disincentive to further rural-urban migration in the same way as an actual reduction in money wages. Moreover, if the revenue generated from such taxes, as well as from comparable taxes on urban business profits, were to be redirected towards the rural sector in the form of direct transfer payments or rural development projects, then it could be a powerful mechanism for removing some of the present artificial distortions between urban and rural economic opportunities.

Finally, instead of using the tax structure as an incentive for rapid capital accumulation through depreciation guidelines and tax rebates, governments can contribute to the growth of new employment opportunities by instead providing incentives for additional employment creation through these very same tax powers. In any case, the effective formulation and implementation of a well-planned incomes policy can be a powerful potential weapon in the fight against unemployment in urban Africa. It will be most interesting to follow the progress of the comprehensive incomes policy recently instituted by the Government of Kenya, which includes a determined attempt to restrain urban wage increases.

---

[1] See, for example, Ghai: " Incomes policy in Kenya . . .", op. cit.: and Berg, op. cit.

2. ACCELERATING INDUSTRIAL OUTPUT GROWTH

A panacea often prescribed by economists for almost all the ills of developing nations is rapid industrial modernisation. In fact, the dilemma which many of the African nations face today regarding their employment problem can be said to have arisen partially as a result of a mistaken impression about the primacy of industrial development and import substitution at the expense of agricultural progress and export promotion in the over-all growth process. Many treatises on economic development define the success of various programmes in terms of the ability of the country to reallocate a majority of its labour force from agriculture to industry. Implicit in the assumption of almost all these development models is the belief that industrial output growth will be accompanied by comparable employment growth so that the employment problem will be indirectly solved by the expansion of aggregate output.

Unfortunately, most cross-sectional and time series evidence on the relationship between industrial growth and employment generation in less developed countries provides a uniformly consistent picture of a significant employment lag. It is well known, for example, that in the three East African countries this employment lag has not only been significant but for quite a prolonged period (the late 1950s and early 1960s) there was in fact a negative relationship—i.e. employment in manufacturing actually declined absolutely while output expanded. Numerous reasons can be cited to account for this phenomenon, including the rapid rise in urban wages, the increased mechanisation of production, and the improved efficiency of those already employed as a result of learning-by-doing and on-the-job training programmes. The crucial point to be made in this context, however, is that even though rapid industrial output growth, if successfully achieved, might indeed create more employment opportunities, it will also accentuate the influx of rural migrants unless simultaneous steps are taken to reduce rural-urban real differentials. Consequently, as demonstrated earlier, the net result of increased industrial growth might be not only an increase in urban employment but also a concomitant increase in urban unemployment.

Our intention here is not to denigrate policies designed to expand industrial output as a means of creating more employment opportunities, but rather to counter some of the unfortunate euphoric assertions made about the ability of a nation to solve its growing unemployment problem merely by expanding its aggregate level of total output. Clearly, output expansion is a necessary prerequisite for employment creation. But the type of production technology utilised in achieving it as well as the industrial composition of the aggregate expansion can have considerably more impact on the success of employment generation than the mere achievement of the output growth target. More labour-intensive output growth is what is needed in conjunction with a package of policies to increase the economic attractions of rural life concurrently with the expansion of urban job opportunities.

3. INTENSIVE AGRICULTURAL AND RURAL DEVELOPMENT

Policies which operate on the demand side of the urban employment picture such as wage subsidies, direct government hiring, elimination of factor-price distortions, and employer tax incentives are probably considerably less effective in the long run in alleviating the *unemployment* problem than are policies designed directly to regulate the supply of labour to urban areas. Policies of rural development are crucial in this regard. Close and informed observers of the African scene such as Lewis, Harbison, Eicher [1], Frank and Hunter all agree on the central importance of rural and agricultural development if the urban unemployment problem is to be effectively solved. The ultimate objective of almost all proposals for rural development as a means of improving the unemployment situation is the restoration of a proper balance between rural and urban incomes and the elimination of ill-conceived government policies which greatly bias development programmes towards the urban industrial sector.

A plethora of proposals designed to increase rural real incomes and amenity levels have been advanced in recent years. Some of the more basic ones have been concerned with the provision of needed amenities such as electricity, piped water, clinics, cinemas, etc., in rural areas so as to reduce the relative attraction of urban centres, particularly for school leavers. Other proposals have included rural settlement schemes, extension services, and training centres. Still others have stressed the importance of locating industry in rural areas so as to spread non-agricultural employment opportunities. Finally, one of the most common suggestions for creating rural employment opportunities is the creation of extensive schemes for labour-intensive rural works. We may note that all the above proposals essentially have one common denominator—they attempt to reduce the urban-rural disparities in *real* income (where real income includes the effects of amenities) and thus the magnet effect of the city.

While the provision of resettlement, extension services, training schemes, rural amenities, and rural-based industries are likely to be effective in increasing rural incomes and therefore to work towards a reduction of the urban-rural differential, the proposals for extensive rural works programmes are particularly interesting. Such works programmes would very likely reduce urban-rural real wage gaps in a number of direct ways. First, individuals could be employed on such projects during non-peak periods in agriculture. They would thus sacrifice less

[1] C. Eicher *et al.*: *Employment generation in African agriculture*, Institute of International Agriculture, Research Report No. 9, Michigan State University, July 1970.

agricultural income in accepting employment of this sort than in migrating to urban areas. Furthermore, the effect of the feeder roads, irrigation schemes, dams, etc., built through such programmes would be to raise agricultural productivity—thus further reducing real income differentials. However, programmes of this type do require inputs of scarce organisational resources if they are to be successful and they also place substantial burdens on the fiscal system or on external aid sources for their finance.

Extensive rural works programmes appear to have been carried out successfully in a number of countries including Tunisia and East Pakistan. In the case of a country such as Kenya, with its considerable experience of successful self-help efforts that have resulted in the creation of hundreds of new schools, health centres and community halls in rural areas, rural works programmes can be built upon the existing foundation of vigour and initiative of voluntary effort at the local level. With appropriate planning on the part of local authorities and the necessary financial commitment on the part of the central government and external aid agencies, it should not be difficult to mount large-scale labour-intensive rural works programmes, thus providing not only immediate employment and income opportunities for rural workers but also the infrastructure required for the longer-run development of rural areas.

Our discussion of rural development has concerned itself exclusively up to this point with non-agricultural aspects of economic progress. However, there also exists considerable scope for output expansion directly within the agricultural sector itself. For example, in their carefully documented and stimulating analysis of employment prospects in African agriculture, Eicher and his colleagues have observed that "Africa's smallholder land tenure system is remarkably labour absorptive provided incentives are available at the farm level".[1] They argue that as long as African governments avoid premature tractor mechanisation, anti-export agricultural policies, autarkic food policies, and an over-emphasis on government capital-intensive direct production schemes, there is considerable potential for significant increases in labour absorption in the agricultural sector itself. Moreover, they note that it is only a matter of time before the new high-yielding varieties of maize and wheat (and possibly of other food crops), with their dramatic potential for increases in output and income, become widely available and adopted in African nations. With careful planning, these new technologies of food production can be made directly applicable to small as well as to large farmers. Considerable research along these lines is currently being conducted at the International Institute of Tropical Agriculture in Nigeria.

Clearly, the adoption and utilisation of the new high-yielding varieties offer the potential for immediate increases in employment

[1] Eicher *et al.*, op. cit., p. 57.

through the emergence of possibilities for multiple cropping and the increased need for farm labour. The longer-run employment effects of the new technology can be equally significant if effective measures are taken to prevent unwarranted and premature mechanisation of farm production techniques through artificial incentives to import capital equipment.

Long-run policies for employment expansion

In the previous two sections I have explored various short- and intermediate-term policy options available to African governments intent upon expanding over-all employment opportunities and curtailing the disproportionate influx of rural migrants to urban areas. In this final section I shall examine two long-run objectives whose achievement is, in my opinion, a necessary part of any general programme for successful economic development with significant labour participation. The first, and more obvious, of these policies relates to the establishment and maintenance of an effective programme to limit rapid population growth. The second, less obvious but no less important, long-run policy concerns the necessity for less developed African nations ultimately to free themselves from their current technological dependence on the importation of machinery and equipment designed in advanced countries in accordance with the latter's needs. Long-run efforts need to be initiated to plan for the eventual development of their own labour-intensive capital goods industry whose production can be directly responsive to the resource needs and requirements of the African countries themselves.

1. LIMITING POPULATION GROWTH

Although most nations of tropical Africa are not at this time faced with the severe population pressures that are currently being experienced by many countries of south and south-east Asia, the rate of population growth in Africa is currently the highest in the world. Population growth rates in excess of 3 per cent per annum are common south of the Sahara. At such rates of growth, it is only a matter of time before the awful spectre of overpopulation becomes clearly visible.

A successful programme of population control can make a significant contribution over the long run not only to the achievement of the major social and economic objectives of development plans, but more specifically to the ultimate elimination of the problem of unemployment. For example, in Kenya the current rate of population growth is adding 126,000 persons to the labour force every year; the annual increment in the labour force associated with a 2.5 per cent, 1.5 per cent, and a 1 per cent increase would be 95,000, 57,000, and 38,000 additional people respectively. These figures illustrate quite clearly how even small reductions in over-all rates of population growth can significantly affect prospects for reducing or eliminating urban and rural unemployment. While it is true that for the immediate and intermediate period, i.e. the next fifteen to twenty years, the population size and distribution has been fixed by past levels of births and deaths so that population control will have a limited immediate impact on unemployment, it should not be forgotten that a large number of children can represent a severe drain on a family's financial resources and thus be a deterrent to savings and investment. Recent empirical evidence has shown that savings rates are strongly influenced by dependency ratios which in turn are determined by the rates of over-all population growth.[1] Moreover, a country with a lower rate of population growth has less need to invest its scarce resources in schools, hospitals and other elements of the economic infrastructure, and can divert them to more directly productive projects with lower capital-output ratios and higher rates of per unit labour utilisation. Thus we see that even though a declining rate of population growth will have its major labour force impact only in the long run, it can have some immediate and significant effects on employment creation indirectly through its impact on the aggregate level of savings and the allocation of public and private resources.

2. GENERATING DOMESTIC LABOUR-INTENSIVE TECHNOLOGICAL CAPABILITIES

One of the principal inhibiting factors to the success of any long-run programme of labour absorption both in the urban industrial as well as in the rural agricultural sector is the complete technological dependence of contemporary African nations on machinery and equipment developed in the advanced industrial nations. In essence, the developing nations of Africa have no choice but to use the capital-intensive technology which has been developed in, by and for the richer industrial countries and must be imported from them. Moreover, since almost 98 per cent of all research and development on new technologies originates in advanced industrial societies, the less developed countries will remain technologically dependent for years to come if nothing is done about the problem. With most available technology being relatively capital intensive in design, the scope for utilising relatively labour-intensive equipment is limited for the most part to the importation of the used and discarded technology of a previous historical period.

When choosing among the available alternatives, less developed nations should make every effort to find and select those parts of modern technology which are of direct value to themselves and which do not

[1] Nathaniel H. Leff: " Dependency rates and savings rates ", in *American Economic Review* (Menasha (Wisconsin)), Vol. LIX, No. 5, Dec. 1969, pp. 886-896.

inhibit employment creation. Many of the efforts to find and utilise " intermediate " technologies have this aim. The only other alternative is to attempt to adapt imported technology to local needs. As the history of Japanese development and the contemporary records of Korea indicate, there is considerable scope for indigenous capital-stretching through the more intensive utilisation of existing machinery, the handling, transporting and packaging of materials within the plant by human instead of mechanical means, and by the training of skilled personnel to repair and replace damaged machinery parts.

In addition to the actual equipment, there is a range of complementary factors which together give imported technology a capital-intensive rather than a labour-intensive twist. Private foreign investors, as well as aid donors, have tended to emphasise the supply of imported capital equipment of the most sophisticated nature for their own pet projects; and technicians, planners, advisers, contractors and consultants are typically imported from abroad or trained abroad or even when trained at home they still tend to be acquainted with the most modern technologies available and are very unfamiliar with alternative possibilities. Finally, the planners, politicians and even the people themselves in developing countries take a natural pride in big and expensive capital structures which are often looked upon as being synonomous with economic development and modernisation.

Since both the mechanism and the dynamics of technology transfer are such that less developed countries have little or no influence on either the production technique they use today or the technique it would be most desirable to use in the future, the task of effectively absorbing large increments of the labour force into an over-all framework of industrial and agricultural progress is made that much more difficult.

The question then arises as to what are the alternatives. I have recently argued that the only real and viable long-run alternative is for the developing countries themselves, either singly or preferably in co-operation, to begin the task of generating their own technology through the creation of a capital goods industry that will be responsive to the unique needs of labour-surplus societies.[1] The creation of indigenous capital goods industries will require for the most part the training of engineers and scientists with creative as well as technological capabilities. It will be a long-run process and will of necessity require the co-operation and the technical and financial aid of advanced societies. One possible way of overcoming the initial administrative, financial and skill requirements of such an enterprise might be through the creation of a series of Regional Institutes for the Development of Labour-Intensive Technologies along the lines of the very successful programmes sponsored by the

[1] Michael P. Todaro: " Some thoughts on the transfer of technology from developed to less developed nations ", in *Eastern Africa Economic Review*, op. cit., June 1970, pp. 53-64.

Rockefeller and Ford Foundations establishing research institutes for the development of new high-yielding food varieties. If such institutes had links both with the government and private industries so as to identify important potential growth areas with significant capacity for labour absorption, and if the necessary training component were built into the over-all operation, then the direct income and employment benefits could begin to accrue relatively soon. Just as the operations and research within the international agricultural institutes have gradually been taken over by indigenous personnel, so too the ultimate technological capacities within these regional research institutes might be assumed by indigenous scientists and engineers. Clearly, serious thought needs to be given immediately to the feasibility and possibility of the creation of such technological institutes. The alternative of continued technological dependence is, to say the least, very grim.

Conclusions

I have attempted in this article to set forth the economic basis for rural-urban migration in tropical Africa and have tried to explain the reasons for the continued influx of rural migrants in spite of rising levels of urban unemployment. My examination of alternative short-, intermediate- and long-run policies for relieving the urban unemployment problem had as its common focus and theme the gradual elimination of the wide disparities between " expected " urban and rural real incomes.

Clearly, what is needed if any real impact is to be made on the unemployment problem is not a single policy but a " package " of policies including those whose effects are more immediate, as well as those whose impact will be felt in the longer run. If I were asked to identify and put together such a package of policies, my inclination would be to argue for the immediate elimination of factor-price distortions, especially with regard to the price of capital, a comprehensive incomes policy in which urban wage restraint is an important element, a redirection of present development priorities towards concentrated and comprehensive programmes of rural development including efforts to repatriate and resettle unemployed urban migrants, and a major effort on a regional basis focused on the establishment of indigenous capital goods industries capable of designing and developing labour-intensive technologies for both agriculture and industry. Finally, some programme for controlling excessive population growth is necessary even though this is unlikely to be welcomed by all African governments at the present time. Without such a package of policies, the ubiquitous problem of growing urban unemployment in Africa promises to become economically more severe and politically more explosive in the coming years.

APPENDIX

A Mathematical Model of Rural-Urban Migration

Consider the following formulation of the theory of rural-urban migration used in this article. I begin by assuming that individuals base their decision to migrate on considerations of income maximisation and that their calculations are founded on what they perceive to be their expected income streams in urban and rural areas. It is further assumed that the individual who chooses to migrate is attempting to achieve the prevailing average income for his level of education or skill attainment in the urban centre of his choice. Nevertheless, he is assumed to be aware of his limited chances of immediately securing wage employment and the likelihood that he will be unemployed or underemployed for a certain period of time. It follows that the migrant's expected income stream is determined both by the prevailing income in the modern sector and the probability of being employed there, rather than being underemployed in the traditional sector or totally unemployed.

If we let $V(0)$ be the discounted present value of the expected " net " urban-rural income stream over the migrant's time horizon; $Y_{u,r}(t)$ the average real incomes of individuals employed in the urban and the rural economy; n the number of time periods in the migrant's planning horizon; and r the discount rate reflecting the migrant's degree of time preference, then the decision to migrate or not will depend on whether

$$V(0) = \int_{t=0}^{n} \left[p(t) Y_u(t) - Y_r(t) \right] e^{-rt} dt - C(0)$$

is positive or negative, where

$C(0)$ represents the cost of migration, and

$p(t)$ is the probability that a migrant will have secured an urban job at the average income level in period t.

In any one time period, the probability of being employed in the modern sector, $p(t)$, will be directly related to the probability π of having been selected in that or any previous period from a given stock of unemployed or underemployed job seekers. If we assume that for most migrants the selection procedure is random, then the probability of having a job in the modern sector within x periods after migration, $p(x)$, is:

$$p(1) = \pi(1)$$

and

$$p(2) = \pi(1) + [1 - \pi(1)]\pi(2)$$

so that

$$p(x) = p(x-1) + [1 - p(x-1)]\pi(x)$$

or

$$p(x) = \pi(1) + \sum_{t=2}^{x} \pi(t) \prod_{s=1}^{t-1} \left[1 - \pi(s) \right]$$

where

$\pi(t)$ equals the ratio of new job openings relative to the number of accumulated job aspirants in period t.

It follows from this probability formulation that for any given level of $Y_u(t)$ and $Y_r(t)$, the longer the migrant has been in the city the higher his probability p of having a job and the higher, therefore, is his expected income in that period.

Formulating the probability variable in this way has two advantages: (1) it avoids the " all or nothing " problem of having to assume that the migrant either earns the average income or earns nothing in the periods immediately following migration: consequently, it reflects the fact that many underemployed migrants will be able to generate some income in the urban traditional sector while searching for a regular job; and (2) it modifies somewhat the assumption of random selection since the probability of a migrant having been selected varies directly with the time he has been in the city. This permits adjustments for the fact that longer-term migrants usually have more contacts and better information systems so that their expected incomes should be higher than those of newly arrived migrants with similar skills.

Suppose we now incorporate this behaviouristic theory of migration into a simple aggregate dynamic equilibrium model of urban labour demand and supply in the following manner. We once again define the probability π of obtaining a job in the urban sector in any one time period as being directly related to the rate of new employment creation and inversely related to the ratio of unemployed job seekers to the number of existing job opportunities, that is—

$$(1)\ \pi = \frac{\gamma N}{S-N}$$

where γ is the net rate of urban new job creation, N is the level of urban employment, and S is the total urban labour force.

If w is the urban real wage rate and r represents average rural real income, then the " expected " urban-rural real income differential d is—

$$(2)\ d = w \cdot \pi - r$$

or, substituting (1) into (2)—

$$(3)\ d = w \cdot \frac{\gamma N}{S-N} - r$$

The basic assumption of our model once again is that the supply of labour to the urban sector is a function of the urban-rural *expected* real income differential, i.e.—

$$(4)\ S = f_S(d)$$

If the rate of urban job creation is a function of the urban wage w and a policy parameter a, e.g. a concentrated governmental effort to increase employment through a comprehensive programme of industrial import substitution or, as in the case of Kenya, the 1964 and 1970 Tripartite Agreements to raise employment levels, both of which operate on labour demand, we have—

$$(5)\ \gamma = f_d(w; a)$$

where it is assumed that $\frac{\partial \gamma}{\partial a} > 0$. If the growth in the urban labour demand is increased as a result of the governmental policy shift, the increase in the urban labour supply is—

$$(6)\ \frac{\partial S}{\partial a} = \frac{\partial S}{\partial d}\frac{\partial d}{\partial \gamma}\frac{\partial \gamma}{\partial a}$$

Differentiating (3) and substituting into (6), we obtain—

$$(7)\ \frac{\partial S}{\partial a} = \frac{\partial S}{\partial d}\, w \frac{N}{S-N} \cdot \frac{\partial \gamma}{\partial a}$$

The absolute number of urban unemployed will increase if the increase in labour supply exceeds the increase in the number of new jobs created, i.e. if—

$$(8)\quad \frac{\partial S}{\partial a} > \frac{\partial(\gamma N)}{\partial a} = \frac{N\partial\gamma}{\partial a}$$

Combining (7) and (8), we get—

$$(9)\quad \frac{\partial S}{\partial d} w \frac{N}{S-N} \cdot \frac{\partial\gamma}{\partial a} > \frac{N\partial\gamma}{\partial a}$$

or—

$$(10)\quad \frac{\partial S/S}{\partial d/d} > \frac{d}{w} \cdot \frac{(S-N)}{S}$$

or, finally, substituting for *d*—

$$(11)\quad \frac{\partial S/S}{\partial d/d} > \frac{w \cdot \pi - r}{w} \cdot \frac{(S-N)}{S}$$

Expression (11) reveals that the absolute level of unemployment will rise if the elasticity of urban labour supply with respect to the expected urban-rural income differential, $\frac{\partial S/S}{\partial d/d}$, (what I have called elsewhere the " migration response function ") exceeds the urban-rural differential as a proportion of the urban wage times the unemployment rate, $\frac{S-N}{S}$. Alternatively, equation (11) shows that the higher the unemployment rate, the higher must be the elasticity to increase the level of unemployment for any expected real income differential. But note that in most developing nations the inequality (11) will be satisfied by a very low elasticity of supply when realistic figures are used. For example, if the urban real wage is 60, average rural real income is 20, the probability of getting a job is ·50 and the unemployment rate is 20 per cent, then the level of unemployment will increase if the elasticity of urban labour supply is greater than ·033, i.e. substituting into (11) we get—

$$\frac{\partial S/S}{\partial d/d} = \frac{\cdot 50 \times 60 - 20}{60} \times \cdot 20 = \cdot 033$$

Clearly, much more needs to be known about the empirical value of this elasticity coefficient in different African nations before one can realistically predict what the impact of a policy to generate more urban *employment* will be on the over-all level of urban *unemployment*.

The Manpower and Employment Aspects of Selected Experiences of Agricultural Development in Tropical Africa

John C. de WILDE [1]

I. Introduction: the nature of the problem

It is now generally recognised that agriculture will for a long time have to absorb most of the available labour force in the less developed countries.[2] This is particularly true of tropical Africa, where the somewhat limited markets for manufactured products together with the application of modern methods of industrial production are likely to generate only slow increases in non-agricultural employment.[3]

The maximisation of employment on the land is not, however, always a conscious objective of development strategy. The primary emphasis has usually been on achieving the greatest possible increase in output, and this is not always reconcilable with maximum expansion of agricultural employment in the country as a whole. International and bilateral agencies financing agricultural development concentrate on the project approach, and in calculating the economic returns of projects they frequently regard labour as a cost of production. On occasion they

---

[1] Special Adviser, Western Africa Department, International Bank for Reconstruction and Development.

[2] See, for instance, Werner Bauer and Michel E. A. Hervé: *Employment and industrialization in developing countries* (Center Paper No. 80, Yale University Economics Growth Center, New Haven, 1970); and Elliot J. Berg in *Wages and employment in less developed countries* (Center for Research and Economic Development, University of Michigan, Discussion Paper No. 13, OECD Conference on Unemployment, Montebello (Quebec)).

[3] Carl Eicher, Thomas Zallas, James Kocker, and Fred Winch: *Employment generation in African agriculture* (Institute of International Agriculture, Michigan State University, East Lansing (Michigan), July 1970).

do take into account the " opportunity cost " rather than the nominal market value of labour and when this happens they may even evaluate such opportunity cost at zero or close to zero. This is, however, still a long way from regarding the creation of additional opportunities for the employment of labour as a positive benefit. There may accordingly be a need, in appropriate circumstances, to take into account the " value added " by an agricultural project. Moreover, the project approach may lead to excessive emphasis on schemes with the highest rates of economic return. This would be a perfectly justifiable procedure if one could assume that rural populations were free to move both within a country and across the boundaries of countries to areas where the highest economic returns can be achieved. Unfortunately, such an assumption is hardly realistic. For the most part agricultural development must take place where people are settled, since opportunities for permanent migration are limited. In these circumstances the minimum rate of return required must vary in accordance with the opportunities available. If in any country projects with only the highest rates of return are accepted, this may well result in neglect of comparatively poor and yet populous agricultural regions and thus aggravate the pressures towards urban migration and urban unemployment.[1]

Complexity of the employment problem

It should be recognised from the outset that the agricultural employment problem is extremely complex. Many regions in Africa are characterised simultaneously by severe seasonal labour bottlenecks and by chronic underemployment of labour over most of the year. Complete rural unemployment does not, to my knowledge, exist to any significant degree. Seasonal labour bottlenecks and seasonal labour surpluses characterise particularly the savanna areas of Africa, where the rainfall pattern permits only a single cropping season and severely limits its duration. Labour requirements are therefore telescoped. Immediately following the advent of the rains, the land must be prepared and the crops planted, so that they can properly mature during the brief growing season. During this time all or virtually all of the available labour resources must be mobilised. Then, very soon after planting, there is a burgeoning of weeds, leading also to the full utilisation of labour for weeding. There may be another labour bottleneck during harvesting,

---

[1] In this connection it should be noted that recent investigations have shown that it becomes rational to migrate to urban areas even if there is only a 50 per cent or even a 33 per cent probability of obtaining a job, because urban wages are generally so much higher than agricultural wages. See J. R. Harris and M. P. Todaro: *A two sector model of migration with urban unemployment in developing countries*, Massachusetts Institute of Technology Working Paper No. 33 (Cambridge (Massachusetts), 1968), and " Migration, unemployment and development: a two-sector analysis ", in *American Economic Review* (Menasha (Wisconsin)), Vol. LX, No. 1, Mar. 1970, pp. 126-142, and Todaro's study above.

although in most cases harvesting can be stretched over a longer and more flexible period of time. During some parts of the agricultural season, however, and more particularly during the dry season, there is little or no work.

Under such conditions attention must be focused on cropping patterns and methods of production which will, on the one hand, avoid an aggravation of labour bottlenecks or facilitate their removal and, on the other, bring about fuller employment during more of the year and command higher incomes. It is idle, for example, to urge farmers to plant both their food crops and such cash crops as cotton early in the season even though agricultural research stations can demonstrate that yields increase in proportion to early planting. Farmers adjust their pattern of production and the timing of their farm operations to the availability of labour. They will generally concentrate first on planting food crops on which their basic livelihood depends and only afterwards on the crops which provide them with cash income.

Coping with seasonal labour bottlenecks

Seasonal labour constraints can be alleviated or removed in only three ways. One of these is through the development, with the help of agricultural research, of cropping patterns providing for the cultivation of crops taking different lengths of time to mature and making possible a better utilisation of labour. In the Bouaké region of the Ivory Coast, for example, the development and introduction of the shorter-maturing yet high-yielding Allon varieties of cotton have made possible the extensive cultivation of cotton during a period that does not conflict with the period of production of yams, the staple food, when labour is also in heavy demand.[1] Elsewhere the development of short-maturing varieties of ground-nuts has made it possible to plant this crop after food grains without a significant sacrifice of yields. Further agricultural research is necessary, however, to achieve improvements in the sequence of cropping such as will smooth out labour peaks and bring about a fuller utilisation of the available labour supply. For this purpose research will need to be oriented less towards specific crops and more towards the modification of farming systems as a whole.

The second method of dealing with labour constraints is through the introduction of appropriate implements and machinery. African farmers still work predominantly with a few simple hand tools—the hoe, the axe and the cutlass. This obviously limits the productivity of labour as well as the amount of land which can be tilled and utilised for cash crops as well as for subsistence. The proper equipment of African

---

[1] J. C. de Wilde *et al.*: *Experiences with agricultural development in tropical Africa* (Baltimore, The Johns Hopkins Press, 1967), Vol. II, pp. 408-410.

agriculture remains to a large extent an unresolved problem.[1] New implements which have been introduced have often been ill-adapted to the farmers' requirements. There have been many ill-starred ventures involving tractor cultivation, and the experience with them has not been analysed sufficiently to indicate more precisely under what conditions it is feasible to employ tractor-drawn implements in an economic fashion. The wider use of animal-drawn implements has also been beset by many problems, particularly those relating to the proper feeding and care of draught animals and the training of both men and animals in methods of cultivation using animal traction. Yet experience shows that equipment can be used effectively to alleviate labour bottlenecks. For example, in the case of the Office du Niger irrigation scheme in Mali, the use of tractors for ridging in the dry season before water becomes available has facilitated earlier planting of cotton. The same is true of the Gezira irrigated cotton-growing scheme in the Sudan. In the case of the Mwea Tebere rice-growing project in Kenya the introduction of tractor-mounted rotavators has made it possible not only to put the land in optimum condition for the growing of rice through a single operation but, above all, greatly to improve the timing of the cultivation. In the savanna areas of west Africa the introduction of animal-drawn ploughs and cultivators has often permitted quicker preparation of land and assisted in improving the sequence of operations. While the role of the plough has sometimes been greater in extending the area under cultivation than in bringing about earlier planting, the expansion of the cultivated area has often been beneficial in that it has made available more land for cash crops and to the extent that the mechanisation of land preparation has made it possible not to aggravate seriously labour bottlenecks such as those caused by weeding. In Mali, for example, cotton cultivation has been considerably facilitated by the use of animal-drawn ploughs. In certain areas, such as the Bokoro region of Chad, it was also found that the use of an animal-drawn cultivator for land preparation, followed by the employment of a seed drill, enabled farmers to plant ground-nuts despite a simultaneous demand for labour for the weeding of previously planted millet.

The third method of overcoming seasonal labour shortages is by supplementing the family labour supply [2] with hired labour. Such labour may come both from within the region where agricultural development is taking place and from other regions where there is a surplus of manpower in relation to profitable employment opportunities. Agricultural

[1] See de Wilde *et al.*, op. cit., Vol. I, Ch. 6: " Implements and machinery ".

[2] It may be remarked here that the full utilisation of family labour is often still impeded by the traditional division of tasks between men and women. Women, who are traditionally responsible for cultivating food crops, for assisting men in the cultivation of cash crops and for discharging manifold household duties, are frequently overburdened while men are comparatively unoccupied.

innovations which raise production and create an additional demand for labour tend to be adopted initially by a relatively small percentage of " progressive " farmers. Many farmers fail to introduce improved methods of production or to engage in the cultivation of new crops either because they are very conservative and disinclined to take risks or because, under some conditions, they suffer from a shortage of land. The successful innovators who are increasing their cash income therefore find it possible to draw on the less progressive and poorer farm families for wage labour. Thus in the highlands of Kenya the larger farmers who are successfully growing such crops as coffee and tea and practising modern dairy-farming have had access to the labour resources of the smaller farmers, many of whom do not have enough land to till. However, as agricultural progress becomes more generalised, the labour resources available within the region tend to become a constraining factor. To the extent that a further increase in output depends upon additional labour supplies, what matters is the availability of migrant workers from other areas within the country or even from outside the country. Many cases can be cited where migrant workers from poorly endowed agricultural regions have greatly facilitated the expansion of cash crops in the richer agricultural areas. For instance, cotton production in the Gezira is heavily dependent as regards sowing, weeding and particularly picking on a large supply of migratory labour from the less favoured regions of the Sudan and also from such relatively distant areas as north-eastern Nigeria, the Central African Republic and Chad. In Uganda the early development of cotton and robusta coffee production owes much to the availability of migrant labour from Rwanda and Burundi. The rapid expansion of cocoa and coffee production in the Ivory Coast and of cocoa cultivation in Ghana and Nigeria would have been impossible without the help of migrant workers from the northern parts of these countries as well as from Upper Volta and (in the case of the Ivory Coast) Mali. The extent to which current projects for the rehabilitation and improvement of cocoa and coffee production in the Ivory Coast and of cocoa cultivation in Ghana will be successful depends largely on the continued adequate supply of migrant workers, particularly since the rehabilitation process will entail an additional demand for manpower.

Varying population pressures on land

The complexity of the employment problem in African agriculture is due not only to the coexistence of seasonal labour bottlenecks and underemployment but also to the large variations in the degree of population pressure on the land. Existing patterns of settlement and differing demographic pressures are the result of historical circumstances. Because of past population movements, tribes and even clans and lineage groups within tribes have been able to establish paramount claims to land, and this tends to perpetuate large disparities in the amount and quality of land available. Some tribes and groups have more than enough land; others are crowded by historical accident into limited areas and have to struggle to maintain a bare subsistence. The " local sovereignties " over land often seriously inhibit more efficient utilisation of land resources and a more equitable distribution of land in relation to population. In some cases, to be sure, the people suffering from an increasing shortage of land have managed to meet the resulting pressures by progressively intensifying cultivation. This is true, for instance, of the Kara on Ukara Island in Lake Victoria, the Chagga on the slopes of Mount Kilimanjaro in Tanzania, and the Gishu and the Kiga in the mountain regions of Uganda. However, experience has shown that adoption of most of the intensive practices involved—such as terracing, cutting and storage of fodder, stall-feeding of cattle and the use of compost and manure—can at best stabilise incomes at a very low level unless this approach is accompanied by the cultivation of a profitable cash crop, such as coffee among the Chagga and the Gishu.

Some African governments have tried to deal with " local sovereignties " over land by formally nationalising unoccupied land. In practice, however, such a measure is difficult to enforce as long as tribal rights and loyalties can be effectively asserted against national rights and loyalties. Tribal claims to land are likely to be broken down only gradually, as African countries progress towards true nationhood. Meanwhile, they must be recognised as constituting a real constraint on agricultural development. They will impede but may not altogether prevent resettlement aimed at providing some relief for areas with excessive population pressure. In Kenya it has not in practice been possible to use the approximately 1 million acres of land purchased from European settlers exclusively for the settlement of African farmers from those tribal areas experiencing the most serious demographic pressures. The purchased land has had to be apportioned among tribes in accordance with established zones of influence, and this has meant in many cases the allocation of additional land to people who had relatively little need for it and little incentive to cultivate it intensively. The paramount national interest constituted by the utilisation of this land reform measure for maximising employment on the land and relieving population pressure thus had to be partially sacrificed to practical politics. In Upper Volta the central Mossi plateau, characterised by poor soils and declining soil fertility, remains seriously overpopulated, while other tribal areas are relatively underpopulated. The Mossis have been driven by necessity to infiltrate to some extent other tribal areas on their periphery, but for the most part they remain there as " guests " without permanent rights, and the other tribes involved are likely to restrict such migration as soon as the Mossis threaten to become sufficiently numerous to contest the absolute control of any of their lands. Thus the principal demographic " safety valve " of the Mossi plateau continues to be temporary labour migration to the Ivory Coast and Ghana, particularly since ecological conditions on the plateau are singularly unfavourable for the introduction of remunerative cash crops which would more adequately support the existing population.

The variations in population pressure on available agricultural resources have important implications for the approach to development. Where people do not consider the availability of land to be a limiting factor on their output, their concern is to maximise the return to labour rather than to the land; and this often remains the primary consideration even after the shortage of land has become a serious constraint according to objective criteria. In such conditions efforts to raise yields per unit of area by intensification, i.e. by greater inputs of labour or other means of production, may well be resisted. This is not to say that an increase in yields cannot in many cases be reconciled with the objective of maximising the return to labour. Instances can also be cited, however, where " extensive " cultivation practices have proved more remunerative and attractive to farmers than the more intensive practices.[1]

The availability of manpower has been a particularly crucial determinant of the success of irrigation schemes in Africa. The substantial investment required for such projects is seldom justified unless high yields per unit of area can be obtained. This entails a rather high density of settlement and/or access to outside labour supplies. The comparative lack of success of the Office du Niger irrigation scheme was undoubtedly due to a variety of factors. One of the most important, however, was the inability to settle in the area a sufficient number of cultivators. The surrounding lightly populated areas provided an inadequate reservoir of settlers, and part of the tenants under the scheme had to be in effect conscripted from among the Voltaics. The rather low level of net income achieved was not conducive to the attraction of more Mali tenants, particularly after cotton was successfully introduced in the rain-fed areas and provided Mali farmers with a good source of cash income. Nor was it possible in these circumstances to recruit much paid labour to supplement the manpower resources constituted by the tenants. The Gezira scheme, on the other hand, proved much more successful. While the land allocations under this scheme considerably exceeded the capacity of the tenants to manage them with their own family labour, the tenants were able to earn higher net incomes and could both find and pay for necessary additional labour from the poorer neighbouring areas. An even sharper contrast is afforded by the success of the Mwea Tebere scheme in Kenya. This scheme was located in a densely populated zone where it proved possible to find not only an adequate number of tenants but also the paid labour needed at the time of the transplanting and harvesting of rice.

* * *

[1] For some examples, see de Wilde *et al.*, op. cit., Vol. I, pp. 74-77.

If in accordance with projected requirements most of the population increase must be provided with a livelihood in the rural areas, efforts must be made in two principal directions. First of all, a broad programme is needed to keep people on the land and increase attractive employment opportunities in the rural areas through the modification of educational systems, the expansion of the production of profitable cash crops, the improvement of rural amenities and the quality of rural life, and the diversification of activities. Secondly, there must be a more particular effort to improve the opportunities of the inhabitants of the poorer and overcrowded areas, either by greater concentration on the development of these areas or through the provision of facilities for resettlement. The various aspects of this dual approach will now be considered.

II. Keeping people on the land

Reform of rural education

The prevailing system of education is often accused, and quite rightly, of alienating people from their rural environment. The type of schooling offered tends to facilitate and encourage an exodus from the rural areas to the cities. Unfortunately no very satisfactory way of providing an education better adapted to rural requirements and calculated to encourage people to take advantage of employment opportunities in the rural environment has yet been devised.

One of the more interesting alternatives to normal primary education are the centres for rural education established during recent years in Upper Volta. By 1969-70 about 28,000 boys and girls were enrolled in these centres, which are intended as a replacement for formal primary education. They take boys and girls from 13 to 15 years of age and provide them with three years' instruction that in theory would qualify them to take up farming careers. Although some basic academic education is provided, the principal emphasis is on practical training—agriculture and associated rural crafts for the boys, and agriculture, child rearing, hygiene and home economics for the girls. On leaving the centres the boys are intended in principle to obtain land to start farming in accordance with improved techniques.

While the underlying concept seems sound, the centres have in practice largely failed to live up to the original expectations. First, both the parents and pupils have tended to consider the centres as an inferior substitute for primary education and increasingly pressed the Government to make them more like primary schools. Second, boys leaving the centres between 16 and 18 years of age have often been unable to obtain land for farming, since under the prevailing custom young men are not normally allotted land until they get married. To meet this problem the

Government has organised a number of co-operative farms and established supplementary post-school training centres, but neither have these measures been conspicuously successful. Consequently many of the boys have migrated to the Ivory Coast. Third, the teachers at the centres have not for the most part been sufficiently trained, particularly in the practical subjects of the curriculum. Finally, the farms attached to the centres have not been large enough or sufficiently well-equipped to provide a real training ground for practical farmers. Despite their deficiencies, the rural education centres appear to reflect a sound approach and to be capable of improvement. Greater efforts are needed to explain their objectives to parents and to enlist the latter's co-operation. The pedagogic training of the teachers could be improved and better facilities provided for practical farm work. Arrangements for close collaboration between the centres and the agricultural extension service could help to make the instruction more practical and to integrate those leaving the centres into rural life.

The role of commercial farming

Other experiments with the reform of rural education could probably be cited. In the last analysis, however, their effectiveness depends in large part on the possibility of providing attractive employment opportunities in the rural areas. The development of commercial farming capable of furnishing incomes in line with the rising aspirations of the younger generation is thus of crucial importance. In the past, considerable success has been achieved through the introduction and expansion of a wide variety of cash crops including arabic and robusta coffee, cocoa, tea, oil palms, cotton and ground-nuts. In limited areas where ecological conditions have been particularly favourable, as in the highlands of Kenya, a profitable dairy industry has been developed. Bilateral and multilateral aid has greatly facilitated the development of commercial farming. The International Bank for Reconstruction and Development (IBRD) and the Commonwealth Development Corporation, for example, have participated prominently in the development of tea production in Kenya and Uganda [1] by establishing an integrated programme to this end, including credits for training in tea cultivation and picking, the building of roads and the provision of other facilities for the collection of tea, and the setting up of tea factories. In the savanna areas of west Africa, French bilateral aid, the European Development Fund and, more recently, the IBRD have financed a substantial expansion of cotton growing, which has created a new source of cash income for thousands

[1] In 1971 the IBRD's affiliate, the International Development Association, also provided a credit for tea development in Mauritius. This project, which will create permanent employment for 4,000 persons, is particularly important for this island, which is extremely densely populated.

of farmers. Other projects have been concerned with the expansion and rehabilitation of oil palms, cocoa production and rubber plantations (e.g. in Dahomey, Ghana and the Ivory Coast).

The increase in wage employment in agriculture

Farming for cash has not only benefited the farmers themselves but also generated a considerable demand for paid labour, albeit at rather low levels of remuneration. This has happened not just because the cultivation and harvesting of cash crops require more labour. It is also a reflection of the fact that the income elasticity of demand for labour among African farmers is high. Once farmers experience a considerable increase in income, they prefer to spend part of this increase on labour in order to purchase for themselves more leisure or opportunities to engage in other occupations. In Kenya land consolidation and the related development of cash crops and dairy farming have brought about a

PROPORTION OF CASH INPUTS ALLOCATED TO LABOUR

Area	%
Northern Katina, Nigeria (ground-nuts):	
Farmers with ploughs	65
Farmers without ploughs	65
Akim Abuakwa, Ghana (cocoa)	86
Mazabuka District, Zambia (maize):	
Progressive farmers	10
Teso District, Uganda (cotton and ground-nuts)	67
Kisii District, Kenya (coffee, tea, pyrethrum):	
Progressive farmers	69
Other farmers	58
Geta District, Tanzania (cotton)	73

Source: Food Research Institute, Stanford University: " Economic, cultural and technical determinants of agricultural change in tropical Africa ", Preliminary Reports 2 to 6 and 8 (Xeroxed, 1969).

substantial increase in employment [1] and helped to arrest the rising tide of migration to the cities. Surveys undertaken by the Farm Economic Survey Unit and others in Kenya have stressed the large labour inputs involved in many of these commercial farming activities.[2] As already

[1] See Eric S. Clayton: " Agrarian reform, agricultural planning and employment in Kenya ", in *International Labour Review*, Vol. 102, No. 5, Nov. 1970, pp. 431-453.

[2] On this aspect see the case study " The experience in Nyeri District ", in de Wilde *et al.*, op. cit., Vol. III, Ch. 2.

noted, the development of coffee, cocoa and palm oil production in the Ivory Coast and of cocoa production in Ghana has been of great indirect benefit to Upper Volta by providing employment for several hundred thousands of Voltaics. In the Sudan the Gezira scheme, which has been expanded with IBRD financing, provides part-time employment for 300,000 or more workers annually.

Studies of experiences with agricultural development in a series of selected areas carried out under the auspices of the Stanford University Food Research Institute have illustrated once more the tendency of farmers in developing areas to allocate a significant portion of their cash outlays to labour. The table provides the relevant information on this subject as obtained in interviews with a presumably representative number of farmers. It is significant that the only area surveyed by the Food Research Institute where there were virtually no cash outlays on labour was Bawku District in Northern Ghana. There, the failure to devise practical and profitable innovations in agriculture meant that the necessary cash income was not generated.

Evaluation of efforts to promote commercial farming

It must be conceded that commercial farming in tropical Africa is far from being a universal phenomenon. Only a minority of farmers engage in it and then in many cases only as an ancillary or supplementary activity to subsistence cultivation. Yields, particularly on annual crops, are still low. There is a considerable lag in the introduction of fertilisers, insecticides and fungicides and in the adoption of improved seed and cultivation practices which would help to raise productivity. Much further progress should be possible with the help of agricultural research, more effective extension and credit services, improvements in transport and appropriate pricing policies. More agricultural research should be devoted particularly to means of raising the yields of subsistence food crops so that more land can be spared for cash cropping and so that grain surpluses can eventually become available for feeding livestock, which is now inadequately nourished. Studies to evaluate the reasons for success or failure in introducing innovations should be multiplied. In many cases where little or inadequate progress has been achieved, there is a need to acquire a fuller understanding of the prevailing farming systems that have to be modified and of the factors which constrain farmers to adhere to them. These may include ecological considerations, the availability of land, manpower and implements, the structure of society and its sense of values and networks of social obligations, markets and prices and the availability of transport and government services. It is vital to identify the critical constraints and to determine to what degree they are susceptible of modification by appropriate measures. Without understanding why farmers and livestock breeders adhere to certain practices and cropping systems we cannot devise and secure the adoption of innovations which are considered by producers to be both feasible and profitable. Although existing and traditional farming patterns have been studied much more in recent years than heretofore, our knowledge of them, particularly considering the wide variety of conditions in Africa, is still far from complete. Even where these patterns are known, the curricula of agricultural schools often pay no attention to them; and agricultural officers and farm-level extension workers are sent out without fully understanding what farming systems they are expected to modify and why. There is a need to put more emphasis in the curricula of agricultural schools at all levels on a knowledge of the whole milieu in which the farmer operates. Ways and means of retraining agricultural officers and extension workers should be explored and opportunities created to enable such personnel to assist in adapting curricula to meet the practical problems encountered in the field.

Alleviation of farm drudgery

Life in rural areas can also be made more attractive and supportable in a number of other ways. For many farmers dependent on the hoe and axe agriculture means a " grubby ", unattractive occupation. The younger generation, which has enjoyed some measure of formal education, seeks largely to escape from it. Consequently the introduction of implements and machinery which take some of the drudgery out of farming assumes increasing importance. It has already been noted that types of equipment which would be both economic and practical under African conditions are by no means easy to find. The use of equipment which simply alleviates labour burdens without significantly contributing to production can hardly be defended.

Improving rural amenities

Improvement of the amenities of rural areas also presents a challenge. The provision of safe and convenient supplies of drinking water, of better health facilities, of social centres and of improved housing can play a significant role in making rural life more attractive. The installation of articulated water systems in some of the wealthier and rather densely populated areas of Kenya has proved a considerable boon to the population concerned; and in a number of countries, including Upper Volta, extensive programmes for the digging of wells have aroused sufficient popular support to result in a considerable contribution of free labour on the part of the local population. In the Ivory Coast substantial efforts are being made to improve the standards of rural housing. In Togo the Housing and Building Centre established in 1969 and financed by the United Nations Development Programme (UNDP) has launched a broad programme for the development of model low-cost housing utilising cheap native materials and for the training of building entrepreneurs and workers. The Centre plans eventually also to foster the creation of co-operatives for the financing of rural housing.

It can be argued that investments in social welfare should be made with great caution so as to avoid the creation of facilities and standards which cannot be supported by the " production base " of the local economy. While concern with this problem is justified, it can be exaggerated. Investment in a pure water supply and in health facilities may make an important indirect contribution to productivity by eradicating or reducing the incidence of debilitating diseases such as Guinea worm, malaria, schistosomiasis and onchocerciasis which curtail the productive capacity of the people affected. Moreover, some subsidising of investment in social welfare in the rural areas may well be justified if the amenities provided help to avert migration to the cities. Investment in similar social infrastructure and facilities in the urban areas is likely to prove more expensive.

Diversification of rural production

The diversification of the rural economy has been increasingly emphasised as another method of creating additional employment opportunities in rural areas. It is usually promoted, consciously or unconsciously, as part of a broad integrated approach to rural development comprising the improvement of agriculture, the provision of rural amenities, a measure of " rural industrialisation " and the related adaptation of rural education. Typical of this approach is the Pilot Project for Rural Employment Promotion started late in 1969 in a small area of Western Nigeria with UNDP financing and the help of personnel of the International Labour Office and the Food and Agriculture Organisation. This project focuses more or less simultaneously on improvements in local agriculture, the provision of feeder roads, the training and promotion of local craftsmen and entrepreneurs and pre-vocational training. In Kenya plans for the development of rural industry through rural industrial centres and small rural industrial estates are being drawn up.

It is important to explore carefully the possibilities for and limits to rural industrialisation. It is by no means easy to find economic and feasible projects. While there may be additional opportunities for the processing of local agricultural and livestock products and locally available raw materials, such processes as cotton ginning, coffee hulling and palm fruit oil extraction have already been developed as an indispensable corollary of efforts to expand the production of the commodities concerned. The establishment in rural areas of undertakings producing for a wide market, including the major urban areas of the country, is often not economically viable. Market-oriented industries are more economically located in or near their major market areas, which means in or close to the cities where purchasing power is concentrated and where such amenities as power and water, as well as skilled labour, are likely to be more readily available. Rural handicraft or quasi-industrial undertakings which have been enabled to develop a level of production in excess of the requirements of the local market may well be tempted to move their operations to the cities, which afford a larger market for their products. On the other hand, as and when agriculture becomes more prosperous and local purchasing power increases, there will be opportunities for the development of trade and commerce in consumer goods and farmers' production requisites and for the setting up of undertakings producing a range of goods and services particularly tailored to the needs of the growing rural market. Undertakings producing building materials and engaged in contracting, as well as woodworking and metalworking establishments, may be especially necessary. While, as already noted, agricultural mechanisation has in many respects made but slow progress, there are areas in Africa utilising various types of equipment, including tractors, ploughs, cultivators, sprayers and dusters, ground-nut shellers, etc. Under existing conditions much of this equipment is poorly maintained and is often wastefully discarded before its normal useful life is exhausted. Proper repair and maintenance services are accordingly an acute need in many areas.

Training for rural crafts and industries

The above remarks highlight the problem of providing proper training for rural craftsmen and entrepreneurs. A number of efforts have been made in this respect. In Kenya, for example, the Christian Churches, supported by the Government, have set up so-called " village polytechnics " for training primary school leavers in various crafts.[1] The first of these was established in 1966 and there were seventeen in operation by early 1971. The polytechnics have very modest operating budgets and appear to rely largely on a volunteer teaching staff. The emphasis in the two-year training course is entirely on hand-work and no attempt is made to qualify trainees for certificates or the passing of trade tests. The objective is to train people who will be self-employed. Difficulties have been encountered in getting sufficiently qualified staff, and consideration is now being given to the establishment of a staff training centre. It is evident also that insufficient attention has been paid to the selection of crafts which are in demand in given rural areas and in which training should accordingly be provided.

---

[1] See also Walter Elkan: " Out-of-school education and training for primary-school leavers in rural Kenya: a proposal ", in *International Labour Review*, Vol. 104, No. 3, Sep 1971, pp. 208-210.

The ILO has also been actively engaged in training programmes of the kind required. Apart from the above-mentioned Pilot Project for Rural Employment Promotion in Nigeria, it has, for example, implemented projects aimed at providing advice and guidance in the training of rural craftsmen in Senegal and Upper Volta and focusing on the training of teachers. Such schemes respond in principle to a real need. Unfortunately, however, they are not very spectacular and thus often fail to obtain constant and vigorous governmental support. Experience also indicates that training alone is not enough. It must be complemented by assistance to craftsmen to install themselves and particularly by facilities to enable them to acquire the equipment they need but cannot make or be trained to make themselves. It must be recognised also that in many of the rural areas of Africa craftsmen cannot as yet find sufficient remunerative work to support themselves solely by practising their trade. They often need to engage also in farming. Some type of combined training in agriculture and crafts may be appropriate under such conditions.

III. The approach to development in the poorer areas

I have already commented on the disparities in the availability of natural resources in various areas of Africa and on the constraints which prevent a more equitable distribution of the population in relation to those resources. There are accordingly enormous differences in the rate of development. The inhabitants of the well-endowed forest areas of the Ivory Coast have experienced a rapid rise in incomes; those in the northern part of this country and in most of Upper Volta have been left far behind. This situation is characteristic of much of Africa. For the poor and overpopulated areas the only palliative in many cases is labour migration. But however important labour migration may be as a means of supplementing meagre local incomes, it can hardly provide a solution to the problem. While, for instance, Voltaics may still find employment in Ivory Coast agriculture, there is already evidence of considerable resistance in the cities to migrant workers. In Ghana steps have been taken to reduce the employment of foreign labour. For the countries and areas providing the migrant workers, such migration is by no means an unmixed blessing. Not only does it create social problems through the disruption of family ties but, above all, it deprives areas of the most able-bodied and vigorous men, thus handicapping the effective implementation of development projects which could in the future reduce the need for migration.

What then can be done for these poorer areas? A few prerequisites for their development may first be mentioned. To begin with, bilateral and multilateral financing agencies should exercise discrimination in determining the minimum rates of economic return acceptable for projects. The required rate of return simply must be lower for the less promising areas. Then there should be somewhat greater flexibility in determining the ecological conditions under which various types of crops may be promoted. Technical agricultural experts tend, not unnaturally, to urge that a particular crop should be grown only where these conditions will result in the highest yields. However, in some circumstances it may be desirable to promote the cultivation of a given crop even under less than optimum conditions where farmers do not have a more attractive alternative. In such circumstances the farmers concerned may well be willing to accept a lower return for their labour than their counterparts in more favoured regions where other options are available. Thus opportunity costs of production should be the determinant in selecting areas where particular crops can be developed.

Above all, every attempt should be made to explore whatever development opportunities may exist in the less favoured areas which nevertheless must support large populations. In the savanna cropping areas more emphasis should be placed on the development of higher yielding sorghums and millets so that a large portion of these grains can be marketed (whether for food or fodder) and some portion may become available for on-farm fattening of cattle. In Upper Volta the financial assistance provided by the French Government and, more recently, the World Bank Group has been of great help in achieving the expansion of cotton cultivation, although unfortunately the best conditions for cotton growing exist for the most part in the less densely populated areas of the country. There are, however, opportunities for the development of small irrigated rice schemes in the poorer areas. In Malawi, which has a large population relative to its resources and where people have long been compelled to seek a cash income through migration, the World Bank Group is financing two projects for the development of the Shire Valley and the Lilongwe Plain in the central region which appear to be promising. The Lilongwe scheme provides for a rather comprehensive approach to agricultural development and will eventually affect some 76,000 farm families with holdings totalling about a million acres. Included in the programme are the development of land use and conservation plans and works, the provision of roads, water supplies and markets, the registration of land, progressive increases in the planting of synthetic and hybrid maize instead of the low-yielding indigenous varieties, improvement of tobacco yields and the stall-feeding of cattle. While the limited experience with this project does not yet permit a definitive judgment, the preliminary evidence indicates that it will significantly enhance the attractiveness of farming in this area.

Another approach is to resettle people from overpopulated areas. While we have already noted that " local sovereignties " over land often interpose serious obstacles to the transfer of populations, this is not always the case. For example, the Sakuma in the Lake Victoria region of Tanzania have been able to escape population pressures by progressively moving westward into virtually unoccupied areas. In Upper Volta this opportunity is not available to the Mossis to the same degree. Even there, however, there appear to be possibilities for facilitating the progressive movement of part of the Mossi population into the comparatively unpopulated region of Fada N'Gourma in the south-east. In Senegal the World Bank Group has recently undertaken to finance a pilot project designed to resettle some of the people from the densely populated ground-nut basin in the new lands *(terres neuves)* of eastern Senegal. This is a small-scale project but it may serve to demonstrate the feasibility of resettling larger numbers of people, particularly through spontaneous migration once the basic infrastructure of the new region has been developed.

Other opportunities for resettlement may be created through the reclaiming and development of insalubrious areas. In the savanna areas of west Africa, for example, the prevalence of onchocerciasis, or river-blindness, which is transmitted by a black fly breeding in the foamy waters of rivers, has been an important factor in driving the population out of the river valleys affected. In such valleys the land is often more fertile than in the higher areas. A pilot programme for the eradication of the vector through the treatment of its breeding sites with insecticides has been conducted for some years, with the help of financing from the European Development Fund, in an area comprising parts of south-eastern Mali, south-western Upper Volta and the northern region of the Ivory Coast. This project has already demonstrated the possibility of controlling the vector and provided evidence that people will move spontaneously into the reclaimed areas. The World Health Organisation, in co-operation with other agencies, began in 1971 a year's study with a view to launching a more comprehensive campaign against the disease. Simultaneously the French Government is financing a feasibility study on the development, with a view to population resettlement there, of the White Volta River Valley in Upper Volta which promises, once the vector of onchocerciasis has been eradicated, to provide some relief for the hard-pressed population in contiguous areas inhabited by the Mossi and Bissa peoples. A comprehensive campaign against the vector could also alleviate pressures in pockets of excessive population in northern Ghana and the Korhogo district of the Ivory Coast.

It must be conceded, however, that resettlement opportunities are limited in relation to the overpopulation problem characterising certain parts of Africa. Experience also shows that resettlement often entails excessively heavy investment unless the primary emphasis is placed on spontaneous resettlement assisted to some extent by the provision of absolutely necessary infrastructure. In some cases, too, sociological problems impede the resettlement of populations far from their ancestral homesteads.

IV. Some conclusions

On the basis of the preceding analysis and previous experience of tropical Africa, the following points can be emphasised:

(1) Employment opportunities in the rural areas must be multiplied so that these areas can accommodate during the discernible future the major increase occurring in the labour force.

(2) Approaches to the rural employment problem must take into account the existence in many areas of both seasonal labour shortages and seasonal labour surpluses. There must accordingly be a co-ordinated effort to alleviate labour bottlenecks, provide fuller employment throughout the season and create additional attractive employment opportunities.

(3) Commercial farming in Africa has made considerable progress in recent decades and has not only provided attractive sources of cash income but generated a considerable increase in wage employment. More attention, however, must be paid to the various types of constraints which still prevent many farmers from introducing new crops and adopting new cultivation practices. To identify and deal with these constraints, a better knowledge of prevailing farming patterns must be acquired and disseminated among agricultural officers and extension workers who are supposed to modify these patterns.

(4) Practical reforms of rural education are necessary if the tide of migration to the cities is to be arrested. Existing experiments in this field should be evaluated with a view to their improvement where necessary, and every effort should be made to develop new and imaginative approaches.

(5) Living conditions in the rural areas must be made more attractive by relieving some of the drudgery of farming through judicious introduction of implements and machinery and by making better provision for rural health, housing and water supply, which can incidentally enhance labour productivity and obviate the need for even more costly investment in infrastructure and services necessary to accommodate rural migrants in the cities.

(6) Additional employment opportunities ancillary to agricultural development must be created in the rural areas. While large-scale rural industrialisation is hardly feasible, there are possibilities for the development of undertakings providing services and goods tailored to the needs of growing local markets. In this context the training of rural craftsmen and entrepreneurs and the implementation of measures to help them to establish themselves and to obtain the necessary equipment are particularly important.

(7) Special efforts are necessary to cope with the problems of the poorer agricultural regions which have considerable populations to support but which have largely been left out of the mainstream of development. These efforts must proceed from a realisation that lower rates of economic return must be accepted for projects in such regions and that the opportunity costs of production are low in view of the limited alternatives. They will need to focus also on the possibilities of resettlement. In this connection attention will have to be paid to the obstacles to population transfers and to the possibility of progressively attenuating " local sovereignties " over land.

II. Approaches

Unemployment in an African Setting

Lessons of the Employment Strategy Mission to Kenya

Hans SINGER [1] and Richard JOLLY [2]

LIKE EARLIER MISSIONS undertaken within the framework of the ILO World Employment Programme [3], the ILO mission to Kenya soon discovered that Kenya did not have one employment problem but many, and that the nature and causes of these various employment problems could not be investigated without making a broader analysis of the structure of the economy at large and the trends in its development. Extreme differences in incomes, productivity, access to resources and government services created imbalances between the structure and location of the jobs in demand and the type and location of available work opportunities. The

[1] Fellow of the Institute of Development Studies, University of Sussex. Chief of the Kenya Mission.

[2] Director of the Institute of Development Studies, University of Sussex. Joint Chief of the Kenya Mission.

[3] For an outline of the World Employment Programme, which aims principally to make productive employment for large numbers of people a major goal of national and international policies for development, see David A. Morse: " The World Employment Programme ", in *International Labour Review*, June 1968, pp. 517-524. The report of the first mission, to Colombia, was published by the ILO in 1970 under the title *Towards full employment. A programme for Colombia, prepared by an inter-agency team organised by the ILO.* The participating agencies and organs besides the ILO were the IBRD, the FAO, UNESCO, the WHO, UNIDO, UNCTAD, UNOTC, the ECE, ECLA, the OAS and the IDB. The report of the second mission, to Ceylon, was published by the ILO in 1971 under the title *Matching employment opportunities and expectations. A programme of action for Ceylon.* The participating agencies and organs besides the ILO were the IBRD, the FAO, UNESCO, the WHO, UNIDO, UNCTAD, the GATT/UNCTAD International Trade Centre, ECAFE and the Asian Development Bank. Finance was provided by the United Nations Development Programme. The report of the Kenya mission was published by the ILO at the end of 1972 under the title *Employment, incomes and equality. A strategy for increasing productive employment in Kenya.* The participating agencies and organs besides the ILO were the IBRD, the FAO, UNESCO, the WHO, UNICEF, the UNDP, UNIDO, UNCTAD and ECA. Finance was provided by the United Nations Development Programme.

rapid growth of the total population, not to mention that of the urban population and of school outputs, has far exceeded the growth of wage earning employment. These internal imbalances are linked to extreme imbalances between the Kenyan economy and the world economy—in trade, technology, and the conditions governing private foreign investment. Many of the imbalances were inherited at the time of independence, others have grown up since. All of them underlie Kenya's employment problems.

Just as the causes of the problems are broad and fundamental, so is the strategy to deal with them. Thus, of necessity, the report of the Kenya mission takes into account a wide range of policy measures with implications for virtually every sector and group in the economy. The underlying theme is, however, a coherent strategy for moving on from the post-independence policies of growth and Kenyanisation formulated within the inherited economic structure to policies designed to diminish the imbalances through a complete restructuring of the economy. The resources for this restructuring would be found from a redistribution of the fruits of growth.

The emphasis is on growth as well as redistribution because of the low level of income per head in Kenya and the high proportion of the population living in the rural areas at near subsistence level. In view of these two facts neither growth nor income redistribution alone would be adequate. Both are needed and must be linked in a comprehensive strategy.

The employment problems of Kenya differ from those encountered in previous missions in a number of respects. Kenya's problems are, in fact, probably characteristic of African countries in general, though this would need to be ascertained on the basis of further experience, discussion and empirical research.[1]

The most striking consideration is the overwhelmingly rural character of employment: the rural population accounts for some 90 per cent of the total population, and the urban population until recently maintained strong links with the countryside, as was borne out by a survey showing that about 20 per cent of all urban wage earnings were remitted to the rural areas, the proportion being even higher in the case of the lower wage incomes. This factor places the question of the disparity between urban wages and rural incomes in a somewhat special context, and means also that rural/urban terms of trade and the nature and sources of rural incomes must be viewed in a different light. In one sense, the preponderance of the rural sector lays the basis for a positive employment policy: small farms in Kenya show both larger labour inputs and higher output

[1] It is intended to hold a six-week study seminar in Nairobi during 1973, when the applicability of the findings and recommendations of the Kenya mission to other African countries will be discussed with officials and other participants from those countries.

per unit of land—and this applies to food crops as well as cash crops. Thus, there is here and in a number of other areas a welcome harmony between more employment, greater equality and higher output. This provides a powerful reinforcement for the over-all strategy of redistribution from growth.

However, one reason why the employment problem has become (or has been felt to have become) so much more acute in recent years is that the traditionally strong links between the countryside and the urban population are beginning to weaken. Historically, the employment system evolved from the tendency towards a high labour turnover in urban employment due to the return to their villages of middle-aged and even younger workers after a period of urban employment, which created numerous vacancies for new entrants to the labour market. To counteract this tendency, a tradition of high urban wages was established—high relative to rural incomes—in order to induce the workers concerned to stay on in regular employment. This earlier policy of high urban wages has, as a result of changed circumstances, led to the " distortion of factor prices ", creating dualism and inequalities in the economic structure. The high wages have in fact served their purpose of reducing labour turnover only too well, in the absence of a corresponding rise in rural incomes; they have attracted young jobseekers far in excess of the quantity justified by the reduced number of job vacancies; and they have been both caused and supported by the prevalence of capital-intensive technologies in the modern urban sector. This in turn has resulted in the growth of an " informal " urban sector, which represents society's way of reconciling the limited number of jobs in the modern urban sector with the increasing number of jobseekers and the inadequate rural incomes. Positive policies based on the existence and potential of this informal sector are proposed in the report of the Kenya mission, as is explained below.

In many other ways, also, recent history has placed its stamp upon the employment problem in Kenya. The question of productive employment for the mass of the African population is inextricably linked with the question of Kenyanisation of the economy. As an over-riding national objective, this must form part of any employment strategy. One approach to Kenyanisation is to change the old racial structure—with Europeans on top, Asians in the middle and Africans at the bottom—simply by changing the people occupying the jobs in the various income strata, which is roughly what has happened since independence. However, this has simply perpetuated the problem of finding productive employment for the masses and has maintained existing inequalities where it has not actually intensified them or sown the seeds for increasing them in the future. A different approach to Kenyanisation is to change the entire economic structure, by reducing the present stratification, so that the whole economy is more closely geared to the achievement of productive employment and the reduction of unemployment.

Dimensions and nature of the problem

Applying the conventional definition of " unemployed " in the Kenyan context, i.e. taking into account persons lacking identifiable urban full-time employment—people working zero hours and having zero income—the mission estimated that the level of urban unemployment was between 11 and 12 per cent among men and considerably higher among women. In fact it was not possible on this basis to estimate the number of unemployed women in a satisfactory way; the usual methods of assessing labour force participation rates did not work, so that the mission felt compelled to use quite different methods. This was even more necessary as regards women in the rural areas, where the demarcation line between activities classifiable as " economic ", which stamp the person performing them as being in the " labour force ", and other " non-economic " activities, performed by persons outside the labour force, is statistically arbitrary and, for purposes of indicating living standards, meaningless. Allowing for a higher level of urban unemployment among women than among men, the average urban unemployment rate may be said to be around 15 per cent. The situation is made all the more serious by the fact that this urban unemployment tends to hit hardest the younger people, who, on balance, are better educated than those currently employed. This creates a special problem in that it implies the frustration of the aspirations not only of the younger, better educated people, on whom the hopes for the development of the country must rest, but also of their parents and families who have invested in their school fees often desperately hard-earned capital. Taken together these two groups represent a powerful political force.

But though the urban unemployment rate is serious, it is only the tip of the iceberg. The " working poor ", i.e. those whose efforts do not earn them even the modest income needed to bring them above the threshold which marks the poverty level in a generally poor country, account for a much higher proportion of the urban population than the 15 per cent or so found to be directly unemployed. The mission did not define this group as " underemployed " because in fact those involved are often working long hours in arduous activities. Again, this is particularly true of the women, when the artificial distinction between " economic " and other activities is disregarded. Nor are the people in this category predominantly engaged in marginal or parasitical sham occupations. In fact, the mission placed great emphasis on the intrinsic value and vitality of a lot of activities in the " informal sector ", where many of the working poor are to be found. Without arriving at a precise estimate, the mission concluded on the evidence collected that those without sufficient productive employment accounted for at least 25 per cent of the urban population of working age, and probably for a higher proportion of the working age rural population.

TABLE I. PROPORTION OF UNEMPLOYED PERSONS AND OF THE WORKING POOR IN THE ADULT POPULATION OF NAIROBI, BY SEX AND HOUSEHOLD STATUS, 1970

	Males		Females	
	Heads of households	All members of households	Heads of households	All members of households
Unemployed [1]	4.9	10.0	10.8	22.8
Working poor	13.8	13.6	40.7	31.8
Unemployed [1] persons and working poor jointly	18.7	23.6	51.5	54.6

[1] Unemployed persons are those with zero incomes who are seeking work.
Source: ILO: *Employment, incomes and equality . . .*, op. cit., p. 64.

Though this article is not a summary of the mission's report, or of its recommendations—these can be found in the report itself [1]—it may be useful to pursue a little further the findings of the mission in respect of the informal or unenumerated sector just referred to. Mention of this sector often conjures up a picture of fictitious, marginal, parasitical or illegal activities—those of the beggar, the shoeshine boy, the thief, the prostitute. For the analytical economist the picture is one of " underemployment " or " disguised unemployment "; for the planner it is one of undesirable slum areas, of messy, uncontrolled and uncontrollable activities; for a newly independent country, it is one of reversion to primitive conditions, a denial of modernisation and progress. The mission found that when applied to the informal sector in Kenya this picture was essentially unhelpful and misleading.[2]

The chief element of truth in this jaundiced view of the informal sector is that many of those active there are among the " working poor "; they are unable to reach a minimum acceptable standard of living; but this is also true of many of the small farmers, or indeed of people working in the modern or formal sector (though here the incidence of poverty is less marked). The mission found that the informal sector, both urban and rural, represents a vital part of the Kenyan economy and that its existence reflects a necessary and, on the whole, beneficial adjustment to the constraints imposed by the prevailing economic situation. If a country like Kenya, which has to find jobs for a population increasing by almost

[1] See ILO: *Employment, incomes and equality . . .*, op. cit., pp. 9-30.

[2] This is not to say that disguised unemployment, undesirable activities and other obstacles to progress do not exist there. But the mission felt that fastening on these aspects tended to obscure the real role and dominant activities of the informal sector and all too often led to the healthy and promising elements being jettisoned along with the noxious elements.

3½ per cent a year (four to eight times as many proportionately as would have to be found in a developed country), with such a limited national income and with an even more limited capital formation potential (perhaps only one-twentieth proportionately of that of a developed country), tries to do so by using a technology broadly similar to that of the rich countries and requiring broadly similar amounts of capital per worker, the inevitable consequence is that the " modern sector " thus created must exclude the bulk of the population. A number of adjustments can be made by reducing capital intensity even within the framework of conventional technology, or by changing the product mix in the direction of more labour-intensive products, particularly where there is a high proportion of rural employment, but these measures will not be sufficient to provide jobs for all the jobseeking population. The unemployed who cannot be maintained by the earnings of relatives or friends or who have no family farm to fall back upon, who cannot draw social security benefit or be assisted by the community in other ways, have to make a living by catering for the needs of their fellow citizens, who are frequently in a similar situation to themselves. This often means self-employment, using methods and resources within their grasp in the absence of a command of capital, access to credit, business know-how, etc.

The informal sector in Kenya, when looked at in this way, appears as a sector in which the adjustments to a prevailing situation have been made with a high degree of intelligence, entrepreneurship, ingenuity and appropriateness. The sector has served as a basis for the development of technological adaptations to actual circumstances which are often admirable. All this has been achieved in the face of frequent government neglect or even harassment due to the prevailing planner's belief in the supreme virtue of " modern "—and thus high-cost—approaches and standards. The report of the mission recommends a major shift in government policies concerning the informal sector—a shift towards active encouragement and support. This would require a new look at health standards, housing standards, licensing policy, access of the sector to loans and technology, policies relating to industrial estates and rural industrialisation, government contract policy and specifications, technological research decisions on products appropriate to the Kenyan economy, the development of subcontracting by larger-scale enterprises (specifically including foreign investors), etc.—all of these being relevant to any fundamental re-orientation of existing policies.

The above reflections also show why reports such as the one on Kenya have to take a comprehensive look at the economy as a whole. Simply to try now to extend the " modern " standards of the formal sector to the informal sector—an attempt which would be hopeless in any case—by introducing everywhere the same " modern " practices (minimum wages or other conditions) would be worse than mere neglect. What is needed are positive new policies for promoting the informal sector and linking it with the formal sector. This attitude ties in with the mission's belief that the informal urban sector in Nairobi, Mombasa and other Kenyan towns has come to stay and is certain to expand rapidly. It does not, as planners often assume, consist of temporary migrants who can be persuaded to return to the countryside, nor does the mission expect, or try to base itself on the assumption, that the rate of migration or urbanisation in the future can or will be reduced by more than a small margin.[1]

There is also a very important rural and small-town informal non-agricultural sector which can be greatly strengthened. Although 90 per cent of Kenya's population still lives in rural areas, this in no way means that all of its income (other than the important urban remittances already mentioned) is derived from agricultural activities. The diversification of rural and small-town activities is, however, largely dependent on increasing agricultural prosperity. In any case, with Kenya's rapid rate of population growth and small urban population, even if the present rate of increase in the African population in the larger towns, amounting to between 8 and 10 per cent per annum, continues, the increase in the rural population will still account for most of the actual total population increase. That is why the mission's recommendations concerning the informal rural and urban sectors had to be formulated in the context of an intensification of labour use in agriculture. In Kenya the evidence suggested that smaller farmers were generally more efficient as well as more labour-intensive in the sense of producing more per acre and employing more persons per acre than larger farmers.

The agricultural strategy which the mission proposed has four main thrusts:

(a) the intensification of land use both for crop and livestock production with the major concentration of effort directed to the poorer families;

(b) a redistribution of land towards more land/labour-intensive farm units;

(c) the settlement of unused or underutilised land in both high potential and semi-arid areas;

(d) the creation of non-agricultural employment opportunities through rural works and the development of the rural informal sector.

Under this strategy the recommendations of the mission centered on promotion of the cultivation of labour-intensive cash crops (coffee, tea, pyrethrum, rice, cotton, sugar, wheat, etc.), particularly by smaller farms. This presupposes the release of land for such cash crops by using less land for food crops, which in turn would have to be achieved by raising the

[1] The mission did recommend policies which it expected would reduce somewhat the net flow of rural-urban migration, particularly the net growth of the larger towns.

productivity of food crop cultivation (still desperately important, in particular as regards high protein foods) through the rapid introduction of hybrid maize and related improved husbandry practices.

As regards the industrial sector, the mission paid particular attention to Kenya's relations with foreign investors, who account for the bulk of modern industrial employment and investment. Its recommendations in this connection, if accepted, would again call for considerable shifts in policy: greater selectivity as to the types of investment to be encouraged; greater initiative on Kenya's part in formulating its own investment proposals and priorities through more active seeking out of investors and "shopping around" among them, instead of just waiting for all the proposals to come from them; a sharply increased effort to enable Kenya to negotiate with foreign investors on more equal terms, on the basis of a better knowledge of the technological problems involved and available alternatives; and a new taxation structure which would be more effective in preventing the drain of capital out of Kenya. At the same time the mission recommended a re-shuffling of the incentives or disincentives in the Kenyan economy for foreign investors, deriving from the tariff structure and price policies and from the exchange rate and fiscal policy. It found that Kenya's export policies also stood in need of considerable re-examination, and the report makes wide-ranging recommendations in this respect.

As already indicated, changes of policy were found to be necessary outside the agricultural and industrial sectors. Two vital areas are education and the labour market—linked because they have operated together as a way of channelling the lucky few into the better paid wage-earning jobs, thus aggravating the distortion in incentives already caused by the gross imbalances in the wage and salary structure. The mission suggested a chain of linked reforms, beginning with major changes in the wage structure and fundamental changes in the process of selection within the educational system and from the school system into jobs. These changes, if implemented, would help redirect the existing aspirations of students and their parents, and thus make possible long overdue shifts within the educational system, away from the white-collar, academic orientation towards a more flexible and diversified system comprising formal education, training and informal education, which would be better suited to the real needs of the country.

The need for a reform of the wage and salary structure is well known and will not be further elaborated on here. On the other hand, it would seem to be worth indicating briefly why a reform of the system of educational selection was seen as a crucial step towards the other reforms.

In Kenya, as in so many other countries, the school examination system has increasingly become the dominant device for deciding who will go on to secondary and higher education and who, in turn, will get the good jobs. Given the very rapid rate of educational expansion when compared with the rate of growth of well-paid jobs, the task of selection has year by year become more burdensome and the backwash effect on the earlier stages of education has grown ever more disastrous. Increasing numbers of children leave shool labelled as rejects or failures, so that the psychological tension to which students are subjected at examination time is extremely severe; even those who succeed do so to an increasing extent by learning to qualify rather than by learning to understand or by developing the initiative and inner resourcefulness which would be useful to them in tackling any one of a thousand practical problems in their locality, their homes, or their farms. The pernicious effects of examinations are not confined to a few weeks a year—being the dominant influence, they interfere with and destroy the whole pattern of what is learnt throughout the year.

The mission felt that nothing less than a radical change in the entire examination system would be adequate. First, the extreme inequalities between districts and between good and bad schools would have to be tackled by introducing a basic quota under which a certain proportion of primary-school leavers from every school would be given secondary school places. (Detailed statistical analysis of past examination results showed that the examination as a selection device had virtually no predictive validity.) Second, a number of bonus quotas could be made available for the schools within each district whose over-all examination results were well above average—thus providing school-focused incentives to spur teachers, parents and students to raise the quality of schools. Third, the examination itself would have to be changed, so as to improve its content and reliability and to supplement the " book learning " parts with tests designed to assess grasp of local problems, as well as ability to deal with them.

Redistribution from growth

The basic decision of the mission to give priority in examining Kenya's employment situation to the problem of the low level—in fact the poverty level—of returns from work, which meant taking into account all those whose employment was not productive enough to earn them an income which was up to a modest minimum, had important repercussions on its whole approach to its task and on its recommendations. The full range of income distribution had to be considered and, at its lower end, the many different groups below the poverty line. This range is illustrated in the table overleaf, taken from the report.

For the 1970s and 1980s the mission proposed that Kenyan development strategy should focus on ensuring that all households achieved minimum income targets by specified dates. The targets proposed by the mission were, for rural households, 120 shs. a month, or £72 a year, by 1978 and £108 a year by 1985, and, for urban households, 200 shs. a

TABLE II. HOUSEHOLD INCOME DISTRIBUTION BY ECONOMIC GROUP AND INCOME SIZE, 1968-70

Economic group	Annual income (K£)	Number of households [1] (thousands)
Owners of medium-sized to large non-agricultural enterprises in the formal sector of commerce, industry and services; *rentiers*; big farmers; self-employed professional people; holders of high-level jobs in the formal sector.	1 000 and over	30
Intermediate-level employees in the formal sector; owners of medium-sized non-agricultural enterprises in the formal sector; less prosperous big farmers.	600-1 000	50
Semi-skilled employees in the formal sector; prosperous smallholders; better-off owners of non-agricultural rural enterprises; a small proportion of owners of enterprises in the formal sector.	200-600	220
Unskilled employees in the formal non-agricultural sector; a significant proportion of smallholders; most of the owners of non-agricultural rural enterprises.	120-200	240
Employees in formal-sector agriculture; a small proportion of unskilled employees in the formal sector; better-off wage earners and self-employed persons in the informal urban sector; a small proportion of owners of non-agricultural rural enterprises.	60-120	330
Workers employed on small holdings and in rural non-agricultural enterprises; a significant proportion of employed and self-employed persons in the informal urban sector; a sizeable number of smallholders.	20-60	1 140
Smallholders; pastoralists in semi-arid and arid zones; unemployed and landless persons in both rural and urban areas.	20 and less	330
Total		2 340

[1] Very approximate.

Source: ILO: *Employment, incomes and equality . . .*, op. cit., p. 74.

month, or £120 a year, by 1978 and £150 a year by 1985.[1] A glance at the above table will show the main categories of people at present below this poverty line. In addition there is the regional dimension: income dispari-

[1] At 1972 prices. At the time of writing the Kenyan £ was worth about 20 per cent more than the £ sterling.

ties between different regions are very considerable in Kenya and the poverty problem tends to be concentrated in the areas outside Nairobi, Mombasa and the Central Province. There are also considerable variations in income levels even among the various districts and localities within the same province. Generally speaking poverty is especially severe in the semi-arid and arid areas—precisely those areas whose settlement will become increasingly imperative as the population continues to expand. The small holdings below the poverty line are concentrated in areas of high population pressure around Lake Victoria and elsewhere, and they also include a high proportion of farms managed by women in the absence of their husbands and other male family members in Nairobi. This situation in turn raises special problems of farm management, together with the question of who should benefit from extension services and have access to the cash income to be earned through the transition from food crop to cash crop production—all of which are very relevant for an employment strategy.

Essentially the report suggests a series of diverse but inter-related measures for ensuring more equal access to the opportunities provided by the expanding Kenyan economy for those now at a disadvantage in this respect and unable to obtain productive employment. This would require a reorientation of government expenditure towards the poorer regions and poorer elements of the population as well as the adoption of an over-all economic policy which would shift employment and earning opportunities in the direction of these poorer groups. One device recommended by the mission for use in various contexts is the system of quotas; quotas for government expenditure in various regions (maximum quotas for Nairobi and minimum quotas for poorer regions); quotas for access to primary and secondary education, with special consideration for girls; quotas for entry into the civil service; regional quotas for access to health services, etc.; and quotas to enable the poorest farmers and women farmers to benefit from extension services.

The over-all strategy of the report is described as being one of redistribution from growth. The Kenyan economy has been expanding regularly at the high rate of 7 to 8 per cent per annum in terms of aggregate production ever since independence. The mission did not make any specific quantitative analysis of the likely future growth rates but many of its recommendations would have the effect of raising the rate—for instance those aimed at raising the incomes of the lower income groups through more productive employment, at intensification of land use, at promotion of the informal sector, at easing balance-of-payments pressures through changed products, changed technology and revised economic policies, and at retention of a higher proportion of the profits of foreign enterprises. While measures to improve the position of the lower income groups might have the effect of reducing the growth rate at least temporarily, in the special circumstances of Kenya there is no reason why these measures should necessarily outweigh others tending to raise the growth rate.[1]

The model of redistribution from growth reproduced in the mission's report [2] is based on the assumption that the rate of growth of production will remain at 7 per cent per annum, that the real incomes of those in the top income bracket, i.e. the 1 per cent of the total population receiving 10 per cent of total income, can be stabilised for a number of years, and that the resources gained from this freeze of top incomes can be switched to a special labour-intensive investment package in favour of those in the bottom income bracket, i.e. the almost 40 per cent of the total population also receiving 10 per cent of total income. The content of this labour-intensive investment package can be derived from the recommendations of the report as a whole. This approach involves the additional assumption that, prior to redistribution, the benefits of economic growth at the rate of 7 per cent per annum would be equally spread over the poor and other sections of the population. There is little evidence as to whether or not this has been the case in the Kenyan economy as a whole [3], but income distribution among the African population has almost inevitably become more unequal since independence, as a result of the Kenyanisation of jobs (commanding incomes far above the average) and of land previously held by expatriates.

Through redistribution from growth, the incomes of the poorer 35 to 40 per cent of the population could be doubled within the relatively short span of a decade or less. The model demonstrates that the period required is not highly sensitive to the capital/output ratio of the special investment package. This doubling of the incomes of the lower income groups could make a real impact on the proportion of the " working poor " in the total population, especially if further refinement reoriented the measures towards improvement of the position of the neediest within the lower income groups, a notion which is central to the whole report.

If applied to all the aspects of development strategy, redistribution from growth would have a profound effect on the programme of each government department and in every area of the country. Full implementation would require a shift from central to local planning in order to permit adjustment in the allocation of government resources,

[1] A comparative analysis of the situation in different developing countries fails to show any connection between the growth rate of GNP and the degree of income inequality, a point made also by the President of the World Bank Group in his address to the 1972 meeting of the Board of Governors; see Robert S. McNamara: *Address to the Board of Governors*. 25 September 1972 (Washington, IBRD, 1972).

[2] See ILO: *Employment, incomes and equality . . .*, op. cit., Technical Paper 6, pp. 365-370.

[3] If this assumption is not correct and the poor sections do not participate in general progress, redistributive action would have to be that much greater. It is very likely that the position of the poorer groups in terms of access to public services—health clinics, water, roads, transport—has improved not only absolutely but also relatively.

as required, to meet the specific priority needs of each area for abolishing poverty.

The real issue is, of course, the political feasibility of the strategy proposed. Already the post-independence structures of incomes and land ownership, power and position, have become more firmly based, though the patterns of privilege and class are still affected by traditional family and other ties. Local interests are bound in important ways to interests abroad through the links of trade and private investment, particularly as regards the developed countries. This constellation of local and overseas interests, of which there are many but not all of which are concordant, makes it difficult to effect the change of strategy required. However, the objective of the Government, as stated in Sessional Paper No. 10 submitted to the National Assembly in 1965 [1], is clear: the benefits of growth must be equitably distributed. The question remains whether the changes required to achieve this objective can be set in motion before the interests inhibiting them strengthen to the point of obstructing all reform.

The rationale of redistribution from growth resides in the low levels of income in the country as a whole, together with the patterns of extreme inequality inherited from the colonial period. These characteristics Kenya shares with the majority of the African countries. That is the basic reason for supposing that the strategy proposed in the Kenya report, with appropriate modifications, may have relevance for other countries in Africa faced with similar problems of unemployment and poverty and gross imbalances in incomes and opportunities.

---

[1] Republic of Kenya, National Assembly: *African Socialism and its application to planning in Kenya*, Sessional Paper No. 10 of 1965.

Employment Policy in Tropical Africa

The Need for Radical Revision

Guy HUNTER [1]

EMPLOYMENT, in its full sense, covers the whole range and style of the economic activities of a society—how people make their livelihood, and the social relations and rules of behaviour within which the economic process is embedded. "Wage-paid employment", as the statistics define it, in the African societies with which this article is concerned, constitutes a tiny fraction of this process, accounting for not more than 10 per cent of the labour force in most of the countries of Tropical Africa; until fairly recently wage earners in Nigeria amounted to about 600,000 out of a population of over 50 million. Before plunging into the details of the current dilemma of existing and prospective "unemployment", it is essential to look at the whole picture of how African peoples made a livelihood and at the changes which have taken place in the last 150 years.

The theme of the first part of this article can be stated in three propositions. First, the main direction of economic growth and the burden of economic advice have been disastrously inappropriate for the *general* development of African societies, and this error has been compounded by political as well as economic choices in the post-independence period.

Second, the economic analysis of the present situation, based on the experience of modern industrialised societies, has presented the "problems" in misleading and inappropriate terms, leading either to the adoption of unattainable targets or to the propagation of unnecessary despair—" full employment " in the Western sense is not either a possible or an appropriate goal for African societies even in the medium term, whereas a marked improvement in the general level of livelihood *is* possible.

---

[1] Overseas Development Institute, London.

Third, the effects of the economic policy pursued have been particularly unfortunate in the field of education and the resulting distortion has now recoiled on the economic policy in question.

The second part of the article will turn to a more detailed analysis of conventional economic policies which might now be available to achieve a better balance, while the third part will suggest a more radical alternative.

I

The reservoir philosophy

Labour shortage, not unemployment, was the problem which concerned the early colonial administrations, particularly in Central and East Africa (Southern and Northern Rhodesia, Nyasaland, Tanganyika, Kenya, Uganda [1]). There were bitter disputes between district commissioners and missionaries about measures designed to force Africans out of their traditional economy to work in more " modern ", European-run undertakings and in clerical jobs in the government sector or elsewhere. This was one early symptom of the long process of substituting wage employment for the traditional livelihood; for, as President Nyerere once remarked, " in the old Africa everybody worked "—or to put it more accurately, everyone had a function in society and a source of livelihood. There was not only local pressure; the *African Labour Survey* [2] prepared by the International Labour Office in 1958 and the First African Regional Conference of the ILO, held in Lagos in December 1960, were much concerned about the vast amount of labour migration which was by then taking place—from Southern and Central Africa to the mines, north and eastwards to Uganda and to the sisal plantations of Tanganyika, and from the dry savannah of West Africa to the coastal forest. It was then estimated that, of the 12 to 13 million adult, able-bodied African males (i.e. healthy and between 16 and 45 years of age) in Southern, East and Central Africa, 5 million were absent from their tribal areas. Such migration should not be taken as a whole-hearted acceptance of the dual economy. The movements within the agricultural sector reflected rather the long dry season, during which the men could move without local loss of production; many of them, in West Africa and Uganda, worked for other small farmers. The movements to the mines came to be partly assimilated into the tribal system of values—a man went to earn his bride-price and to some extent to show his manhood. One social anthropologist [3] has described

[1] See in particular Philip Mason: *The birth of a dilemma* (London, Oxford University Press, 1958), and Roland Oliver: *The missionary factor in East Africa* (London, Longmans, 1952).

[2] ILO: *African Labour Survey*, Studies and Reports, New Series, No. 48 (Geneva, 1958).

[3] W. Watson: *Tribal cohesion in a money economy* (Manchester, Manchester University Press for Rhodes-Livingstone Institute, 1958).

these movements as those of " peasants raiding the cash economy for goods ". The real home society remained the traditional society. Thus, if we take a reasonably long time-span, say from Livingstone's Africa of 1850 to 1950, it will be seen that a considerable dent had been made in the traditional African way of life, impoverishing the rural areas and building up mines, plantations and westernised capital cities.[1]

The philosophy of this colonial period might well be called the " reservoir " philosophy—with its strangely apt echo of " African reserves ". According to this philosophy, out of the poverty-stricken subsistence economy African labour would enter modern wage-paid employment (until they were all absorbed?). Until the 1950s there was little real attempt to raise the existing rural society from where it stood to a significantly higher level. The dual economy was deeply embedded in Africa, not only in fact but in philosophy. Certainly, there were soil conservation measures, anti-starvation regulations for planting cassava, local attempts at cash-cropping; but, with few exceptions, there was no radical agricultural development policy for small farmers—the Swynnerton Plan for Kenya's Central Province came into being in the last half of the 1950s. The main exceptions were the result not so much of government action as of the action of the commercial companies—the much earlier development of the palm oil trade in West Africa, of cotton and later coffee in Uganda, of plantations in the Congo, and of ground-nuts in Northern Nigeria.[2] In the 1950s more effort began to show: co-operatives were pushed, revolving funds or credit and savings banks to help African traders began to be set up, and there were some (mainly small and hesitant) attempts at irrigation. But on the whole more determined (and more expensive) attempts were made to create industries, and by 1960 a limited number of industrial undertakings (electric power, cement, textiles, biscuits, soft drinks, breweries, flour mills) could be found, in plan or in fact, in a large number of countries.

Alongside this " reservoir " economic system, education had to have its place. Primary schools were set up on a growing scale, and at first greeted with little enthusiasm by the African villager. Not only was it often hard to get the children to school at all (there were many apologies from the local administration about this) but it was even harder to keep them there; there was an enormously high " drop-out " rate after two years, or four years at the most. But by the late 1950s (earlier in West Africa), a revolution had taken place. Largely thanks to the idealism of the missionaries, high-quality secondary grammar schools were established and then governments added the first few university colleges. Suddenly,

---

[1] For example, the African population of Leopoldville grew from 39,700 in 1938 to 282,000 in 1956.

[2] A few non-company schemes stand out—e.g. Kilimanjaro coffee (co-operative), Mwanza cotton (co-operative), the much earlier Sudan Gezira irrigation scheme, and the ill-fated British ground-nut scheme in Tanganyika.

with Independence not far off, the huge rewards of secondary and higher education were well within sight. Moreover, even the 7- or 8-year primary school leaver in the late 1950s stood a good chance of obtaining a wage-paid job (teacher, clerk, extension worker, policeman, hospital assistant, factory worker). Some time in the 1950s—again, earlier in parts of West Africa—Africans really accepted the dual economy and set themselves to leave the lower and enter the upper half of it.

Finally, as Independence was achieved, there was a sharp intensification of the factors which have created our present problem. There was a renewed emphasis on industrialisation—for industry had made the rich world rich. Economists (with a few honourable exceptions [1]) supported African politicians in this policy, partly no doubt on account of their own belief in " structural transformation ", based mainly on their experience of the transfer from agriculture to industry which had marked the recent growth of Western Europe in wholly different conditions and from a wholly different starting point.

Simultaneously, there was renewed strong emphasis on creating an élite (new and expanded universities and secondary schools), supported by a flood of " high-level " manpower surveys and by the enthusiasm of (particularly) British and American universities. Africans had to be found to fill government posts and to man the new industries. Possibly, if this had been all that had happened, the present situation would at least appear less difficult, although it would in fact be worse. But it was not all. Under the influence of the United Nations Educational, Scientific and Cultural Organisation (UNESCO), a major campaign for the rapid expansion of primary education also developed. Since education by now had, in the African mind, the connotation " qualification for a job ", the faster primary education expanded, the greater became the dissatisfaction and frustration within the " reservoir ", because the jobs available for primary school leavers were few, and rapidly becoming fewer per head of the fast expanding output of the schools. The continued neglect of the agricultural economy made life there an increasingly unacceptable alternative.

In the decade of 1960-70 this psychological and physical movement gained momentum and volume with the speed of an avalanche. Relatively huge numbers of Africans were pouring out of the schools; the modern sector was far too small to absorb them; the cities were growing at an alarming pace; and the demand for jobs was growing even faster. Employment became the planner's nightmare.

Thus by 1970, as a result of the policies both of former colonial powers and of the successor African governments, supported by United Nations agencies and many other outside influences, Tropical Africa found itself the victim of two grave miscalculations. The first was economic.

---

[1] For instance Sir Arthur Lewis, W. W. Rostow, W. B. Reddaway.

There are at least three clear reasons why the modern sector, based on advanced technology, should never have been expected to absorb the labour from the reservoir at an adequate rate. First, there was hardly any external market for African industrial goods; Africa lacked the comparative advantage which enabled European industry to expand its exports so fast, and indeed, at the equivalent stage of its development, Europe would have been hard put to it to industrialise on the basis of the market provided by its own internal agricultural population. Second, the African rural economy was in any case very little developed—far less so than the European rural economy at the equivalent period; 80 per cent of all consumers—in some countries over 90 per cent—belonged to the rural population, with virtually no cash purchasing power; they provided no adequate internal market for industrial growth. Third, the technology used absorbed relatively little labour per £10,000 of scarce capital invested. On top of these difficulties is piled a population growth rate rising quickly to 2.5 or 3 per cent per annum—three times the rate of growth of nineteenth-century Britain. The inescapable conclusions to be drawn from this situation were noted by Bruce Johnston [1] when he established the length of time—thirty-five to fifty years according to various assumptions—during which the absolute numbers of the rural population would continue to increase even on the basis of optimistic estimates of urban employment growth. This should have put an end to all talk of " structural transformation " by drawing rural labour into the urban-industrial sector as an employment policy which could be effective in less than two generation ahead.[2]

The second miscalculation, largely a consequence of the economic policy, was educational. It was not perceived early enough that an educational system designed to staff the initially tiny modern sector —first primary schools for junior clerks and mission assistants, then a more literary secondary school system for teachers and junior government staff, and finally a full-scale university at London or Paris levels for senior officials—would be out of style for a population the vast majority of which would consist of smallholders for fifty years ahead. Even technical education in the trade schools of the 1950s was designed to produce modern sector skills—electricians and mechanics. Very quickly the university, because of its immense prestige and the huge rewards promised for its graduates, not only spread its influence downwards to affect the curriculum and examinations of secondary and primary schools,

[1] Bruce Johnston: " Agriculture and economic development: the relevance of the Japanese experience ", in *Food Research Institute Studies* (Stanford), Vol. VI, No. 3, 1966, pp. 251-312.

[2] Keith Marsden dealt very effectively with one of the most recent " structural transformation " arguments put forward by Barend de Vries when he suggested that " the objective [should] be a society in which all are employed in activities in which the most productive methods known to man are used ". See " Towards a synthesis of economic growth and social justice ", in *International Labour Review*, Vol. 100, No. 5, Nov. 1969, p. 391.

but began to suck upwards every African boy or girl who could make the grade. One secondary school, technical college, medical college, or agricultural college after another managed to become a university faculty. There appeared to be some justification for this in the need for high-level manpower, and indeed both British and American policies urged a lowering of university entrance standards (to Form IV instead of Form VI, as in Zambia) in order to speed up university output.

But what was not perceived was that simultaneously both the government and the physical structure in capital cities were deliberately being made more sophisticated and complex, increasing the demand for high-level skills. Planning departments, with first one, then three, then a dozen economists and statisticians became fashionable. Huge modern buildings, tarmac roads and airlines were in demand; probation officers, educational planners and psychologists, electronic engineers, physiotherapists and cine technicians were needed; the requirements for sought-after sophisticated skills and the tables of shortages seem unending. This was, of course, only natural. Developed economies are almost insatiable consumers of graduate manpower. If African countries were to have a cap-à-pie modern sector and modern capital city, both their ambitions and their advisers from developed economies would see the need for such things. But all the while the gap between the government services and the capital city on the one hand and the 80 per cent rural population on the other was growing; the educational system was increasingly focusing on preparation for sophistication, but the number of jobs for the ordinary African was stagnating. Thus at the primary level of education an insoluble problem was created: no amount of " rurally biased " curricula could persuade young people to remain in an unimproved agricultural sector or in a rural economy deprived of even minor investment—feeder roads, telephones, electricity, storage space for agricultural produce, water supply, health services, and transport and petrol for the extension and other staff trying to improve the situation. That is why I have called the educational problem consequential—it is largely a consequence of the " reservoir " economic philosophy.

Finally, it is indeed unfortunate that this whole situation should have been analysed in terms of unemployment—with a large and murky penumbra of underemployment, disguised unemployment, etc.—and on the basis of some very extraordinary definitions of the labour force, drawn from Western experience, which excluded sometimes those who were " not seeking work " because they knew there was no work to find, sometimes women, despite the hours which most African women spend working on the farm, or in trading, or in pounding grain into flour (this is, of course, " employment " if it is done in a flour mill). These definitions and concepts have been so unsatisfactory and controversial because the categories and conventions found in developed countries are unsuited to the African context, and to make use of them is as if a constitutional lawyer were to analyse the actions of the Norman kings in terms of conventions governing the British monarchy of 1972.[1]

In fact, whether in Asia or in Africa, the great majority of people find a livelihood, in a family unit, through a host of miscellaneous and petty activities—partly from a landholding of perhaps two or three acres, partly from a little market or street trading, partly from a day here and there of casual or seasonal employment, in ways so elusive that they slip through the crude net of statistics unnoticed. Nearly 50 per cent of Indians are said to live on a per head income of less than 1 rupee (13 US cents) per day.[2] At the root of this rural poverty is the low level of production on the land, and the consequent low purchasing power of the average villager.

In sum, there has been a failure to develop the economy from its original state of being a wholly rural economy; a failure to invest adequately in such development; a failure to learn, whether from seventeenth- or eighteenth-century Europe or from parts of contemporary India, what an enormous number of livelihoods (and even "jobs") can be generated in services, trade, minor production, construction, distribution, and processing in a rural economy and its small market centres, provided that the productive base of farming is intensive and flourishing.

Even today, when employment has begun to supersede growth of GNP as the target of economic planning, one finds, for example in the report of the international team of development experts organised by the ILO to study the causes of unemployment in Colombia [3], not only a significant title—" Towards full employment "—but also a set of highly theoretical calculations of the rates of growth in the agricultural, industrial and other sectors which would generate enough " jobs " for the whole labour force. If the employment programmes of the decade of 1970-80 are to be framed in these terms, we shall continue to stare aghast at report after report recording 10 or 18 or 25 or 30 per cent unemployment [4], population growth of 3 per cent, employment growth of 2 per cent, insufficient capital or " projects " to achieve the enormous expansion of wage-paid jobs which appears to be necessary, and a few despairing recommendations for rural works or youth brigades, which are, by clear

---

[1] See in particular Gunnar Myrdal: *Asian drama* (London, Allen Lane, 1968), and in an interview with FAO: *Ceres* (Rome), Vol. 4, No. 2, Mar.-Apr. 1971, p. 32: " We must discard entirely the concept of 'unemployment' and 'underemployment' as inadequate to reality. We have to base our analysis of labour utilisation on simpler behavioural concepts: which people work at all; for what periods during the day, week, month and year do they work; and with what intensity and effectiveness."

[2] V. M. Dandekar: *Poverty in India* (New Delhi, Ford Foundation, Dec. 1970). See also B. S. Minhas: *Mass poverty and rural development in India* (New Delhi, Government of India, Mar. 1971).

[3] ILO: *Towards full employment*. A programme for Colombia prepared by an inter-agency team organised by the International Labour Office (Geneva, 1970).

[4] The differences in figures reflect chiefly the confusion and variation in definitions of the " labour force ", " employment ", " underemployment ", etc.

admission, wholly inadequate to achieve the assumed goals. We can avoid despair only by remembering that both the analysis and the goals are put in the wrong terms: " full employment ", in the normal sense of this term, is not yet a realistic aim for most of Africa.

II

So far the picture has been painted in bold and rather dark colours —bold because it is essential to make clear the need for fundamental review rather than tinkering; dark because in total the situation is dark. Necessarily, exceptions have been omitted; there is no tribute to good intentions and local achievements, no allowance for hindsight—for the district commissioners of 1900 did not foresee 1960, although many of them did view with concern the disturbance of values and disciplines in the old society by a modernising process which could only affect so small a proportion of it. I have so far used few detailed references, because the results of the policy followed are now known and documented and will, I think, support the thesis of the first part of this article. We can now turn to some general facts about the labour force and employment; to some of the suggestions, made mainly by economists, for improving the situation, largely within the existing tradition of economic thinking; and, finally, in the third part, to some more positive and radical suggestions for turning development policy upside down and starting, not from the modern sector, but from the potential of the great mass of the population, both as producers and as consumers.

The labour force and employment

David Turnham [1] has estimated the growth of the labour force as follows:

Type of country	1965-80		1970-80	
	Total	Annual	Total	Annual
			%	
Less developed countries	39.0	2.2	25.2	2.3
Developed countries	15.8	1.0	10.0	1.0

A fairer comparison with developed countries might be made by reference to the period of most rapid growth—

[1] David Turnham: *The employment problem in less-developed countries*, Employment Series, No. 1 (Paris, OECD Development Centre, 1971), p. 31.

(% per annum)

Germany		*France*	
1860-90	1.4	1820-70	0.4
1890-1913	1.6	1870-1913	0.4
Great Britain		*United States*	
1870-90	1.4	1850-83	3.0
1890-1914	1.2	1883-1914	2.5

Only the United States, with its enormous resources, equalled the rates for less developed countries today. In Europe, despite rapid economic growth and huge external markets, the rate of growth of the labour force never moved above 1.6 per cent per annum (in Germany).

At the present time Elliot Berg [1] estimates that, outside Latin America, the proportion of the total population in wage-paid employment is less than 10 per cent; and this estimate is partially supported for Tropical Africa by the ILO [2] figures (wage earners constituting less than 9 per cent of the labour force in about half of thirty-four African countries).

Labour force figures are rather questionable, since there is much argument about which categories of workers should be included; but the LDC labour force growth rates are lower than the possibly more reliable LDC population growth rates, and there is no reason to suppose that the labour force will grow more slowly than the population. With high population growth there is a high proportion of young people; in 1965 young people under 15 years of age made up 45 per cent of the total population of Africa, and the 15 to 59 year old age group constituted about 50 per cent.[3]

The LDC labour force is, of course, primarily in the rural sector. The ILO estimates for Africa that 75.4 per cent fall in the category " farmers, fishermen, hunters, loggers and related workers ".[4] Moreover, as Bruce Johnston's calculations [5] imply, the rate of structural change is extremely slow. Turnham [6] gives a figure for all LDCs—including those of Latin America where the percentage in agriculture is far lower in some cases—of 73.3 per cent in the agricultural sector in 1950, falling to 70.7

[1] Elliot J. Berg: " Wages and employment ", in OECD: *The challenge of unemployment to development and the role of training and research institutes in development* (Paris, 1971), p. 102.

[2] ILO: *Employment policy in Africa*, Report IV (1), Third African Regional Conference, Accra, December 1969 (Geneva, 1969), p. 18. The percentage for *all* Africa is given as 19.2. But this includes 63.3 per cent for the Republic of South Africa and 33.2 per cent for North Africa. East and Central Africa each has about 15 per cent, West Africa only 6.1 per cent.

[3] Ibid., p. 11.

[4] Ibid., p. 17.

[5] Johnston, op. cit.

[6] Turnham, op. cit., p. 35.

per cent in 1960. Sir Arthur Lewis [1] has quoted figures for Kenya showing an average per annum growth of private real output of 4 per cent, and a negative figure of −1 per cent for wage employment, over the period 1954-64. Figures varying from 11 to 15 per cent per annum have been given as the GNP growth rate necessary to provide jobs for the *increase* in the labour force—Robert Shaw, for example, quotes an 11 per cent rate as the minimum required to stabilise present unemployment in a " typical African country ".[2] An additional misfortune is that, as both Turnham and Berg confirm, there is a much higher proportion of unemployment among the better educated than among the illiterate, and this is probably partly explained by the much higher proportion of literates who emigrate from rural to urban areas [3]; in the rural areas their number might be concealed in figures for underemployment or self-employment. Turnham [4] also draws attention to the high proportion of the 16 to 17 year old male age group shown in sample survey data for India as " students " (55 per cent as compared with 17 per cent of the male and female population of that age group, according to UNESCO figures, in the Federal Republic of Germany), a sign of concealed unemployment.

To the concern aroused by these over-all figures must be added the anxiety felt about rural-urban migration. The often quoted thesis on this subject by Todaro [5], suggesting that the rate of this migration reflects a balance between the differential between rural and urban wages and the chances of finding employment in a town, can be somewhat expanded by taking into account other factors—Berg [6] emphasises the motive of escape from the tyranny of rural tribal society, and others have pointed to attractions of urban life in negative form (e.g. escape from agricultural drudgery) as well as to the *social* pressure put on young men with any education to provide a return on their parents' investment and gain the approval of their local society by getting a paid urban job. Berg notes that migration continues even when urban wages fall quite sharply.

---

[1] W. Arthur Lewis: " Employment in Nigeria ", in *Development Digest* (Washington, DC, National Planning Association for the United States Agency for International Development), Vol. VII, No. 4, Oct. 1969, p. 15.

[2] R. d'A. Shaw: *Jobs and agricultural development* (Washington, DC, Overseas Development Council, 1970), p. 3.

[3] Cf. Louis Roussel: " Measuring rural-urban drift in developing countries: a suggested method ", in *International Labour Review*, Vol. 101, No. 3, Mar. 1970, pp. 229-246, and in particular the figures quoted on p. 240 for the Ivory Coast, for the 15 to 29 year old age group:

Educational level	*% of males leaving the village*
Illiterate	8
Literate	42
Primary school-leaving certificate	61

[4] Turnham, op. cit., p. 42.

[5] M. P. Todaro: " A model of labor migration and urban unemployment in less-developed countries ", in *American Economic Review* (Menasha (Wisconsin)), Vol. LIX, No. 1, Mar. 1969, pp. 138-148.

[6] Berg, op. cit.

Naturally, migration from the countryside creates urban unemployment problems of increasing intensity, worrying to governments because the urban population is more politically vocal and because urban relief and welfare are so expensive. Economists are now apt to call this " open, urban unemployment ", perhaps with a sigh of relief that here is a problem, similar to that of Western economies, which can be measured (?) and understood, unlike the unfamiliar and unclassifiable problems of rural underemployment. It would be just as unfortunate if this problem attracted too much attention as if it were disregarded; for the causes of urban unemployment lie largely in the neglect of the rural economy.

Perhaps these few highly condensed references to the general " employment " position will be enough to point up the basic situation described in the first part of this article—over-reliance on structural transformation and wage-paid employment as a development method; the inability of the modern sector to meet expectations in this respect; the disastrous effect of the consequential educational system in creating expectations which the economic policy followed could not fulfil; and the dilemma of urban unemployment, which is positively *increased* by efforts to create more urban jobs, since the 70 per cent " reservoir " of rural labour will simply flood into the towns in greater volume.

Conventional remedies

1. The urban wage level

In the past few years economists have increasingly stressed the effects of certain economic policies, viewing these as a cause of the slow rate of employment growth. I prefer the view, recently expressed by John Weeks [1], that they are symptoms rather than causes—symptomatic of the whole reservoir-modern sector approach. But even symptoms deserve treatment.

High urban wages come in for much attack in this analysis, as encouraging capital intensity in industry, decreasing service and other unskilled employment, and accelerating the rural-urban labour flow. Berg [2] has observed that urban incomes are three times higher than rural incomes in West Pakistan, four times higher in Egypt, two-and-a-half times higher in Kenya. Elkan [3] mentions an average wage increase of

[1] John Weeks: " Does employment matter? ", in McGill University, Centre for Developing Area Studies: *Manpower and Unemployment Research in Africa* (Montreal), Vol. 4, No. 1, Apr. 1971, p. 69.

[2] Elliot J. Berg: " Wages policy and employment in less-developed countries ", in R. Robinson and P. Johnston (eds.): *Prospects for employment opportunities in the nineteen seventies* (London, HMSO, 1971).

[3] Walter Elkan: " Urban unemployment in East Africa ", in *International Affairs* (London, Oxford University Press for the Royal Institute of International Affairs), Vol. 46, No. 3, July 1970, p. 525.

10 per cent per annum for unskilled urban workers in Kenya between 1960 and 1966 and a rise in the urban statutory minimum wage in Uganda from Sh.EA 75 to 152 between 1959 and 1964; similar high figures could be given for many African countries. An ILO mission to an East African country put forward the suggestion that a 10 per cent increase in wages might imply a 2.5 per cent decrease in employment; but the evidence for this statement is not clear.[1] Both Todaro and (for Latin America) J. A. Eriksson [2] and many others have traced a direct relationship between wage increases and employment.

2. Other factors

Many writers have listed policies tending to induce high capital intensity and low employment rates. Berg [3] suggests overvalued exchange rates, subsidised credit arrangements, industrial incentive legislation, fiscal policies for industry, duty-free imports of capital goods, spares and materials for industry, accelerated depreciation and investment allowance provisions. Higher capital intensity has in fact increased the productivity of the industrial labour force, estimated by Singer [4] to be rising at from 4 to 5 per cent and by Clark [5] (for Uganda) at from 5 to 6 per cent per annum. Artificially cheap capital imports are therefore assisting a certain type of GNP growth but very substantially checking direct employment in the industries concerned. Moreover, the Colombia report [6] stresses that the goods bought by industrialists, managers and relatively highly paid urban workers tend to be imported and Western style (this is also true of foodstuffs and building materials), resulting not only in a foreign exchange drain but in less possibility of expanding local manufacture; whereas peasant communities have a type of demand more easily met from local industries and crafts. Even the argument that accumulation of capital in relatively few hands is likely to favour savings and investment is of doubtful validity in developing countries; apart from profits remitted overseas by expatriate commercial companies, local gains are often spent on overseas travel, overseas investment, or imported luxury goods.

Many writers, from Peter Bauer onwards, have drawn attention to the system of heavy taxation of agricultural surpluses as a means of aiding modern sector investment, as practised, for example, through

[1] ILO: *Employment policy in Africa*, op. cit., p. 44.

[2] J. A. Eriksson: " Wage change and employment growth in Latin American industry ", in *Manpower and Unemployment Research in Africa*, op. cit., Vol. 3, No. 2, Nov. 1970.

[3] Berg: " Wages and employment ", op. cit., p. 109.

[4] Hans Singer: " Agricultural unemployment and underemployment, with some implications for land reform " (unpublished).

[5] P. G. Clark: " Development strategy in an early stage economy: Uganda ", in *Journal of Modern African Studies*, Vol. 4, No. 1, 1966, pp. 47-64.

[6] ILO: *Towards full employment*, op. cit.

West African and Ugandan marketing boards: this has helped to keep down rural purchasing power and consequently rural employment. Eicher [1] and others have listed a number of employment-reducing agricultural policies, such as the subsidising of large tractors, food self-sufficiency policies (resulting in rising prices and higher urban wages), and government capital-intensive schemes (e.g. settlements) aimed at providing short cuts to agricultural development and avoiding the "unresponsive" small farmer. In fact ambitious plans for capital-intensive modern sector development, by raising wages in towns, by decreasing the rate of employment growth, and by robbing the agricultural economy of both purchasing power and development funds, have contributed very greatly to the present alarming situation. It may be useful to add two small reminders of the costs and results involved. The ILO [2] gives the following investments costs per worker in Egypt:

	US dollars
1 industrial job	5 070
1 agricultural job	616
1 building job	206

In the same report [3] it is mentioned that the agricultural sector (70 per cent or more of the labour force) ought to get 25 per cent of total investment—a fairly modest claim. At the time of preparation of the report in question this was the case in only four out of nineteen African countries and in more than half of them the share of the agricultural sector was less than 20 per cent.

To close this part, I would like to include two longer quotations. The first questions whether rectification of fiscal, exchange and wage policies would in fact have a dramatic effect:

> The favourite prescription of the economists—besides doubling or tripling of growth rates—is to correct the price system, particularly exchange rates, interest rates, terms of trade between agriculture and industry and prices of all factors of production. But has this faith in the price system been tested empirically? When various developing countries corrected their exchange rates or interest rates at various times, was this followed by a great surge in their employment situation or merely by better utilisation of capital, larger output and higher labour productivity? In any event, how large a segment of the economy does the price adjustment affect, when there is a large subsistence sector in these countries and the modern industrial sector generally contributed less than 10 per cent to total output? No one will dare suggest that price corrections will not move these economies in the right direction. But are they decisive? Or do they make only a marginal impression on the unemployment problem?

. . . .

---

[1] C. K. Eicher, Thomas Zaller, James Kocher and Fred Winch: *Employment generation in African agriculture*, Research Report No. 9 (East Lansing, Institute of International Agriculture, Michigan State University, July 1970).

[2] ILO: *Employment policy in Africa*, op. cit., p. 45.

[3] Ibid., p. 69.

We are more aware now that the very pattern and organisation of production itself dictates a pattern of consumption and distribution which is politically very difficult to change. Once you have increased your GNP by producing more luxury houses and cars, it is not very easy to convert them into low cost housing or bus transport. A certain pattern of consumption and distribution inevitably follows. We have a number of case studies by now which show how illusory it was to hope that the fruits of growth could be redistributed without reorganising the pattern of production and investment first.[1]

The second quotation is from a most thoughtful article on technologies by Keith Marsden.

It is significant that, during the historical growth of the now advanced countries, a close harmony was maintained in the development of one sector and another, and between capital intensity and income levels. In the United States, for example, average capital intensity per worker in industry was equivalent to only 1.7 times the average net output of the entire labour force (all sectors) in 1880. In 1948 it was 1.8 times. Variations from one industry to another were relatively small (mostly within a range of 3 : 1). In other words, industrial investment never " ran ahead " of the society's ability to save out of past and current incomes.

. . . .

The scale of organisation and the kind of technology which goes with it should match the economic and social characteristics of a country. Artisan workshops and small factories using simple equipment may be the most suitable first stage of industrialisation in a subsistence economy with low purchasing power and little monetary exchange, with bad communications and a predominantly peasant population where authority is vested in tribal chiefs or large landowners. In more advanced societies with a developed exchange economy, a more homogeneous, mobile population and a basic infrastructure, more highly mechanised small and medium factories will take the lead. In the process of time, some of these will grow into large-scale enterprises as they acquire experience, as markets expand, as the level of education and scientific skills rises and as a professional managerial cadre can be developed.[2]

Both these passages point to the need for the more radical thinking which this article is urging. In the third part an attempt will be made to put forward a positive alternative.

III

This article, so far, might be taken as a one-eyed attack on the development of a modern sector in developing countries. It is not. It is an attack on the particular ways in which a modern sector has been

---

[1] Mahbub ul Haq: " Employment in the 1970s: a new perspective ", paper presented to the Twelfth World Conference of the Society for International Development, Ottawa, May 1971.

[2] Keith Marsden: " Progressive technologies for developing countries ", in *International Labour Review*, Vol. 101, No. 5, May 1970, pp. 475-502, and in particular pp. 484 and 487. See also S. H. Frankel: *The economic impact on under-developed societies* (Oxford, Basil Blackwell, 1952), where he states on page 24: " . . . the machine and capital goods in general never exist in the abstract but always only in the relatively fleeting form suited to the momentary situation ".

developed and on the neglect of the much larger non-modern sector. Its object is to stress the need for a direct attempt to tackle the development of the major part of society by methods and by types of technology which can utilise both the physical potential of the land and its human potential, i.e. the muscles and skills of the people on it. Such a programme would need administrative, scientific, industrial and infrastructural support and investment of many modern kinds. Indeed, while agreeing with Marsden on the need for general adaptation of technology to stages of economic evolution, I would also stress that in the twentieth century there are certain advanced technologies, such as electric power, radio, herbicides, modern plant genetics, to give only a few examples, which can be married to a more dispersed, small-scale, simple type of economic activity.[1] In "turning development policy upside down" the point is to develop and use a modern sector to meet the needs and achievements of a vitalised rural sector and not to build a modern sector first, hoping, irrationally, that it will absorb the reservoir of villagers into wage-paid employment.

A new policy implies not only a change in the direction of investment and of price policy in broad terms: it implies a change of definitions and objectives.

In his conclusions Turnham [2] inclines towards adopting a criterion of incomes gained as a measure of the level of labour utilisation. This has the advantage of measuring both poverty and, to some extent, the intensity and effectiveness of work; for few will work really hard over long periods without any reward, except perhaps women engaged in domestic work! I would prefer to speak of "livelihoods" instead of employment or individual incomes in this context, and preferably "family livelihoods", because both in Africa and India the family is a real economic unit. The evening meal may have been earned by three or four members by means of different activities—from the family acre, selling a few cigarettes, and half a day's casual labour. The falsity of employment as a criterion can be shown, for example, when a large estate is broken up into ten-acre plots for "settlement" purposes. The employed workers disappear and statistically the level of employment falls; but family livelihoods are almost certainly increased—part of the apparent drop in the level of employment in Kenya is certainly due to the break-up of European farms into smallholdings. If agriculture is efficient, incomes may well rise substantially, and so may total production.

Secondly, a new policy would need a much bigger element of sociological and even historical understanding—it is partly the monopoly of economists in planning which has led to the present situation. A clearer understanding of how societies grow and change and a far deeper socio-

[1] I argued this at some length in *The best of both worlds?* and in *Modernising peasant societies* (London, Oxford University Press, 1967 and 1969).

[2] Turnham, op. cit.

logical *knowledge* of the present African situation are required. Indeed, a short list of our deficiencies in knowledge and some hints of possibly fruitful directions of research may be the best way to start this inquiry.

Ignorance of the traditional sector

First, we do not know nearly enough about farmers, farming systems and the motives or constraints which have led to the huge gap between what it is possible to grow—say 1,800 lb. of cotton per acre in Northern Nigeria—and what farmers do grow—about 350 lb. on average; this applies to an increasing range of crops, as research forges ahead of performance.

Second, we know far too little about the service, small-trading and workshop sector, both in rural and urban areas. In the discussion of the paper presented by Berg [1] to the OECD Development Centre's Meeting of Directors of Development Training and Research Institutes (Montebello, Quebec, July 1970), attention was drawn by the working group concerned [2] to " the significance of a large area, especially in services, that was neither ' subsistence ' nor part of the modern labour-employing sector ", and which the working group qualified as " murky " ! Yet, as Sir Arthur Lewis long ago observed, this area is a major source of livelihoods. We get a hint of the weight of the service sector in Latin America from Frank [3], when he quotes the following figures from studies undertaken by the United Nations Economic Commission for Latin America (ECLA):

Sector	Year	Share of GNP	Share of employment
		%	%
Industry	1925	11	14
	1969	23	14
Construction and services	1925	. .	26
	1969	.	43

Out of the 43 per cent employment in construction and services, 23 per cent was in " other services and unspecified activities " and was described by ECLA as " nothing more than unemployment or marginal services of lowest productivity ". Dantwala [4] quotes the Indian National

[1] Berg: " Wages and employment ", op. cit.

[2] " Summary of discussion by Working Group No. 3 ", in OECD: *The challenge of unemployment to development*..., op. cit., p. 140.

[3] André Gunter Frank: "Employment structure in Latin America", in *Manpower and Unemployment Research in Africa,* op. cit., Vol. 3, No. 1, Apr. 1970, p. 45.

[4] M. L. Dantwala: " The definition and measurement of unemployment in developing countries", in OECD: *The challenge of unemployment to development*..., op. cit., p. 30.

Sample Survey (17th Round, 1961-62) as showing 37 per cent of the gainfully employed in India as being " own account " workers and 25 per cent as being unpaid family workers—i.e. 62 per cent of the total gainfully employed. Even in urban India these two categories in 1959-60 together accounted for 47 per cent of the total gainfully employed (15th NSS Round). It is significant that in Tanzania the labour force survey by Robert S. Ray and the detailed regional planning surveys, by careful enumeration, made about a 300,000 addition to the official employment figures of just under 600,000, the vast majority of the persons concerned being employed in tiny undertakings, such as tailoring establishments, in the rural areas. Dharam Ghai [1] draws attention to the rapid growth of wage employment in Kenya in the traditional sector by means of the following comparison between the modern and traditional sectors:

Sector	1964	1968	Annual growth rate
	Thousands		%
Non-agriculture:			
Modern sector	381	436	3.4
Traditional sector	25	38	11.0
Agriculture:			
Modern sector	201	173	3.3
Traditional sector	301	410	7.8

He comments: " There has been an extremely rapid growth since Independence in small-scale African enterprises in trade, transport, construction, manufacturing and services. These enterprises typically use simple techniques, are largely unaffected by minimum wage regulations, and consequently tend to have relatively high marginal employment/output ratios, probably in the neighbourhood of unity."

Space does not permit more references, but the implications are that we do not know enough about this " murky " area of self-employment and small enterprise, which none the less John Weeks [2] has described as " the basis of the economy ", and that, where basic farm incomes are rising (as in parts of Kenya), the multiplier effect on local employment and enterprise can be very large. No one seems to have done any accurate work on this multiplier effect. The 1969 spring review prepared by the United States Agency for International Development (AID) says airily: " The proper multiplier effect between agriculture and GNP is not known ". Ozay Mehmet [3], in an interesting article emphasising the low

[1] Dharam P. Ghai: " Employment performance, prospects and policies in Kenya ", in Robinson and Johnston, op. cit., p. 48.

[2] Weeks, op. cit., p. 67.

[3] Ozay Mehmet: " Benefit-cost analysis for employment creation ", in *International Labour Review*, Vol. 104, Nos. 1-2, July-Aug. 1971, pp. 37-50 and in particular p. 44.

social costs of employment in the traditional sector and the importance of the multiplier effect, cannot provide an exact figure for the multiplier, although he believes it would be at least 5. The experience of the parts of India and Pakistan where the Green Revolution has been most successful suggests a rapid growth in non-agricultural employment close to areas where there are high farm incomes (especially in the West Pakistan Punjab). It may be observed, particularly from Dharam Ghai's statement, that small enterprises and services are not only labour-intensive but *naturally* use " intermediate technologies ". In fact, the view that the intermediate technology movement has failed to achieve large-scale results is based on the assumption that it ought to be applied to modern sector enterprises—but this is extremely difficult. The multiplication of traditional sector enterprises and services will result almost automatically in the use of simple technology, particularly if the temptation to invite foreign mass-production firms to supply simple consumer goods which could be made by local labour using local materials is resisted. Foreign exchange rates, inducements and concessions to capital-intensive industry, high minimum wages, etc., are all particularly significant in this connection.

Agricultural development

Perhaps the main point emerging from the foregoing discussion is the prime importance of agricultural development for improved employment prospects.[1]

Given the relative weights of agricultural and non-agricultural sectors . . . it is obvious that the nature and dimensions of the unemployment problem in LDCs is strongly influenced by the rate of growth of population, and its resolution primarily involves agricultural development and transformation. The arithmetic on this score is devastating.[2]

There are plenty of such statements. I have chosen only two from *employment* economists rather than from agriculturists. Why has this advice, which has been given so often lately (and much earlier by a few economists), not been effectively adopted?

The proposition which it involves goes somewhat as follows:

First, rural-urban labour force distribution, combined with population growth, implies a rising absolute number of people in rural areas for at least a generation and perhaps fifty years. Second, production per acre on small farms is higher than on large farms. More, and probably better, family livelihoods can be generated by intensive rather than extensive farming.[3] Third, the findings of modern research, if effectively

[1] Turnham, op. cit., p. 114.

[2] Berg: " Wages and employment ", op. cit., p. 103.

[3] There are many sources of reference. The Indian farm management surveys have found that there are higher yields on smaller farms. Marsden confirms this (" Towards a synthesis of economic growth and social justice ", op. cit., p. 411), as do J. W. Mellor, T. F. Weaver, J. J. Lele, and S. R. Simon (*Developing rural India—plan and practice* (Ithaca,

applied, can ensure a considerable rise in small farm production and incomes. Fourth, the purchasing power so generated will create a dispersed demand for labour, not only on farms but also in connection with distribution, construction, maintenance and transport, and for the supply of consumer goods, farm inputs, and minor farm investment. This employment can be augmented by rural works programmes (irrigation, roads, power lines, levelling, etc.), by public or co-operative investment in storage, market facilities and processing plant, and by an increase in personal and social services in market centres. As agriculture gains momentum and sophistication, larger " modern sector " industries will be stimulated for the production of fertilizers, tools and equipment, agricultural chemicals, and small-scale agricultural and other machinery.

There are, indeed, some difficulties, apart from the alleged conservatism and obstinacy of small farmers, which have been shown to be a myth whenever a really feasible and profitable opportunity is offered to them. There is, first, the problem of the market for agricultural produce. In fact, many parts of Africa are faced simultaneously with a limited food market and with malnutrition due to a diet which is deficient in quality and quantity. This situation will be cured by greater specialisation and efficiency and by better market communications. Fruit, vegetables, meat, fish, eggs and poultry, and milk are examples of produce offering large opportunities for expansion; the outlook for the export market is not as gloomy as is often thought, and the possibilities for more processing and packaging (higher value added) are still vast.[1]

Second, there is the fear that mechanisation in the course of agricultural development will reduce labour requirements. Studies of the Green Revolution in India and Pakistan do not bear out the contention that this danger is general. An AID study [2] of different levels and types of mechanisation, in various combinations, in the Punjab and in Maharashtra, concluded that a full range of mechanical equipment, including combine harvesters, might reduce on-farm labour requirements in the Punjab, but that requirements would grow in the different farm and crop condi-

New York, Cornell University Press, 1968)). Turnham provides startling figures for minifundios in Latin America. Taking the yield per acre of farms of an average size of 1 acre as equalling 100 (index), he compares this with the figure of 51 for family farms (12 hectares average) and of 49 for large farms (269 hectares average) (op. cit., p. 106). E. S. Clayton gives the cost of intensifying existing holdings in Kenya as being Shs. 100 per hectare, of subdividing large units as being Shs. 1,000 per hectare, and of creating new settlements as being Shs. 7,160 per hectare (" Agrarian reform, agricultural planning and employment in Kenya ", in *International Labour Review*, Vol. 102, No. 5, Nov. 1970, pp. 431-453, and in particular p. 443).

[1] Kusum Nair observed that farmers operating less than 0.3 hectare each in Japan marketed 38.4 per cent of their produce (cf. " Modernisation or obsolescence of the Indian farmer ", in *Development Digest*, Vol. VII, No. 4, Oct. 1969, pp. 42-48, and in particular p. 45).

[2] Martin H. Billings and Arjan Singh:" The effect of technology on farm productivity in India ", ibid., Vol. IX, No. 1, Jan. 1971, pp. 89-107, and in particular pp. 105-107.

tions of Maharashtra. This proposition has been put in general terms by Ridker [1]:

> The extent to which the positive employment effects offset the negative ones depends strongly on the particular mechanical device being considered (e.g. tube wells vs. combines) and the particular soils and cropping patterns to which it is applied.

In fact, in the early stages of intensive agricultural development, especially where double or treble cropping is involved, labour demand almost always rises. By the time a suitable and complete form of mechanisation is available, and can be afforded by African farmers, their prosperity will have created so much *off-farm* employment that this will more than offset falls in on-farm labour requirements. It may be useful to mention that the highly mechanised, highly intensive Japanese farms use twice as much labour per hectare of rice as the less mechanised Indian farms.

I have left to the end the gravest difficulty—agricultural administration.

> Sustained rapid increase in agricultural production requires a large number of highly complementary inputs. These inputs are perhaps best thought of as institutions —institutions for research, education, input supply, incentives and so on. But they also include a large quantity of physical inputs such as fertilizer, water, and pesticides, each of which requires various complex institutional structures if it is to be supplied in the appropriate time, place and form. . . . Indeed, the magnitude of the task and the range of things to be done is consistently underestimated, which in turn explains the paucity of successes in agricultural development.
>
> . . . .
>
> This public role is particularly crucial in the early stages of agricultural modernisation, when there may be many things to do and the returns to any one alone may be quite low.[2]

The problem of agricultural administration and institutions has been grossly neglected. This neglect is particularly due to the influence of " received opinion " (mythology), which, for example, constantly stresses " co-operatives " as a solution, without reference to the 60 to 70 per cent failure rate of agricultural co-operatives that has been recorded both in Africa and India; constantly repeats the need for official rural credit schemes, without reference to the surveys of how they have worked out and to the part played by private credit; cheerfully accepts a proportion of 1 extension worker to 1,500 farmers, without reference to the fact that the sponsors of almost all donor-aided projects find this proportion wholly inadequate. There are now some signs that a more careful and objective study is being made of these problems. But it cannot be denied that the lack of an effective, co-ordinated, administrative and institutional system for the development of smallholder agriculture is responsible for the gap between the production and employment potential revealed by research and the actual performance within LDCs all over the world.

---

[1] Ronald G. Ridker: " Agricultural mechanisation in South Asia ", ibid., p. 113.

[2] Mellor, Weaver, Lele and Simon, op. cit., pp. 368-369.

The need for a knowledge of farm systems has been neglected; adult education, as Myrdal remarks, has been scandalously neglected; the undertaking of an objective comparative study of administrative and institutional performance at various stages of agricultural advance has been neglected.

It remains for me to underline the paucity of investment in the agricultural sector. The experience of the Special Rural Development Programme in Kenya is indicative not so much of the failure of large schemes as of a mass of minor weaknesses—not enough transport, no telephone link with the Divisional Agricultural Office, inadequate petrol allowances, vacancies in agricultural establishments, missed opportunities for river control, lack of holding grounds for cattle, a shortage of cattle dips, late delivery of seeds or fertilizer as a result of inadequate systems. The Kenya administration is one of the more efficient ones; these petty shortcomings could be multiplied, and worse things found, in almost any African country. Members of the mission sent to Nigeria in connection with the UNDP-ILO pilot project for rural employment promotion there found that 70 per cent of farmers had never seen an extension worker, six general extension workers had 27,000 farms to look after, and that, even if the personnel of special government programmes were included, this proportion only came down from 1: 4,500 to 1: 2,000.[1]

Rural investment, marketing, far more research into the social and economic problems of the farming, self-employed and minor employment sectors, a greater effort as regards the training of rural administrative and institutional staff, their proper use and the co-ordination of their activities —these measures, together with the revision of the financial framework of the modern sector, represent a large but feasible programme of action which would at least turn the economies of Tropical Africa in the right direction.

But there needs also to be a change in the attitude and approach to the whole style of development. There are skills and potential in the rural economy which are being almost deliberately neglected by the centralising policy of governments and by mythologies. For example, despite the fact that it has been established on the basis of detailed and careful work, particularly by the Food Research Institute of Stanford University in Africa and by Cornell University in India, that the profit margins of small traders are not excessive, private traders and middlemen come in for a constant stream of abuse. One finds, even in some FAO reports, sentences such as the following with reference to Nigerian traders:

> The reduction in the number of unproductive middlemen can hardly be a matter for regret in a country with a progressive social policy.[2]

---

[1] P. Mueller and K. H. Zevering: " Employment promotion through rural development: a pilot project in Western Nigeria ", in *International Labour Review*, Vol. 100, No. 2, Aug. 1969, pp. 111-130, and in particular p. 127.

[2] FAO: *Agricultural development in Nigeria, 1965-1980* (Rome, 1966), p. 365.

is . . . the distinct economic advantage of bypassing a number of middlemen.[1]

This is followed by a suggestion that, where co-operatives have 75 per cent of the trade in some crop, they should be given a 100 per cent monopoly. It is this monopoly which can lead to the creation of marketing boards with multi-storey buildings, low prices to farmers, and diversion of farmers' profits into urban expenditure. Finally, there is an adjuration:

. . . strenuous efforts by the government to indoctrinate its unemployed population with the concept of the dignity of agricultural labour would seem to be called for.[2]

The attitude which I am trying to encourage is one which is determined to help the bulk of society to grow—be they farmers, traders, tinkers or tailors. The trader who collects a few bags of surplus produce from a village miles from a good road inevitably has high costs. When roads are better and storage available, and when the volume of surplus is greater, his costs will be lower; and this applies equally to marketing boards, which are not noted for their convenient service or the attractive prices they offer to isolated farmers. What farmers need is not a " concept of the dignity of agricultural labour " but a better reward for their efforts, and a better framework within which to work.

Social transformation

Let me end with four quotations, which go back to the first sentence of this article:

The growth of Gross National Product captures only imperfectly, if at all, the essence of the development process. This is a process of social transformation which can only be effected by a myriad of micro-economic changes, not simply by macro-economic additions of domestic and foreign resources. These changes have to be effected largely—if not exclusively—by the government and citizens of developing countries themselves, and primarily by the private enterprise (in a very broad sense) of the private citizens—operating of course in an environment set by government policies.[3]

Economic development cannot be understood in isolation. It is part of a more general process of transformation. . . . Each nation will have to develop its own vision of the future, out of the materials of its own history, its own problems, its own natural make-up.[4]

The problem is not to wipe the slate clean in underdeveloped countries, and to write our technical and economic equations on it, but to recognise that different peoples have a different language of social action, and possess, and, indeed, have long

[1] FAO: *Agricultural development in Nigeria, 1965-1980*, op. cit., p. 361.

[2] Ibid., p. 336.

[3] Harry Johnson: " Objectives and strategies for development ", statement made on 18 May 1970 to the Sub-Committee on Foreign Economic Policy of the Joint Economic Committee of the United States Congress (Washington, 1970).

[4] H. E. Soejatmoko: " Religions and the development process in Asia ", paper presented to the Asian Ecumenical Conference for Development, Tokyo, 15 July 1970.

exercised, peculiar aptitudes for solving the problems of their own time and place; aptitudes which must be further developed in the historic setting of their own past to meet the exigencies of the present and the future.[1]

. . . the structure of education which alienates the resident from the actual jobs which his simple society can offer.[2]

The reservoir of the " reservoir philosophy " is the bulk of society. If it seemed necessary to provide leadership, a government, electric power, a university and communications for this society, even at high cost, well and good: it has been done. But if we are to talk of employment, in the sense of using the full energies of this society, we must go back to where the people are, both geographically and, in the broadest sense, culturally. We must learn better how they contrive to make a livelihood and, indeed, thus sustain the nation. We must learn to build upon the real virtues and skills which they possess and to widen their humble opportunities. If that can be done, it will be possible to think in terms of an education which does not alienate but assists both adults and children; and it will set in motion, from the potential of land and people, a dispersed, granular, yet massive economic and social transformation. This is what we should mean by development; " unemployment " is a symptom of a partial and faulty approach.

---

[1] Frankel, op. cit., p. 96.

[2] H. W. Singer: "Employment problems in developing countries", in *Manpower and Unemployment Research in Africa*, op. cit., Vol. 4, No. 1, Apr. 1971, p. 30.

The Work of the Intermediate Technology Development Group in Africa

E. F. SCHUMACHER [1]

Origins and aims

THE CREATION OF THE Intermediate Technology Development Group in 1966 was the result of an initiative by people from the professions and industry in the United Kingdom, all with extensive overseas experience, who found a common basis for action in the approach of " intermediate technology ". This Group, which is keenly aware of the world-wide dangers inherent in the build-up of unemployment taking place in virtually every poor country, is a company limited by guarantee and a registered charity endeavouring to furnish the poor and the unemployed in developing countries with the means to work themselves out of poverty.[2]

The concept of intermediate technology was first introduced by the author in a report prepared for the Indian Planning Commission (1963) and subsequently presented in a paper to the Cambridge Conference on Rural Industrialisation in 1964.[3] The *raison d'être* of the Group was, and continues to be, that the source and centre of world poverty and under-

---

[1] Chairman of the Intermediate Technology Development Group Limited, 9 King Street, London WC2.

[2] The author feels it appropriate that this article should appear in the *International Labour Review* because the ILO is concerned with people rather than with the instruments of mass production and because it has consistently advocated and promoted job-creating programmes in the developing countries—because, in short, it has been among the first to recognise the significance of the ideas that have informed the ITDG since the creation of this Group. See, for example, Keith Marsden: " Towards a synthesis of economic growth and social justice ", in *International Labour Review*, Vol. 100, No 5, Nov. 1969, and " Progressive technologies for developing countries ", ibid., Vol. 101, No. 5, May 1970.

[3] See also my " Social and economic problems calling for the development of intermediate technology ". This paper and other basic material have been incorporated into an " IT Kit ", obtainable from the ITDG headquarters.

development lie primarily in the rural areas of poor countries, which are largely by-passed by aid and development as currently practised; that the rural areas will continue to be by-passed and unemployment will continue to grow, unless self-help technology is made available to the poor countries with assistance in its use; and that the donor countries and agencies do not at present possess the necessary organised knowledge of adapted technologies and communications to be able to assist effectively in rural development on the scale required.

It is now widely acknowledged that the most urgent need of the developing world is employment—productive employment measured in millions of new jobs every year. It is also increasingly recognised that for jobs to be created on anything like the required scale, the technologies and methods of production must be appropriate to the conditions of poor people in poor countries; that is, they must be cheap enough for jobs to be provided in very large numbers and simple enough to be used and maintained by rural and small-town populations without sophisticated technical or organisational skills and with very low incomes. It follows that equipment of this kind will have to be provided largely from indigenous resources and employed largely to meet local needs.

The labour-saving, capital-intensive technologies of the rich industrialised countries do not meet these conditions. Even on the simple test of capital cost per job [1], leaving aside all other considerations, the high-cost technology of the rich countries would condemn the third world to mass unemployment on an unimaginable scale. The choice between new work positions costing £1,500 each and, say, £150 or £100 each may be the choice between half a million jobs and 5 or 7.5 million jobs. It is no exaggeration to insist, as the Group has done from the outset, that the choice of technology is the biggest single collective decision facing any developing country today. It was—and still largely is—the denial of such a choice to the developing world that brought the Group into existence—to make it known that the possibility of choice exists and help to introduce techniques that poor communities can afford to use and operate for themselves. What, in short, the Group identified is a major gap in aid and development: the virtual absence of organised, systematic efforts to provide the poor countries with a choice of low-cost, self-help technologies, adapted to meet their needs for labour-intensive and small-scale development. This deficiency cannot be made good by accelerating conventional aid programmes any more than, say, a housing shortage can be alleviated by building more supersonic aircraft.

The Group therefore set out to compile practical data on intermediate technologies, to test them under operating conditions, and to make them widely known and freely available. It started by producing *Tools for*

[1] That is, the cost of " equipping " a work position, excluding the cost of land and buildings.

progress, a guide to relatively simple tools and equipment made in the United Kingdom. Since 1968 it has embarked on more searching and detailed investigations into the basic technologies required for rural development—those concerning building, agricultural equipment, water, food technology, rural health, small industry, power, education and training, co-operatives and women's activities. Each work programme seeks to identify basic needs for simple technologies, to document appropriate techniques and equipment and to demonstrate their practical application through overseas field projects.

Each subject is tackled by a panel of experts—engineers, scientists, architects, building technologists and others with wide overseas experience, who serve in a voluntary capacity, guiding and supervising teams of full-time research and development officers. This work organisation has brought to bear on the task of filling the intermediate technology gap not only the expertise of the hundred or so senior professional people who serve on the Group's advisory panels but also that of many industrial concerns. Close working links have also been formed with institutions specialising in different aspects of technology.[1]

From the start the Group's aim has been not merely to supplement the existing aid and development programme but to change its emphasis: to move it away from treating the poor countries as if they were already rich towards recognising and acting upon their need to develop methods of self-help and self-reliance. One thing that emerges from the Group's few years of existence is that it has demonstrated how such a change can be brought about and what needs to be done and can be done to discover, devise and make known a new range of self-help techniques adapted to the actual conditions and resources of developing countries: technologies that they can afford and that make possible the mobilisation of their labour power for productive activity (both for capital creation and for consumption).

A second conclusion founded on the Group's experience is that, for this kind of work to be fruitful, a considerable part of it must of necessity be done in the developed countries. There are several reasons for this. The basic work of assembling and systematising knowledge of low-cost technologies can be started and promoted most readily in centres where: (i) the required technical and organisational knowledge and facilities exist or can be relatively easily mobilised; (ii) communications—internal and external—present few obstacles; (iii) world-wide coverage can readily be achieved; (iv) there can be freedom from " project " pressures.

The first three reasons require little elaboration. The industrialised countries have the necessary technical knowledge and research facilities

[1] For example, the agricultural equipment project is based at the National College of Agricultural Engineering, Silsoe; the food technology project in housed at the National College of Food Technology, Weybridge. Other research work is based at the Department of Applied Physical Sciences, University of Reading, and the Royal College of Art.

at their command. The direction of research and development requires changes of emphasis and scale, but the essential knowledge and the effort are readily available there to be mobilised. The need for efficient communications, among centres of knowledge within a country and internationally, is a precondition for organising knowledge and expertise [1]; and so are ease of access to and contact with the developing world, if knowledge is to be adequately obtained and disseminated. The fourth reason may be less obvious but it is crucial; the task of producing generalised information requires freedom from the pressures generated by " country " projects. To take an example, the Group's Co-operative Panel recently produced a manual on simple accounting techniques for co-operatives. This has already been adopted by Sierra Leone, and may well appeal to other countries without an established system of co-operative accounting. There is a need, that is, to make known the *kinds* of choice that exist before the detailed work of local adaptation can take place. The same would apply to the industrial profiles now being prepared by the Group on woodworking, metalworking and agricultural equipment capable of local manufacture.

The question is often asked: is the demand for intermediate technologies forthcoming on anything like the required scale? To this there is a decisive counter-question: can people demand something when they are not aware of its existence? In other words, the primary task is to assemble detailed, practical information on simple techniques and make known the fact that they exist—" making known " here includes both communicating the information and showing how it can be applied with advantage.

The argument for siting the work of mobilising organised data on intermediate technologies in the centres of existing technical knowledge —and bodies similar to the Group in the United Kingdom and VITA (Volunteers for International Technical Assistance) in the United States exist or are foreshadowed in Australia, Canada, the Federal Republic of Germany and India—is little affected by the possibility of some initial overlapping; the potential field of work is so vast that a degree of international specialisation could easily be introduced. Nor, it must be noted, is this an argument for not starting intermediate or appropriate technology centres in the developing countries themselves as points, first, for receiving information about the choices available, making known their specific needs and adapting techniques to their own environments, and then, when their resources allow, for developing their own research and development facilities. This is now happening in India, which already has a considerable industrial sector and well-endowed research facilities, and where an Appropriate Technology Unit has been set up within the

[1] Just as the United Nations and the specialised agencies are located in Geneva, New York, Rome and elsewhere. The need to decentralise their activities once they have built up cadres of specialists and the relevant knowledge simply reinforces the point.

Ministry of Industrial Development. It has been happening—as far as one can gather in a more decentralised way perhaps—in the People's Republic of China for some years past.

The essential point, however, is that the initial drive—the change of emphasis, the mobilisation of technical knowledge for the evolving of self-help techniques—must come from the countries that possess such knowledge now. Only if this occurs can a useful dialogue on technology develop.

The account of the Group's work programme which follows should perhaps be read as an indication of what can—and should—be done on a much larger scale.

The building for development project

The first project to be started was on construction—a basic part of the development process. As development proceeds, the standard of building and construction required by developing countries changes. A greater variety of building *types* is required, in greater *numbers* and *distributed* over a wider area. The traditional demand simply for shelter becomes a demand for schools and clinics, administrative buildings and post offices, roads and bridges. Can the capacity of indigenous construction industries in developing countries meet this growing and changing demand?

Because construction embraces such a wide variety of skills and activities, including design, component manufacture and assembly, and the management of men, materials and plant, it provides a rich field of training and experience for a large number of people struggling to increase their standard of living. Construction is usually the second biggest employment sector in an economy, second only to manufacturing industry in a developed country and to agriculture in a developing one.

The scope for investment, both public and private, in physical infrastructure is so extensive that it should contribute more to the development process than just the buildings and construction works. It should contribute to the formation of an industry which can expand, renew and maintain these buildings; and it can and should, therefore, be planned with the specific aim of developing the local construction industry.

Construction, by enabling people to obtain training and experience, can assist them in making the necessary transition from agriculture to industrial work. In this sense it can provide valuable midway jobs between agriculture and manufacturing for between one-tenth and one-fifth of a country's manpower.

While half of the gross capital formation in most countries goes into construction, developing countries are forced to import most of the necessary construction capacity. Development plans are often little more than " shopping lists " for building and civil engineering projects, and pay no regard to what could be done locally. The Building Panel therefore tackled the question how to assist indigenous construction industries. This work was started in 1969 as the building for development project. Its aim is to help to improve the efficiency of building operations in developing countries by making available to local construction industries guidance on appropriate technologies and business procedures. The project team, comprising an architect, an engineer and an economist, identified the small contractor as being most in need of attention. There is adequate training for the professionals—architects, engineers and the technical staffs of ministries of works. Yet they have to rely on indigenous contractors to an increasing extent to implement their building programmes, and these builders generally receive no training or development guidance. Everywhere the gap is the same—growing construction programmes without the indigenous skills needed to execute them.

Initially the team concentrated on Nigeria and Kenya. In Nigeria it started by identifying the needs of government-registered building contractors in the northern states. With the co-operation of the state Governments it ran a series of six four-day conventions for contractors and government technical officers in early 1970, at the Kaduna Polytechnic. Teaching material covering elementary management skills for small building firms was presented to the contractors in a wide variety of ways: through lectures, seminars, films, exhibitions, dramatisations. The conventions were a test both of the project team's own understanding of builders' needs and appropriate teaching techniques and of the contractors' ability and keenness to learn.

The conventions clearly demonstrated that the great need was for advice on management and business methods. They also showed that contractors, men without formal education, *can* be taught these skills, without which few indigenous organisations can develop into efficient construction firms.

Using the experience of the Kaduna conventions, the project team began work in Kenya to help the National Construction Corporation to provide training programmes for African contractors. The team produced a series of teaching kits which can be adapted to suit the level of the participants. The idea underlying these kits is that the main information barrier in the African situation is not so much between teachers and taught as between those who devise educational material and the teachers. The kits are being developed into a complete elementary management series useful to teachers in many different African countries and situations. The team is currently exploring with a number of East and Central African governments new opportunities for applying and extending its experience in the training of contractors.

Water projects

One of the chief factors influencing development at village level is the availability of water for human, animal, and agricultural purposes. In most tropical and subtropical areas rainfall is seasonal and governs the type and scale of traditional agriculture and animal husbandry.

Before appropriate forms of land use and agricultural practice can be specified, it is necessary to identify existing simple techniques for water storage and handling, and to evaluate these in terms of cost and benefit, efficiency, and the technical skills required.

The Group started by assembling the data available in the United Kingdom on small-scale, low-cost water technologies. This work was completed and the results published early in 1970.[1] The conclusion was that there is a big gap in the knowledge recorded in written form on what might be called the theory and practice of small-scale rural water supplies—the design and construction of the various devices for obtaining, lifting, transporting, purifying and, particularly, storing water which are suitable for individual villages, individual farmsteads, or even individual homes. These include means of catching the rainfall on the spot, of leading it into the tank or cistern, of holding it safely in store, of drawing it out when needed, and of purifying the water, if necessary, to suit the purpose for which it is intended.

At the same time the project disclosed the existence of a great deal of experience and data on the design and construction of dams and reservoirs of the order of a few million gallons, which are customarily filled from the transient flows of streams during the rainy season so that water is available during the long rainless season. This information is well documented and needs no further elaboration. But by their nature these types of reservoir are almost always situated at a distance from the villages. Very often—even usually—these sizeable sources serve the needs of several villages and the villagers and their animals have to carry every drop of domestic water from the source to the home. This imposes a heavy daily workload, particularly since it is the women who carry the water and who very often are responsible for the work of cultivation as well, and it forces villagers to make do with far less water than they need; it denies them the small but vital amount necessary for raising seedlings for the household vegetable garden; it cuts down the efficiency of the animals used for transport, for drawing the plough and for other services, because much of their time is spent walking to the dam or reservoir to drink instead of doing productive work. There can be no doubt whatever that the much-needed improvement in peasant farming productivity in the rain-fed zones would be greatly helped if the techniques for collecting

[1] ITDG: *Bibliography on low-cost water technologies* (London, 1970).

and conserving rainfall were extended to small village units, farmsteads and even households.

In view of the scant amount of information on such techniques that was obtained from written sources, the Group has launched into field trials and investigations. An investigation was carried out in collaboration with the Department of Agricultural Economics at Reading University, which is conducting research into village development around Ho, in Ghana. The purpose was to make a detailed study of village water requirements and to find ways of meeting them.

A further project stemmed from the ITDG's work on water catchment tanks in Botswana, a detailed account of which the Group published in 1969.[1] A project officer with practical experience of the work carried out in Botswana went to Tanzania, Kenya, Malawi and Swaziland, and revisited Botswana, demonstrating the field application of water catchment techniques. As a result of his work in Swaziland his services have been officially requested to carry out an extensive programme of small-scale water catchment development in that country: he will also be training other field officers to do similar work in East Africa.

These programmes of work offer a good illustration of intermediate technology in action. The idea of catchment tanks is of course not new; the construction of a tank or cistern in the ground, with a "catchment apron" alongside, is an ancient way of holding rainwater for use in the dry season. It had largely fallen into disuse but is now coming into its own again, for two reasons. The first is need—there are great tracts of semi-arid territory where population growth is creating pressure on the drinking-water supplies, which in order to be adequate require large numbers of catchment tanks to ensure that water is available just where it is wanted, namely at the farm, at the school or in the household. The second reason is opportunity. Within the last couple of decades modern science has produced revolutionary new materials in the form of cheap impervious membranes. These materials open up the way for a really massive attack on a problem which is becoming more and more acute as the years go by. The techniques are cheap, simple, labour-intensive—ideal for turning underutilised labour into essential capital assets.

Supporting research and development work are being carried out in the United Kingdom to discover the different techniques and materials that can be cheaply and usefully employed to improve traditional methods, and so provide more water of better quality. Much of the work involves trying out new waterproofing materials such as different types of impervious membranes, emulsions derived from coal and oil, and water-repellent dressings. This has been planned as a two-year project, and it started in mid-1971.

---

[1] ITDG: *The introduction of rainwater catchment tanks and micro-irrigation to Botswana* (London, 1969).

Agricultural tools and equipment

The application of adapted technology to agriculture offers wide opportunities for diversifying and upgrading rural life. Many new and improved agricultural inputs—especially farm tools and equipment, means of transport and facilities for the storage of crops—can and must be locally manufactured to an increasing extent. Yet the technology of agricultural development, looked at from the standpoint of local needs and resources—what the farmer's needs and resources *are* as distinct from what foreign experts think should be done—has been virtually neglected until very recently.

The programme of the Agricultural Panel is designed to identify needs for improved agricultural equipment and to promote the local manufacture of such equipment. It is being undertaken in collaboration with Wye College, University of London, the National College of Agricultural Engineering at Silsoe, and the Governments of Zambia, Nigeria and Tanzania.

The first of the field projects now under way in Zambia is based at the Agricultural Research Station at Magoye. Two others are in preparation, in Nigeria and Tanzania. Their essential purpose is to identify the constraints on increased agricultural production and to provide selective mechanisation. There are periods in the farming calendar of most peasant communities when every available pair of hands is fully occupied; the shortage of labour to perform critical tasks during these periods acts as a constraint on farm production. Selective mechanisation of the tasks in question could therefore increase productivity without causing unemployment. Such mechanisation might involve the development of equipment to meet specific needs, the adaptation of existing types of equipment and the use of equipment already developed and appropriate for the job. This approach would not, for example, rule out the introduction of tractors or other forms of mechanisation—the test must always be: what job needs to be done? how can the local community best afford to do it on a permanently improved footing?

The agriculture team has designed the framework for a field project to identify socio-economic constraints on production as a first step towards the introduction of innovations appropriate to local circumstances. The aim is to introduce such innovations and build up indigenous capacity to make and maintain improved equipment by means of on-the-job training of local artisans and craftsmen.

A supporting programme of documentation—detailed specifications and working drawings and the construction of prototypes—is being carried out by the Group's unit based at the National College of Agricultural Engineering. Among the innovations already developed at Silsoe are an improved seed riddle-broadcaster—redesigned to eliminate castings and so make possible local manufacture—now being tested in Botswana, and a hand-operated, multi-purpose metal-bending machine. Contact has been established with some fifty institutions concerned with various aspects of farm machinery research throughout the world, and the systematic compilation of documentation on locally made, field-tested equipment is now in hand. The value of this clearing-house of technical information is already becoming apparent.

The agricultural research staff are also compiling a guide to hand implements and animal-powered farm equipment that are still commercially available in the United Kingdom and other European countries.

Many new tools and pieces of equipment and various forms of improved co-operative husbandry have been designed and tried out in farming systems just because it was assumed that a particular task was limiting or onerous or that current yields would be greatly improved; very often the experiments have failed. The starting point of the Group's work in Zambia—carried out under the auspices of the Zambian Ministry of Rural Development—is that innovation must be based on detailed knowledge of the farmer's problems and needs, and on an accurate picture of the farming calendar and cropping sequence in a locality, taking into account communal customs and obligations and the economic pattern on which the present farming system is based.

The work of identifying needs and building up local manufacture is being carried out by two of the Group's field officers attached to the Magoye Research Station. An investigation of the labour inputs of small farmers cropping from 5 to 20 acres is being made at three sites in the locality.

Meanwhile the engineering field officer is investigating the availability and quality of local timber and steel supplies, the current level of rural craftsmanship and the development of appropriate basic tools for rural blacksmiths.

Although this project is in the early stages, certain types of equipment have already been identified as suitable for local manufacture and testing. These include a single-row, ox-drawn maize planter with fertiliser hopper attachment; single and double-row planters for maize, groundnuts and other common crops, using the notched-wheel principle; equipment to separate groundnut pods from the haulm, and other equipment for grading and shelling groundnuts; low-cost tools for blacksmiths; and improved ox-carts.

As an indication of the utility of linking the Silsoe base in the United Kingdom with field projects, when the Zambian project was launched at the end of 1971 the home base provided it with some forty technical specifications drawn from India, Nigeria, Tanzania, VITA and other sources.[1]

---

[1] See the supplementary note on documentation at the end of this article.

As field projects proceed, the methodology of the tested rapid-survey technique will be passed on to government field extension staff for wider application, and local artisans will be trained in the metalworking and woodworking techniques which are necessary for making farm equipment in each locality. The nucleus of farm machinery units thus created should offer good prospects for establishing a number of rural development centres and extending operations to cover production of a wider range of crop storage facilities, processing and other forms of local manufacture.

Field experiment, demonstration, and local involvement from the outset are, in the Group's view, essential parts of the process of disseminating knowledge of low-cost techniques. The programmes envisaged for northern Nigeria and Tanzania (which, like that in Zambia, are guided and supported by the home base in the United Kingdom) are broadly similar, though in both instances considerable work has already been done by government agencies as regards identifying needs, and the Group's contribution can therefore be largely concentrated on developing equipment and promoting its use and local manufacture.

Small industry

Early in 1969 the Group formed an Industrial Liaison Unit, with the object of linking feasible projects for small-scale industrial development overseas with appropriate technologies adapted from British industry. The overseas end of this project is in Nigeria, where the Group's engineer is identifying products and processes suitable for local manufacture, and has set up a small workshop for the manufacture of prototype equipment. The home-based unit is preparing a series of industrial profiles, starting with woodworking and metalworking, to provide a range of technologies at varying levels of cost and technical sophistication. This is being done in collaboration with universities, technical colleges, industrial research organisations and private firms. The work of the Industrial Liaison Unit is a practical exercise in the transfer of technology. This is a subject on which the literature is rapidly growing. Much of it is of a theoretical kind; it is generally misdirected and beside the point because it is concerned with the largely insoluble problem of how to transfer mass production to the poor with the capital-intensive technologies of the rich. It is surely more practical, and much more deserving of the attention of research workers, to start by considering the needs of poor countries, adapting technologies to meet these needs and helping to introduce new techniques.

By the autumn of 1970 the Group had approached more than a hundred United Kingdom companies in various branches of engineering, food technology, leather and textiles, etc., which expressed interest in helping to develop appropriate machinery and equipment. The first industrial profile, on iron founding, is nearly completed. This will comprise, first, a profile of the simplest possible forms of charcoal-fired crucible foundry, requiring only manual power and very little capital; then an alternative between the oil-fired crucible foundry and a coke-fired cupolet; and finally a more sophisticated unit to indicate the possibilities for expansion. Simple training manuals will accompany these profiles along with guides to sources of equipment.

In addition to answering over 200 technical inquiries a year, the Unit is now providing specific advice on the setting up of industries—for example on the establishment of small-scale barbed-wire production in Swaziland, metal window and door production and a craft unit in Nigeria, and a woodworking shop in Botswana—and is also taking on research and development work to meet specified technical requirements. A simple example is the redesigning of equipment used for weighing babies in the rural areas of East Africa. A much more complex case, arising out of requests from a number of African countries, has involved the complete design and fabrication of a prototype machine for making packaging materials; this involved work by the Unit itself, the Royal College of Art, London, and the Department of Applied Physical Sciences at Reading University.

Food technology

Towards the end of 1970 the Group set up a Food Technology Unit. This started by assisting with a rice storage project in Liberia, and is now engaged in a research and development programme aimed at making better use of traditional foods. Arrangements are in hand to conduct field trials in a group of Tanzanian villages. The home-based unit is at the National College of Food Technology, Weybridge, which will provide research and development facilities for the project.

Consultancy

During the past two years the Group has undertaken consultancy assignments in Africa for the ILO, the United Nations Economic Commission for Africa (ECA), and the United Nations Industrial Development Organisation (UNIDO). These assignments were handled by the Group's consultancy wing, Inter-Technology Services (ITS), a wholly-owned subsidiary.

In the latter part of 1970 the Group helped to man a mission to Botswana, Lesotho and Swaziland to report on small enterprises and entrepreneurial development. In this venture it was working in collaboration with the Research Institute for Management Science, Delft. A request had been made to the ECA by Botswana, Lesotho and Swaziland for a specialist mission to help accelerate the development of local enterprise and job creation and in particular to identify the industrial, managerial and training inputs required. The joint team that carried out the mission issued a report, and it is hoped that in implementing its recommendations the Group can form close links with ILO-assisted small-enterprise programmes in Swaziland, which are breaking new ground in the field of technology transfer.

At the request of the ECA and UNIDO the Group has recently undertaken assignments in West Africa. One was centred on the Kumasi University of Science and Technology, Ghana, where during the previous two years a group of university staff had been voluntarily advising small local business. The University wished to expand this service and the ITS team worked with it to investigate how a permanent technology consultancy centre could be organised and operated. The immediate result was that an experienced engineer, a lecturer in the School of Engineering Science at Edinburgh University and a member of the Group's Power Panel, was sent at the expense of the Inter-Universities Council to Kumasi, where he stayed six months to assist in setting up the new centre.

Another assignment was related to the production of locally manufactured hospital equipment in northern Nigeria. The Group assessed the technical and economic feasibility of setting up manufacturing units to supply hospital equipment on an operational scale in the northern states, and such units are now being established there. The purpose of the feasibility study was primarily to follow up the work already done at the Institute of Health, Zaria, where there has been considerable progress in the design and manufacture of locally made hospital equipment.[1]

It was found that there was a growing potential market for locally made, good-quality products. Their manufacture was encouraged by the federal and state authorities as a means of promoting import substitution, providing an opportunity for local participation in industrial development and making an important contribution to the creation of employment.

In the study of this industry in particular, attention was paid to the training of management and other personnel; methods of design and production; and the vital aspects of local financing and marketing. Investigation showed that good potential in these respects already existed within the country and that, with initial technical help in setting up production units, a viable local small-scale industry could be developed. It was considered important that it should be started at the level of the finance and technical skill that were readily available within the country at present. As skill and competence developed through experience and training, more ambitious small-scale manufacturing ventures could be

[1] An account of this work is given in ITDG: *Bulletin No. 4* (London), Feb. 1969.

envisaged. The method of setting up and developing such an industry is as important as technical know-how and financing, and this venture could become a prototype for many other enterprises.

This type of enterprise encourages the maximum use of local materials, personnel and finance in the badly needed programme of self-help, small-scale industrial development that is being developed for the six northern states for which the feasibility study was commissioned; but it is also relevant to similar situations in other developing countries.

Work done in collaboration with the ILO has resulted in the establishment of two key posts in intermediate technology in Tanzania (financed by the ILO); one is for a technical officer attached to the Tanzanian Agricultural Machinery Testing Unit, the other for a full-time liaison officer between the Group and the Government of Tanzania.

The panels and documentation

The Group's research and development programme relies upon research grants and donations from aid and charitable organisations. The activities described above have all secured short-term grants of this kind. Other panels, which have not yet received financial assistance, have nevertheless produced valuable work. Thus the Power Panel, created to investigate and produce data on simple power sources, has already published a detailed bibliography on a multi-fuel engine.[1] It intends to produce a profile of small power sources already available, setting out their technical capacities and the kind of uses for which they are appropriate, and then to investigate, in particular, power sources derived from wind, water and solar energy. The uneven distribution over the globe of commercially available sources of coal and oil and the not far distant scarcity of oil (even at present rates of consumption) give particular importance to the work of identifying cheap, simple and small-scale ways of using unconventional (but permanent and non-polluting) sources of energy. Here again—and this applies right across the field of intermediate technology—the Group is decidedly not advocating a return to nineteenth-century machinery; the need is to build modern science and technology into methods that may start with old-established principles but emerge as new techniques in terms of both quality and performance.

As an example of the kind of question put to the Power Panel, it has recently been asked to find or devise a method of cane-crushing for northern Nigeria (diesel engines have been specifically excluded) to replace the primitive horse-operated device currently in use. To such problems there may be a fairly readily available answer—something appropriate may already exist—but it may well require considerable

[1] ITDG: *Sterling engine bibliography* (London, 1971).

design and fabrication work in the United Kingdom before field trials are undertaken.

The Co-operative Panel is looking at ways in which co-operatives can function more effectively, especially because they are themselves vehicles for rural change and innovation. It has recently completed a series of three manuals on simple accounting methods for co-operatives. The first of these [1], published by the Overseas Development Administration in 1970, deals with thrift and credit co-operatives and has aroused widespread interest in African countries.

The Panel on Rural Health, set up to explore effective ways of bringing medical care to the rural populations of developing countries, has produced its first piece of documentation, on health manpower and the place and functions of the medical auxiliary.[2] This includes the first-ever annotated bibliography on the subject, and the text, written by three members of the Panel, is a manual or guide to the economic and medical advantages of the medical auxiliary. Drawing on examples from many African countries, as well as from other parts of the developing world, it shows that the system of health care in the rich countries is singularly unsuited to the needs and resources of developing countries, and describes an alternative that is both cheaper and more effective.

Other panels whose work will have an obvious bearing on the needs of rural Africa and are still in course of formation or just starting to identify their tasks are those on women's activities, education, and forestry and forest products.

The panel method of operation is proving remarkably successful as a means of bringing together the three elements essentially affected by the work of identifying the gaps that can be filled by intermediate technology, of assembling the necessary practical data, and of engaging in field trials to demonstrate their uses. We call them the ABC of development—the administrators, the business and industrial community, and the communicators or academic fraternity. In the established, conventional routine of aid-giving and associated research, these three seldom, if ever, work in collaboration. We believe that the work of the panels, multiplied and extended, could begin to redress the existing imbalance in research and development, whereby some 95 per cent of the effort undertaken in this respect throughout the world is of benefit only to the rich countries.

An important supporting activity recently undertaken by the Group consists of the implementation of student projects. These were started largely in response to the growing interest shown by students and by various university faculties in applying themselves to action which could be of use to the developing world. Through these projects the Group

---

[1] ITDG: *Thrift and credit co-operatives* (London, Overseas Development Administration, 1970).

[2] Idem: *Health manpower and the medical auxiliary* (London, 1971).

hopes to widen considerably the range of technical information available to it, for field trials and ultimate documentation.

All the panels referred to have been built up and their work programmes formulated within the past three years. Their experience has shown that the information gap to be filled is a wide one. The need for data on simple techniques can be envisaged as existing at the following three levels, which the Group is using as a general guide, though obviously even such broad criteria have to be modified in real situations:

(1) Home industry: local resources, hand tools, family members, up to £20 per work position, handmade articles generally for local use.

(2) Village industry: more a community operation, small groups of artisans, co-operatives, basic technical terms capable of translation into the vernacular, locally purchased materials, hand and simple machinery, up to £100 per work position, production for the local and surrounding communities.

(3) Small industry: local companies, bigger co-operatives, normal technical terminology, indigenous or imported materials, powered machinery, relatively skilled labour, up to £500 per work position, machine products for district or national markets.

With such categories in mind, the Group's plans for documentation envisage, broadly, the following:

— Technical profiles, which cover a range of technological choices in the intermediate categories, up to small-industry level. These profiles are intended for departments of industry, government planners, international agencies. They will give an outline of the inputs and operations necessary for, say, the three categories shown above, illustrating the technical choices available for each.

— Instruction manuals, containing the detailed information (including technical drawings) necessary to put the available choices into practice.

— Directories, catalogues of equipment in the intermediate range. These may be catalogues of commercially available equipment, or of local self-help equipment and tools.

— Annotated bibliographies, covering intermediate technology applications, on such subjects as water and rural health.

— Special project reports, which give a step-by-step account of field demonstrations of particular techniques.

Conclusion

The importance of technological choice, more particularly the need to make low-cost technologies widely available in usable form, is gradually entering the consciousness of economists and development planners. There would appear to be four stages in the process, judging by reactions to the work of the Intermediate Technology Development Group: the first was widespread rejection of the idea; the second, now in vogue, is widespread acceptance, but with little support or concerted action; the third would be active involvement on a considerable scale to mobilise knowledge of technological choices; and the fourth would be the practical application of such knowledge, again on a significant scale.

There are certain hopeful signs on the horizon. The fact that jobs are needed in their millions by the developing world is now universally acknowledged. The inescapable question of how much can be afforded for providing each job, when millions are needed, must very soon compel equal attention. There are extensive moves by international agencies towards finding labour-intensive methods for public works. These are important not just in themselves but also because of the opportunities they can provide—by increasing rural income—for other forms of rural employment. There are the growing points of action in a few countries on low-cost technologies, to which reference has been made earlier. The only criticism that can be levelled at these—and the Group's—efforts to fill the " technological gap " are that they are on too small a scale in relation to needs. They represent an insignificant fraction of total aid expenditure. (The Group's budget now runs at about £3,000 a month, along with a total outlay on field projects of about £70,000 a year—less than one-twentieth of 1 per cent of the United Kingdom's expenditure on aid.) Yet unless practical, useful work on these lines is rapidly expanded and multiplied, there can be no hope for the poor and the workless; nor any, perhaps, for the rich either.

Supplementary note on documentation

In addition to the publications mentioned in footnotes the Group has produced the following documentation in connection with its building for development project:

The Nigerian building contractor : practices, problems and needs; *An educational strategy for the Nigerian building contractor*; *Construction and reconstruction : towards a policy for the Nigerian construction industry*; *Contractor development : report of the Conference on the Training of Nigerian Building Contractors*; *A management handbook for the Nigerian building contractor*; *The Kenyan building contractor : practices, problems and needs*; *Bradford Seminars I and II* (report on the study seminars on the construction industry held at the University of Bradford's Centre for Project Planning for Developing Countries).

Teaching manuals for the construction industry (in five kits): *How to decide business policy*; *How to do accounting*; *Contracting and the client*; *How to estimate and tender*; *Planning for the contractor.*

The following list of technical specifications provided by the Group from various sources for the Zambian field project gives a further idea of its documentary services:

Indian standards: *3-tined cultivator, animal-drawn* (IS:3342); *V-blade hand-hoe* (IS:3185); *Soil-scoop, animal-drawn* (IS:3360); *Single-row cotton seed drill, animal-drawn* (IS:3310).

From the Industrial Development Centre, Nigeria (figures in brackets refer to special report numbers of the IDC): *The plough bolt* (70-1); *The wood bearing* (69-8); *IDC weeding attachment* (70-2); *The plough gauge wheel* (70-6); *Blacksmith entrepreneurs and their capabilities*; *The IDC singletree* (70-5); *The IDC single ox-yoke* (70-4); *The IDC Clarkson ox-yoke* (69-3.1); *The IDC Bornu groundnut lifter* (69-5).

From other sources: *Workshop designs*; *Hand and workshop tool lists*; *East African timbers list*; *Blacksmith's hearth, COSIRA design*; *Blacksmith's forge, Pearson design*; *Home-made anvil*; " *Thought starters* " *on welded design*; *Steel fabricated vee pulleys*; *Manufacture of harrow tines*; *All-welded steel vice*; *All-welded M.S. vice*; *VITA foot-powered wood lathe*; *Drawings and specifications—" Animal-drawn equipment and basic tools for farmers, suitable for local construction* "; *The Samaru bicycle cart*; *The Samaru ox-cart*; *The fuffle*; *The Shinyanga lift pump*; *Chitedze multi-purpose ox-drawn tool bar*; *Hand-operated flap-valve water pump*; *Animal-drawn tool bar.* Technical drawings of animal-cart wheel and axle jig assembly, universal welding jig, ploughshare welding jig.

III. Aspects

Human Resources Investment and Employment Policy in the Maghreb

André TIANO [1]

The need for human resources investment

THE LATEST PLANNING documents in the various countries of the Maghreb (Algeria, Morocco and Tunisia) show how acutely aware the leaders of these countries have become in recent years of the gravity of their employment problem.

The Moroccan Five-Year Plan, covering the period 1968-72, provides for 97,000 new jobs to be created every year, which compares with an estimated annual increase of 142,000 in the active population. Underemployment, which is probably around the 50 per cent mark at the present time, will consequently rise still further in the years to come.

In assessing the extent of underemployment, a distinction has to be made between the towns, where one can only measure open unemployment, and the countryside, where one can, and should, measure disguised underemployment. In Morocco, where the towns account for 31 per cent of the total population, the figures for the labour force participation rate assumed for the purposes of this article and reproduced in the tables show that the rate among the younger men is slightly lower in the towns than in the countryside; this is attributable to the better facilities for schooling in the urban areas. Some account, however, must also be taken of the potential demand for employment among the female population; 160,000 women are already working in the towns and the number of job-seekers will increase as opportunities for education are gradually extended. To simplify the following analysis, it has also been assumed, perhaps a little arbitrarily, that the numbers of men and women in each age group are the same.

---

[1] Professor at the University of Paris-Dauphine.

TABLE I. MOROCCO: ESTIMATED NUMBER OF JOBS REQUIRED IN URBAN AREAS, 1970

Age group	Participation rate (%)		No. of persons of each sex (thousands)	No. of jobs required by both sexes (thousands)
	Men	Women		
15-19	80	20	240	240
20-59	90	20	905	995
60-64	40	—	45	18

TABLE II. MOROCCO: ESTIMATED NUMBER OF DAYS' WORK REQUIRED IN RURAL AREAS, 1970

Age group	Participation rate (%)		No. of days' work required (millions)	
	Men	Women	Men	Women
15-59	90	90	560	225
60-65	60	—	6	—

A total of 1,253,000 jobs are consequently required, but only 985,000 [1] non-agricultural jobs are currently available, which means that the rate of open unemployment is around 21.5 per cent.

Turning now to agriculture, I have assumed, as in previous studies on the subject [2], that a man is fully employed if he works for 250 days a year and a woman if she works for 100 days a year. Allowance has nevertheless been made for inactivity due to sickness or school attendance. A further assumption I have made is that farming has been somewhat more intensive since 1966, with a consequent 10 per cent increase in the number of man-days required (the calculation being made by taking the area of land devoted to the different types of farming operation [3] and multiplying it by the " normal " number of days' work needed for 1 hectare of each type). This is why the rate of underemployment is shown to be lower than that estimated in my previous studies on the subject.

In all, persons of both sexes required 791 million days' work, but only 330 million were available, giving an underemployment rate in rural areas of about 58.5 per cent.

[1] For purposes of the Moroccan plan, all non-agricultural jobs have been assumed to be in urban areas, although in fact more than 15 per cent of them are to be found in country districts, which implies that the rate of urban unemployment has been underestimated and the rate of rural unemployment overestimated.

[2] See A. Tiano: *La politique économique et financière du Maroc indépendant*, " Etudes Tiers Monde " (Paris, Presses universitaires de France, 1963), p. 11.

[3] Type of cultivation or produce.

TABLE III. ALGERIA: ESTIMATED NUMBER OF JOBS REQUIRED IN URBAN AREAS, 1969

Age group	Participation rate (%)		No. of jobs required (thousands)	
	Men	Women	Men	Women
15-17	.	.	150 [1]	.
18-59	90	20	1 100	240
60-65	40	—	10	—

[1] Allowance for potential demand by out-of-school youths.

TABLE IV. ALGERIA: ESTIMATED NUMBER OF DAYS' WORK REQUIRED IN RURAL AREAS, 1969

Age group	Participation rate (%)		No. of days' work required (millions)	
	Men	Women	Men	Women
15-17	.	.	50 [1]	.
18-59	90	90	385	180
60-65	60	—	2.4	—

[1] Allowance for potential demand by out-of-school youths.

Thus, bearing in mind that the rural population of Morocco accounts for 69 per cent of the total population, the total underemployment rate is clearly in the region of 50 per cent [1] and is going to increase.

In Algeria, the planners expect the situation to develop along much the same lines, because the number of jobs created will be less than the additions to the active population until 1980.[2] Increasing underemployment is consequently likely and the plan for 1970-73 is based on estimates of 23.7 and 51.3 per cent for urban and rural areas respectively. These figures are almost certainly overoptimistic, because they make no allowance for the potential demand from women or from out-of-school boys and girls between 15 and 17 years of age (still numerous, unfortunately). If these figures are compared with my earlier estimates and with statistics compiled for the colonial period of Algeria's history, it will be seen that the level of urban unemployment has remained constant, which is an achievement in itself. The level also appears to have remained the same in the rural areas, despite an increase in the population, but my earlier calculations were slightly overstated. Details are given in tables III and IV.

[1] $\frac{58.5\,(69)+21.5\,(31)}{100} = 47.$

[2] *Rapport de synthèse du Plan 1970-1973*, p. 133.

In all, therefore, 1.5 million jobs are required, while according to the plan 840,000 jobs are available, giving an open unemployment rate of 44 per cent.

As compared with a total requirement of 617.4 million days' work, there are not more than 190 million days available, which yields an underemployment rate of 69 per cent in rural areas.

In Tunisia, the plan for 1969-72 strikes a more optimistic note, since it makes no mention of disguised underemployment, estimates total open underemployment at 15.6 per cent and provides for the number of new jobs created to be 10,000 higher than the demand. Admittedly this optimism was mitigated by the Prime Minister in a speech outlining the official policy on 17 November 1970, in which he stated that there was no real short-term solution to the underemployment problem and that a final answer would take several years to find. In his view, no economy based on the ideals of social justice could tolerate a very high rate of unemployment.

I myself, working on the same assumptions as for the other two countries and using the figures given in the Tunisian plan, was nevertheless surprised to find that at first sight the number of jobs created outside agriculture was higher than the number of workers available for employment in the towns. My own approach has always been to take the figures that are least likely to bear out any point I wish to prove (in this case an underestimate on the planners' part of the scale of underemployment), and I credited the country districts with the surplus number of jobs available. This would mean that any miscalculation on my part of the percentage of the urban population would be of no practical significance. Just as for the other two countries of the Maghreb, I therefore took the figures for Tunisia and analysed the employment situation in the towns and the country districts (which respectively represent 40 and 60 per cent of the total population).

According to the plan, the total number of jobs required is 496,000, as compared with 620,000 jobs available in non-agricultural employment, which means that there is no underemployment in this sector.

The total number of days' work required amounts to 341.5 million, as against an estimated 86 million available, to which should be added a further 30 million to take into account the surplus non-agricultural employment among the active population in the towns. This gives an underemployment rate in agriculture of 66 per cent.

To meet the demand for consumer goods and capital accumulation, the proportion of the population needing to be engaged in open employment in the towns and real employment in the countryside is probably around 60 per cent in Tunisia, the corresponding figures for Morocco and Algeria being 53 and 42 per cent respectively. Furthermore, the employment of some people, admittedly not many,

TABLE V. TUNISIA: ESTIMATED NUMBER OF JOBS REQUIRED IN URBAN AREAS, 1968

Age group	Participation rate (%)		No. of persons of each sex (thousands)	No. of jobs required by both sexes (thousands)
	Men	Women		
15-19	80	20	76	76
20-64	90	20	380	420

TABLE VI. TUNISIA: ESTIMATED NUMBER OF DAYS' WORK REQUIRED IN RURAL AREAS, 1968

Age group	Participation rate (%)		No. of days' work required (millions)	
	Men	Women	Men	Women
15-64	85	85	244	97.5

is more apparent than real; this is the case, for example, in the lower grades of the civil service in all three countries and also in Algerian industry.[1]

Finally, it seems unlikely that all the new jobs due to be created will in fact materialise in the course of the current plans, with the result that unemployment will be greater than expected in Algeria and Morocco and will not be any lower in Tunisia.

The Algerian plan provides for an annual increase of 18,750 jobs in industry, 23,750 in the building trades and public works and 24,000 in transport, services, commerce and government administration. None of these objectives is impossible of attainment and the amount of money necessary does not represent an undue fraction of net investment. On the other hand, the magnitude of the task becomes apparent when the 18,750 jobs that it is hoped to create each year in industry are compared with the 2,000 actually created annually as part of the Constantine Plan and during the first years of Algeria's independence. In agriculture the plan provides for 168,000 new jobs (or 42 million additional days' work) to become available over the four-year period; this seems hardly possible, as the country will be producing less grapes and citrus fruits unless it embarks on a bold investment policy.

[1] See A. Tiano: *Le Maghreb entre les mythes* (Paris, Presses universitaires de France, 1967), p. 404.

The Moroccan plan is very modest in its objectives for the secondary sector (5,800 new jobs a year in mining, manufacturing and the building trades) but is extremely ambitious, in terms of anticipated productivity requirements, as regards the tertiary sector (where there are to be 36,200 new jobs). The target of 55,000 new jobs for agriculture is impossible of attainment without the country's national development programme (i.e. without a human resources investment policy) but too modest if the figures for the programme are included.

The Tunisian plan provides for 12,500 new jobs a year to be created in the tertiary sector, which is a reasonable objective. The target of 4,000 new jobs in industry can be achieved with the amount of money set aside for net investment, and the figure of 4,000 jobs for the building trades also seems reasonable enough. On the other hand, there seems very little likelihood that farming, which is passing through a period of crisis, will be able to absorb an additional 10,000 workers every year in addition to those for whom jobs are found on work sites opened as part of the national full employment policy.

It would be a mistake, however, to pass judgment against the plans because of the numerical imbalance in the employment market. It is perfectly understandable that even a rapid industrialisation programme is not able to redress this situation. With every job created costing an average of 80,000 French francs, even a country investing on the scale adopted in Algeria cannot provide work for every job-seeker. What would be wrong, and indeed disastrous, would be to select industrial projects on the basis of the number of jobs immediately resulting from them, instead of adopting the yardstick of the value added both directly and indirectly to the domestic product as a result of the activity in question. An oversimplified criterion like the number of jobs directly created by a given investment programme cannot be used for the purposes of industrial development schemes. Similarly, Morocco and Tunisia, despite their efforts in the field of family planning, cannot expect any rapid return in the form of an easier situation on the employment market, because the young people looking for a first job in 1986 will have been born in 1970 and, furthermore, while the first results of a birth control programme become apparent after roughly fifteen years, it will not be until about the year 2000 that there will be any real impact on the balance of the employment market.

A lack of employment opportunities is synonymous with an inadequate production potential and the best way of fighting unemployment is to generate *additional* potential. On the other hand, new capital equipment usually requires related installations. New machine tools, tractors, fertilisers, gas mains and dairy product factories cannot be used to full effect unless they are accompanied by other machine tools and the heavy equipment used for public works. All this is part of the normal pattern of productive investment and it is for the planners to strike a balance between the forms of investment that do not immediately result in additional consumer goods and the requirements of an incomes policy and population growth. Similarly, where a plan provides for inexpensive housing to be put up in a new industrial town or for the building of a hospital or school, it earmarks part of the national product for what are usually labelled as unproductive items of investment. Admittedly, the new capital, whether productive or unproductive, will be derived from the work of human beings, either directly because workmen will have driven the machines and received part of the money in the form of wages, or indirectly because the capital equipment used will itself have been produced by the work of human beings. Human resources investment, on the other hand, is something rather different.

Let us take the case of a country where all the opportunities for investment of the normal type have been exhausted, where all the available public works equipment is being fully utilised, where additional machinery cannot be acquired for lack of foreign currency, where all the workers that the public authorities and undertakings can recruit and pay a regular wage out of the available investment funds are on the job and where a vast reserve of labour still remains untapped and men and women are standing empty-handed. What is known as human resources investment begins when this labour force is drawn upon to generate additional potential.

It may legitimately be asked whether the planners in the countries of the Maghreb have been induced to adopt a human resources investment policy as a logical consequence of the imbalance they have come to perceive in their employment markets. The answer is, in fact, both yes and no. No, because only the Moroccan plan, with its national development programme, explicitly adopts human resources investment as a method of development. The Algerian plan contains no more than a passing reference in connection with the construction of rural housing, while the Tunisian plan is completely silent on the subject. The Tunisian Prime Minister's speech outlining his country's programme even goes so far as to relegate human resources investment to the rank of a temporary expedient.[1] Yes, if account is taken of the efforts made in recent years in the three countries and the conclusions that their respective leaders have arrived at. Let us therefore take a look at what they have achieved; we can then put forward some practical suggestions, which should help to raise any future experiments with investment of this kind to the status of a systematic method of national development.

---

[1] His actual words were: " Partial and temporary solutions have been adopted in Tunisia to reduce the burden of underemployment, the most striking examples being afforded by the work sites opened for the unemployed. It has to be conceded, however, that the present state of our finances precludes our going very far in this direction, particularly since more than purely manual labour will be needed for the major projects still outstanding."

Experiments with human resources investment and the conclusions to be drawn from them

The attitude of Algeria's leaders—as far as one can judge in the absence of any official policy statements—has been that the country is not yet in a position to have recourse to human resources investment as an instrument of development policy. They have tended to look upon it as a form of relief and have earmarked credits as part of their expenditure on " rural development " or " full employment " which will not in any circumstances be sufficient to provide permanent assistance for more than about 30,000 unemployed.

On the other hand, about 120 local reafforestation schemes have received assistance under the United Nations World Food Programme since 1966 [1] and form a kind of test-bed whose lessons can be used in the same way as the experiments carried out in 1963 and 1964.[2]

By contrast, the national development programme in Morocco was drawn up as a genuine rural development policy and was introduced as such in 1961 under the direct patronage of the Crown. Since then it has been progressively improved, although there are limits to which the improvements can be taken because the programme is unrelated to any kind of agrarian reform or to any really novel system of financing, as we shall see a little later in this article. Detailed reports on the programme have been drawn up by those responsible for its administration [3] and it regularly figures in the country's planning documents. The programme seems to be increasingly closely linked with the work of the normal technical services of the Ministry of Agriculture. The implications of this are twofold: on the one hand, it is ceasing to be a way of using human resources investment to supplement the ordinary forms of investment and is thus becoming a way of substituting a normal, but more labour-intensive and less capital-intensive, investment procedure for another; on the other, it can be easily co-ordinated with regional plans such as those prepared for the Sebou and the Western Riff.

Tunisia has adopted an unobtrusive policy of " full employment " work sites, which does not appear to have been the subject of any explicit comments by the country's leaders. By comparison with the measures taken in Morocco, these work sites have been organised on a wider scale in absolute terms and on a very much wider scale in relative terms, if account is taken of the country's size. On the other hand, the tendency

[1] These schemes were launched as a result of the joint efforts of the Christian Committee for Algerian Relief and the Algerian authorities.

[2] These experiments have been studied by Régine Dhoquois in a paper prepared for the Occupational Sociology Institute of the Paris Faculty of Law under the title " Les chantiers de plein emploi en Algérie ".

[3] Délégation générale à la Promotion nationale et au Plan: *La Promotion nationale* (Rabat, 1964).

seems to have been the same as in Morocco, namely to use them as a substitute for the normal forms of investment, instead of running the two in parallel, and it may even be that the process of substitution is more marked than in Morocco. And yet the agricultural production co-operatives offered an ideal setting for a policy of this kind and would have enabled it to achieve its avowed purpose of using manpower surpluses to lay down the necessary infrastructure, which, in turn, could provide productive employment opportunities for the unemployed. The future prospects of this policy are as uncertain as those of the co-operative societies, but nothing that has been said by the Tunisian leaders gives any grounds for thinking that they have abandoned the ideal of a partial co-operative sector.

Experiments with human resources investment in the Maghreb have not yet reached a stage where they can be regarded as one of the bases for the development of the area, but they have gone far enough for detailed examination to yield a certain number of conclusions.

For human resources investment to qualify as a method of achieving national development, it must, in terms of scale, reach a certain level of efficiency. Furthermore, it must not operate to the detriment of the normal forms of investment and must trigger off a cumulative process of employment generation.

The level of efficiency to be achieved in mobilising manpower surpluses can only be determined in the light of the number of jobs required to provide work for the unemployed and underemployed and the opportunities for undertaking labour-intensive projects. Enormous opportunities are, in fact, available, since more than 1,000 million days' work can be devoted to minor irrigation projects in Morocco and the same number to land improvement programmes in Algeria.[1] On the other hand, as we have seen, the scale of these opportunities is matched by the employment opportunities required. It is a fair contention, therefore, that the aim to be achieved in the mobilisation of manpower surpluses should be, first, to prevent an increase in unemployment by avoiding an excessive expansion of the tertiary sector (representing about 8 million man-days in Tunisia, 20 million in Algeria and 28 million in

[1] In Morocco 3 million hectares of productive land are affected by erosion and 400 million days' work could be devoted to soil conservation; 75 million days' work could easily be spent on reafforestation and about 30 million on farm improvement schemes, such as scrub clearance and stone picking. About 15 million days' work would be needed to put up cattle sheds, endless work could be done on roads and tracks and 1,000 million days' work could be devoted to minor irrigation projects (for further details see *La politique économique et financière du Maroc indépendant*, op. cit., pp. 39-43). In Algeria 1,200 million days' work are needed for land betterment alone (9.3 million hectares of arable land require attention, 2.1 million hectares could be improved by afforestation or reafforestation schemes and 1.4 million hectares of pasture land require protection). In addition 650 million days' work could be spent on irrigation schemes covering 1.3 million hectares, while there is a substantial amount of work to be done on roads and tracks, which are more numerous than in Morocco, because of the war.

TABLE VII. WORK CREATED BY FULL EMPLOYMENT WORK SITES IN THE MAGHREB, 1958-72

(Millions of working days)

Year	Algeria	Morocco	Tunisia
1958-59	.	.	29.6
1960	.	.	31
1961	.	7.4 [1]	55.5
1962	.	16.4	57.4
1963	10 [2]	10	55.4
1964	8 [2]	15	56.4 [2]
1965	5-10 [3]		31 [2]
1966	.	18	.
1967	3.5-7 [3]		.
1968	7.5-10 [2]	19.6	.
1969	7.5-10 [2]	19.2	.
1970	7.5-10 [2]	20-22	31 [2]
1971	7.5-10 [2]	24.6 [2]	.
1972	7.5-10 [2]	24.6 [2]	.

[1] Second half only. [2] Estimate only. [3] Tentative estimate, made on the basis of total financial allocations, because the estimated cost of a working day was itself tentative.

Morocco [1]) and, secondly, to contribute, over a period of about ten years, to eliminating rural underemployment (representing 25 million man-days in Tunisia and from 40 to 45 million in Algeria and Morocco [2]). Hence, the objective would be to achieve a level of 35 million man-days in Tunisia and 60 to 70 million in Algeria and Morocco. This level was regularly exceeded in Tunisia from 1961 to 1964 and was almost achieved in subsequent years, but it has not even been remotely approached by Morocco or Algeria, especially the latter (see table VII).

A further prerequisite is that the employment resulting directly from human resources investment should be additional to that generated by normal methods. This would not be so if the cost of the operation were so high that it drained off money required for ordinary investment. This might happen if the workers mobilised for employment on a project needed heavy equipment, such as lorries, bulldozers and other machinery used for public works, or if they were paid a normal wage. The project would cease to be a sound financial proposition because, the machinery having been introduced to reduce the cost of the operation, bearing in mind the wage rates prevailing in the country concerned, to ban it would be a backward step. Moreover, the size of the payroll would absorb a substantial proportion of the funds needed for regular out-

[1] Growth of the rural population (taking into account the participation rates indicated in tables II, IV, and VI) and 10 per cent of the increase in the male urban population.

[2] Ten per cent of the surplus active rural population (see above).

lays. To daily wages must be added the irreducible cost of incidental equipment and material such as shovels or pickaxes, cement and gabions, as well as expenditure on transport and essential administrative costs. On this basis the number of days' work fixed as a minimum level of efficiency in terms of scale would absorb more than the total amount of money earmarked for gross investment in agriculture (including irrigation projects) in Morocco and three-quarters of that amount in Algeria and Tunisia.[1] There can consequently be no question of paying the workers concerned a normal wage. It is immaterial whether the wage is paid in kind or even financed out of an international assistance programme; the amount of money devoted to the workers' remuneration in cash or kind could have been used to finance ordinary investment. Even if a normal system of remuneration is incompatible with a policy of human resources investment, however, it does not follow that the persons concerned should work without reward. There is no question of their being employed for nothing, and any work site organised should be able to provide the persons working on it with what they are all hoping for in the absence of a direct wage, namely a chance of lifting themselves out of the rut of unemployment and finding a stable and normally remunerated job. In rural areas this aim is symbolised by the possession or working of a plot of land, and the best way for a work site to galvanise the workers' efforts is consequently for it to give them a feeling of having a claim to the land on which they are employed. Even on the most optimistic assessment, however, there can be no question of answering this claim in the immediate, since it is linked to the development process itself, i.e. to the policy of human resources investment. Assuming normal productivity, about 1,500 man-days must be devoted to a project before there is sufficient improvement in the land to provide a living for one extra worker (or, in other words, before there is a productive infrastructure corresponding to one job). This means that an input of six man-years will be required for every job created, and if it is impossible to find some way of making already developed land available to those concerned, they will consequently have to spend six years working more or less for nothing before they can acquire sufficient land to earn an independent living. This is not impossible, but a better solution could be found as part of a more efficient agrarian structure—a point to which we shall return a little later on. A policy of human resources investment is accordingly linked with agrarian reform, not on account of preconceived ideological considerations but simply because it is the only way of providing work for the peasantry without paying them a wage and without going to the other extreme of having to turn the country into a vast concentration camp.

[1] The respective figures in the national currencies are 720 and 1,035 million dinars for Algeria, 560 and 502 million dirhams for Morocco and 24.5 and 31.9 million dinars for Tunisia.

This has not happened in the Maghreb. The Algerian Government very sensibly decided that agrarian reform was premature and drew the logical conclusion from its own decision by rejecting a manpower mobilisation policy. Persons employed on work sites in the departments of Algiers and Oran are paid a normal wage. Those working in the department of Constantine receive daily compensation in the form of a modest sum in cash (0.75 dinars [1]) and various benefits in kind to a value of between 6 and 8 dinars.

In Morocco the Government did not feel that agrarian reform was a possible alternative, so that the situation there is similar to that obtaining in Algeria. The Moroccan leaders are aware of this, because the authors of the official 1964 document on the national development programme, to which reference has been made above, pointed out that the daily wage rate was too high (although only 4 dirhams [2] at the time) for the country to embark on a general mobilisation programme, which, at this rate, would have been far too expensive for the State.

In Tunisia there has been no connection between the policy of human resources investment and agrarian reform. Each worker has received what is considered to be a normal wage in agriculture (0.35 dinars [3]), which has floated upwards with the general wage level. This explains why the policy has lost impetus with the passage of time; the number of man-days has progressively diminished [4] and, instead of being a net addition to the normal forms of investment, has come to be regarded as a substitution for them.

This is yet another twist of policy which has prevented human resources investment from being an effective way of triggering off the process of economic development. A substantial number of working days have been devoted to projects which were carried out by normal means before the policy was introduced. One way of doing things, and even one form of government responsibility, has consequently not been superimposed upon another but has actually been substituted for it.

Similarly, in Morocco a comparison of the results achieved with the national development programme and those of the services in earlier years [5] shows that many projects would have been carried out without any manpower mobilisation scheme, the exact percentages for the various activities being as follows: minor irrigation projects 25 per cent, soil conservation 72 per cent, infrastructure 50 per cent and community development 40 per cent. The number of working days actually contributed as a net addition to the projects undertaken with normal sources

[1] One Algerian dinar is worth about 1.15 French francs.

[2] One Moroccan dirham is worth about 1.10 French francs.

[3] One Tunisian dinar is worth about 10 French francs.

[4] See table VII.

[5] See *La Promotion nationale*, op. cit.

of investment was only 3.8 million in 1961, 8.4 million in 1962 and 5.3 million in 1963. Subsequently this distinction between addition and substitution was reflected in the administrative procedures and the official documents themselves (second part projects and first part projects).[1] Over the period 1965-67 the additions represented 11 million days a year (62 per cent of the total number of days worked), the corresponding figure for 1969 being 13.9 million (72.5 per cent).

The same distinction has been made in Tunisia since 1963 between regional projects (which are additional to normal forms of investment) and national projects (which replace them); over the years the latter have represented an increasing proportion of the total—48 per cent in 1963, 59 per cent in 1964, 87 per cent in 1965 and 72.5 per cent in 1970. The net addition in 1970 was consequently no more than 11.3 million days, which is very much below the minimum level of efficiency defined above and actually exceeded in 1962.

For human resources investment to be an effective instrument of development policy, it has to set in motion a cumulative process of employment generation. For this to happen, two rules must be observed: first, the projects undertaken have to be productive; and, secondly, they have to be carried out by workers maintaining a normal standard for the productivity of labour.

The selection of the projects is not an easy task, because activities that are likely to turn out to be a labour of Sisyphus have to be avoided. They also have to be productive, so that some of the workers engaged on them can be transferred to actual production jobs in course of time. This would be the case with a minor irrigation project, since the substitution of high-yielding crops for cereals or grazing land will create a greater demand for labour and, through the higher value added, provide funds for the payment of a normal wage. This contrasts with the laying of a water main supplying drinking-water, or even the building of a school, which does not generate any productive employment opportunities, and, when the project is completed, another of the same size is needed to provide employment for the persons who were working on it. Many problems are encountered in connection with the choice of a productive project. In an inhabited locality, and especially in a town, the population or its representatives will not spontaneously vote in favour of a project of this kind; their natural tendency is to favour projects that are devoid of economic value, such as paving the floor of the bazaar, fencing-in cemeteries, laying drains or channels for running water, or even projects that are of long-term economic benefit but not immediately productive, such as hospitals, housing, schools, community

[1] " Cash wages are financed out of the technical services budget and *replace* the expenditure that would have been incurred by those services in connection with the use of plant or machinery " (Délégation générale à la Promotion nationale et au Plan: *Trois années de Promotion nationale* (mimeographed, 1964)).

centres or the building of roads instead of tracks. Admittedly any attempt to base a manpower mobilisation scheme on the good will of the participants must pay the greatest possible attention to their preferences, but overriding economic and financial considerations demand that the project should be immediately productive, so that the persons working on it can enter the normal circuit of production and earn a normal wage as soon as possible. This is a point that takes a long time to bring home to them. Furthermore—and this is most important—the local community provides the wrong setting for a project; the setting chosen must have some direct connection with production. Table VIII lists a number of productive projects that have much to recommend them from this point of view.

TABLE VIII. SELECTED MANPOWER MOBILISATION PROJECTS

Type of project	No. of man-days required to carry out the project	No. of man-days created in the form of permanent employment	Economic effects and time-lag
Protective earthworks and soil conservation (1 hectare)	180	30	Maintenance of cereal crops through better infiltration of rainwater after 1-2 years. Fruit crops after 3-8 years.
Reafforestation (1 hectare)	130-160	6	Production after 12-15 years.
Scrub clearance (1 hectare)	25	30	Value for production purposes variable, depending on the type of farming. Effect may be immediate or only apparent after irrigation or plantation.
Scarifying (1 hectare) . .	10		
Stone picking (1 hectare) .	30		
Minor irrigation works (1 hectare)	450-550	20-105	More even distribution of returns if a low-yielding type of farming is retained. Usually leads to the substitution of a high-yielding for a low-yielding type of farming. Effect immediate.
Laying of tracks (1 kilometre)	18 000-41 000	50-540	Return depends on the economic value of the tracks. Time-lag varies with the level of development of the areas concerned.
Putting up a building for small-scale rural handicrafts	Indeterminate	Indeterminate	Varies with the type of activity.

Source: *Le Maghreb entre les mythes*, op. cit.

TABLE IX. TYPES OF PROJECT CHOSEN FOR THE MOROCCAN NATIONAL DEVELOPMENT PROGRAMME

(In %)

Type of project	1961	1964	1965-67	1968-72 (planned)	1969
Soil improvement and conservation, reafforestation and minor irrigation works	29.7	55	41.7	59.5	55
Local and municipal infrastructure	16	11	18.3	13.8	17
Roads and tracks	54.3	34	40	26.7	28
All projects	100	100	100	100	100

Among the various kinds of projects listed in the table, those with a quick return should have priority (minor irrigation projects and agricultural improvement schemes other than soil conservation). Care should also be taken to ensure that the importance attached to reafforestation is in keeping with the fairly limited effects to be expected of it. Work on new tracks should not be undertaken unless it forms part of a general development scheme and even the improvement of existing tracks should be given careful study to see whether it is likely to yield an adequate return.

In its choice of projects the Moroccan national development programme got off to a bad start, but constant improvements have been made to it, as may be seen from table IX.

A number of welcome changes have been made within each type of project. In the first group, a great deal less importance has come to be attached to reafforestation and to manual irrigation schemes. Progress was also made in the third group during the initial years, since the laying of new tracks accounted for 45 per cent of all the infrastructure projects in 1964; this led to a reduction in maintenance work, which represented 80 per cent of the total programme in 1962-64. In Algeria, the broad types of project have been well selected, but the individual items in each group have not proved to be particularly productive; a lot of time has been devoted to manual irrigation schemes and reafforestation (as an illustration, 64 million trees were planted in the department of Constantine alone between 1963 and 1967). No material would appear to be available from which any conclusion can be drawn in this respect from the projects undertaken in Tunisia.

It should not be imagined, however, that all that need be done is to select productive projects; there is still the problem of getting the work done at minimum cost in terms of labour. A high level of productivity presupposes enthusiasm, supervision, technical guidance and, in some cases, the co-ordination of the project with general employment policy. Enthusiasm is not easily forthcoming without wages, even if the workers can foresee the possibility of enjoying a claim to the land at some time in the future. Admittedly, a solution can be found, as we shall see, whereby they can be encouraged to wait patiently for the six years that must inevitably elapse before they can enjoy this claim and earn a normal living, but the fact remains that the pay-off in the early days is more a question of having something to look forward to than of earning good hard cash. A considerable amount of persuasion is consequently necessary to maintain the workers' interest; this can be achieved, for example, by stressing the value of the project not only to them personally but also to the nation as a whole, by providing evidence of backing from the general population and by arranging for each project to be included in a broader programme. Such methods of persuasion involve recourse to the techniques of rural promotion that have been applied from time to time in Morocco and Algeria, whereby the masses of the population are associated with a given policy by explaining to them the measures decided on at the top and paying heed to their reactions. This objective would be completely attained if, after the explanatory process, the policy—whatever it may be—were the subject of an agreement concluded between the State (or, more usually, the institution which holds the purse-strings, the stocks of equipment or public power) and the community which provides the manpower. But if there is to be a fruitful dialogue, it must proceed at a slow pace and in a form comprehensible to an illiterate and traditional population. This means that those conducting it should belong to the milieu whose sympathy they are trying to gain. The system of rural promotion consists in training non-professional promoters who will continue to share the life of the masses and speak the same language. For the dialogue to be initiated and kept going there must be an organisational framework and the participation of experts. Promotion is a technique and, while it depends upon the support of non-professional agents, these must be trained by professionals. Accordingly technical assistance is involved, but it should be of a very temporary nature in view of the political aspect of the matter. It goes without saying that the desired results can be obtained only if there is a coherent policy. Accordingly, if the workers' interest is to be maintained, they must not be employed on the development of private land unless the improvements resulting from their work are taken over for their benefit. Finally, the public authorities have to fulfil their obligations and ensure that such compensation as is due, however small, is regularly paid and that the work site is properly supplied with the tools and other incidental equipment and transport facilities it needs. All this looks simple enough, but government departments are unfamiliar with the processes involved, which need to be kept flexible, and usually lack the necessary book-keeping and accounting staff. It has also been observed that budgetary considerations have given rise to repeated delays in the opening of work sites at the beginning of the year, which is the very time when human resources investment offers the best prospects of success because normal farming is often at a standstill. If a project is to be undertaken at the local level, therefore, a certain number of changes will also be called for at that level.

To keep up the workers' spirits, arrangements must also be made to give them the necessary encouragement when their enthusiasm flags; this implies certain appropriate forms of supervision. Assuming that the projects are of medium size, an input of about 10 million man-days will require 2,000 team leaders, 700 work site foremen and 300 general work site managers.

Experience in Morocco has shown that the necessary supervisory staff can be trained locally, using illiterate labourers, who are either tried out in supervisory jobs on a temporary basis or given a certain period of training. It takes two months to train a team leader; four months later he will be capable of acting as a work site foreman and four months after that again as an assistant manager. If a suitable period of time is allowed to elapse at each level, any one of the first 200 unemployed taken at random on his arrival at the work site is capable of becoming an assistant manager within two years. The cost of the operation is minimal; in Morocco (where the practice is to pay a wage) it amounted to 0.2 dirhams per working day in 1969. Technical supervision is quite another matter and is, in fact, the most difficult problem encountered in activities of this kind. Drawing up plans and laying down daily standards of performance are not insuperable tasks, but the best possible location must be found for minor irrigation projects and there has to be some kind of co-ordination between the basic programmes for soil conservation, the planting of trees and the laying out of tracks. All this demands a certain amount of study, and it is therefore not surprising that the Moroccan leaders have paid considerable attention to the difficulties involved and have rightly felt that they provide an explanation for the way achievements have fallen short of expectations. Officials have pointed out that the shortage of medium-grade supervisors and technicians and the inadequate participation of the specialised government departments have been among the limiting factors encountered in connection with the national development programme.[1] Some improvement should be possible as a result of technical assistance and the reallocation of technical staff to the most backward areas (which are precisely those benefiting most from a human resources investment policy). Progress along these lines is slow, however, and the level of efficiency of scale referred to earlier in this article can only be achieved by stages.

---

[1] Ministère des Affaires économiques du Plan et de la Formation des cadres: *Plan quinquennal 1968-1972*, Vol. I, p. 14; *Rapport sur l'exécution du Plan en 1969*, p. 67.

To increase the over-all efficiency of the operation, every human resources investment project, irrespective of its scale, needs planning. It must not operate to the detriment of normal farm work and the pace must consequently be kept up even at peak periods. It must not be hampered by a shortage of tools, seedlings or incidental supplies, and any additional production must be marketed.

For all these reasons the countryside provides an infinitely better setting for human resources investment projects than the towns. This has been emphasised by the officials responsible for administering the Moroccan plan in the following terms: " Where projects are undertaken in the towns as part of the national development programme, they only too often look like a form of unemployment relief; the cost is usually prohibitive and the workers' output very low." [1]

Human resources investment is one way of generating productive employment opportunities at very little cost. The basic conditions that it has to meet make it a difficult instrument to handle and, if it is clumsily conceived, it may result in a higher cost per job than is incurred in heavy industry. This, in fact, is what happened in the early years in Algeria, Morocco and Tunisia. A selection of unproductive projects and a low level of labour productivity (40 to 50 per cent of the generally accepted level) involved a cost of between 40,000 and 60,000 dirhams per job in Morocco in 1964-65 and between 100,000 and 130,000 dinars in Algeria in 1965. In Tunisia, with 50 per cent productivity and a choice of projects that were only 50 per cent productive, the cost of each permanent job amounted to 1,620 dinars; with normal productivity and fully productive projects, the cost would have worked out at 405 dinars. Further, if wage payments had been replaced by the lowest possible rate of subsistence allowances, the cost could have been limited to 200 dinars. Unemployment could probably be eliminated over a period of fifteen years at a cost of approximately 150 million French francs a year; given the higher levels of remuneration, the same objective, pursued in the same optimum conditions, would involve an outlay of about 350 million French francs a year in Algeria and Morocco.

All this would seem to show that the experiments made with a human resources investment policy in the various countries of the Maghreb are not particularly convincing, but they do provide a basis for drawing a certain number of conclusions. All that is needed for many of the projects is a team of workers and a certain amount of light equipment, and the problems of administration and supervision have not been all that difficult to solve, once the obstacles encountered in the initial years of independence had been overcome. On the other hand, if human resources investment is to be more than a useful but indecisive expedient and become an instrument in the process of national development, it

[1] *Plan quinquennal 1968-1972*, op. cit., Vol. II, p. 173.

must be linked to agrarian reform. Even in the most favourable circumstances, it will still require a quite considerable amount of capital (roughly 3 per cent of the gross national product), which should, if possible, be raised in other ways than through the normal methods of financing, e.g. in the form of international assistance or a national solidarity campaign. Finally, if it does become a method of development, it should not be used in isolation from the other major methods, namely industrialisation and intensification of farming, but should complement them and support them.

Human resources investment and the general development of the countries of the Maghreb

Human investment and co-operatives

I came to the conclusion many years ago that human resources investment was inseparable from agrarian reform and felt that it should take the form of work sites opened on expropriated land, which would be progressively developed and allocated to some of the participants, the various plots being grouped around a core of fertile land previously belonging to settlers or absentee landlords. Where there was no such fertile land, every year a sixth of the workers could be taken off the work site, and where it represented a third, the workers would only have to wait four years, and so on. Such a procedure proved unrealistic, however: work sites opened at the local level tended to be devoted to unproductive projects and the transfer of the workers concerned to agriculture was delayed accordingly. At the stage when it was decided to implement agrarian reform, how was one to choose between the workers who would be allocated land immediately and those who would have to wait? Of course answers can be found enabling the system to operate. But what has actually happened in Tunisia has led me to rethink the process along entirely different lines. Co-operative societies have been set up all over the country, each one of them with more members than it could possibly support. As long ago as 1964-65, the author of a paper on the subject [1] observed that 9.3 per cent of the total membership of co-operative societies were unemployed; at the time, disguised underemployment was probably much higher, because the value of a working day was rated at no more than 0.44 dinars. Other figures also provide evidence of an imbalance. The area of land available to each member of a co-operative society has steadily diminished, and

[1] Rafika El Hamdi: *La réforme des structures agraires en Tunisie*, paper prepared for the Occupational Sociology Institute, 1969.

directly reflects the number of co-operatives set up.[1] Moreover, at the time, each member was paid for an average of 150 working days a year (the figure ranging from 80 in the case of the poorest societies to 300 in the case of the more wealthy ones); this, in the extreme case, would yield an annual income of only 66 dinars for each worker. Under-employment was undoubtedly rife in the co-operative movement, and yet the principles were very carefully thought out up to the beginning of 1969.

What happened was apparently inevitable. This being so, why not regard it as one of the facts of life and give each co-operative society a certain amount of land to be improved in different ways (through soil conservation, irrigation works and other programmes)? Each co-operative would provide a full-employment work site and would not preclude the possibility of arrangements being made by groups of co-operative societies in connection with more important projects, such as the building of a dam. Each society could conclude a contract with the central authority, which would provide certain consumer goods (representing a minimum allowance for the workers), light equipment and the necessary technical supervision, in exchange for a certain job to be done on its land, rather than for a certain number of days' work. In this way no family would be obliged to rely on the income derived from the work site as its sole source of livelihood. The necessary supervisory staff would be available on the spot and the choice of project would be dictated by the membership's desire to increase the co-operative's income. In any event it is difficult to make a commercial proposition of a co-operative society with too many members, and there can be no question of ordering the excess membership to leave.

What holds true of the traditional forms of co-operative society in Algeria and has inevitably happened to them is equally true and inevitable for the country's self-managed undertakings. Here, disguised under-employment probably affects about a third of the labour force. Why not recognise this fact and use the surplus manpower for human resources investment? However prosperous they may have been, most of the settlers' farms were, and still are, capable of improvement. Action could be taken without waiting for agrarian reform. There would, admittedly, be the possible objection (which would be even more pertinent than in the case of the co-operative movement) that the benefits of the Government's limited efforts would not fall to the people most in need of them. In the case of self-managed undertakings, however, a rapid expansion in gross output would very soon enable the Government (through the various " funds " maintained by undertakings) to recover its modest outlay on the mobilisation of what would be virtually free labour. In the traditional

[1] The following are the figures for the number of hectares per member: 1962-63, 15.5; 1963-64, 12.2; 1964-65, 10; 1965-66, 11; 1966-67, 8.

sector, a solution to the problem would be more difficult to find, because it would be the same persons that would suffer twice—workers who had already been marginal to the work of a co-operative would also find themselves high and dry on the completion of a project. In the short term, their lives while working on a project would not be particularly easy, since their earnings would be almost nil, but family solidarity would probably be instrumental in lightening the burden.

However low the rate of compensation granted, the Government would nevertheless incur considerable expenditure, which would not have to be financed to the detriment of ordinary investment; the answer would be to raise the necessary money by appealing to national and international solidarity.

Human resources investment and civic service

In most of the industrialised countries young people are required to do military service, which, whatever else it does for them, prevents them from continuing with their work or studies and keeps them occupied on low pay for a period ranging from eighteen months to two years. Keeping them occupied is usually the essence of the problem, because while a few of them may admittedly be given training for a future job very few of them ever develop a liking for this kind of life. In the Maghreb the army will sooner or later think of adopting a system of military service for all young people who have undergone some form of training, but there can be no guarantee that it will have more success than the armies of the developed countries in arousing their enthusiasm.

Why not, therefore, forestall this tendency and mobilise young workers on the spot? All persons between the ages of 23 and 30 who are working for an employer or as members of a family business could be required to pay a levy equal to two-thirds of their wages or a flat-rate assessment of their incomes for a period of two years. In this way they would suffer far less inconvenience than their counterparts in the developed countries, since they would spend this period working at their jobs or studies, rather than being divorced from them. Anyone unable to make do with a third of his wages could be housed in a barracks opened for the purpose. Probably the average age for getting married would rise, but the general interest would not suffer. It should be possible to find a solution without too much difficulty to the problem of persons who have been supporting their families for years while continuing their studies.

In Algeria the plan provides for 66,500 new jobs to be created outside agriculture every year. On the assumption, and it is a minimum assumption, that persons under 30 years of age do not fill more than 40,000 of them, a two-thirds levy on wages would bring in more than

500 million dinars over two years.[1] On the assumption that 40,000 young people under 30 years of age enter the employment market, the breakdown in revenue would be as follows:

Wage group (dinars)	Monthly levy (dinars)	No. of workers	Total levy over two years (millions of dinars)
1 200	800	2 000	38.4
900	600	28 000	403.2
600	400	10 000	96
			537.6

Even after deduction of any outlay on the payment of relief and assuming a certain amount of tax evasion or a 20 per cent overestimation on my part, this sum would be enough to finance a number of man-days corresponding to the level of efficiency referred to earlier.

In Morocco, the forecasts for the number of jobs to be created are more modest and I myself have in any event produced adjusted figures; on this basis the scheme could bring in over 200 million dirhams (given the lower wage levels), which would be enough, even allowing for the risk of error, to finance half the outlay on a human resources investment policy. My own assumption is that 36,000 jobs will be created every year in the non-agricultural sector and in modern forms of farming and that two-thirds of these jobs will be taken by persons under 30 years of age. The luckier ones will earn as much as in Algeria, and the others less. The figures thus obtained would be as follows:

Wage group (dirhams)	Monthly levy (dirhams)	No. of workers	Total levy over two years (millions of dirhams)
1 200	800	2 000	38.4
600	400	10 000	96
450	300	12 000	86.4
			220.8

In Tunisia, it would be possible, on the basis of similar calculations, to cover two-thirds of the manpower mobilisation budget. Here, I have reduced the number of jobs created outside the traditional forms of

[1] In case of error due to overoptimism it would always be possible to apply a smaller levy to young persons who had already found jobs in previous years.

farming to 24,000, of which 16,000 I have assumed will be taken by persons under 30 years of age. The wage level is lower than in Morocco for the highest and lowest groups. The detailed calculation is given below:

Wage group (dinars)	Monthly levy (dinars)	No. of workers	Total levy over two years (hundreds of thousands of dinars)
90	60	2 000	28.8
60	40	10 000	96
30	20	4 000	19.2
			144.0

The only purpose of these figures is to give some idea of the scale of the operation, which will not be affected if it is found necessary in all fairness to reduce the levy on the lower wage groups. Some people might consider that the procedure envisaged is unrealistic from both the administrative and political points of view. I do not share this fear, because I believe that compulsory military service will soon be introduced in the Maghreb and that this will require still more cumbersome administrative machinery and will cause greater dissatisfaction among the young people themselves. It could also be argued that the burden of action against underemployment should not be placed on just one category—young persons. But this is not so. The main burden will rest on the mobilised workers themselves, because it will be they who will create a productive base without immediate reward. As for young people with jobs, they are a privileged group and will be the least affected by the social cost of this measure.

The system of financing advocated here would have the advantage of bringing home to the persons working on a project that the nation is actively behind them. It would also serve to encourage international backing for the scheme.

Human resources investment and international assistance

To reach the minimum level of efficiency under a scheme of this kind, Morocco and Tunisia would have to have recourse to foreign aid; given help, Algeria would actually exceed that level. These countries have always been assisted in coping with their food problems, even where the assistance was only needed for the provision of poor relief. They would be in a far better position to obtain support if they came forward with a programme containing a built-in guarantee that the aid requested would be temporary. It might even be possible to dovetail the expected improvements with regional development plans, which international organisations regard with even greater favour. To take the idea further, it is conceivable that a country waiting to demonstrate its solidarity and capable of supplying wheat or of providing French-speaking technical staff, like Canada, might look upon such a programme as presenting a field of action worthy of its good will and of its vocation as a world power.

Human resources investment and industrialisation

So far, we have not found any very definite connection between the twin policies of human resources investment and industrialisation, the former merely being one way of enabling the latter to evade the straightforward problem of direct employment generation. Once the decision has been taken to tackle unemployment along other lines, there is less danger of according systematic preference to investment in labour-intensive projects rather than more capital-intensive ones which create less jobs but are more useful in the longer term. On the other hand, it is possible to conceive of a more positive connection between the two policies, which might supplement each other. One of the obstacles to industrialisation, in fact, is the narrowness of domestic markets. Goods cost too much to produce because they are produced in such small quantities. This state of the market is also an obstacle to sound industrial management, because since most of the French population left the area, many undertakings have not been used to full capacity. This can be seen from the following figures for Morocco:

Item	Production capacity (tons)	1968 demand (tons)	1973 demand (tons)
Fish meal and oil	63 000	32 500	53 000
Seed oil	111 500	71 000	90 000
Margarine	4 250	2 000	2 200
Nails	4 700	3 100	4 300
Woollen yarn	6 000	4 150	5 120
Soap	45 000	30 250	34 200
Candles	10 000	4 900	4 900

Why should the Government not short-circuit the market by buying up products at marginal cost and then distributing them to the persons on its work sites? If assistance in the form of cereals represents no more than half the compensation granted, the Governments of Morocco and Algeria could provide industry with an assured market worth 100 million French francs. This would make it possible for several firms to operate at full capacity and for some industrial projects to be expanded. Through economies of scale, the marginal cost would not be very high and the workers' standard of living would be appreciably improved. Moroccan workers' families would certainly be very glad to be offered the various products listed in the table.

* * *

There is every reason to suppose that a human resources investment policy can effectively contribute to the development of the countries of the Maghreb by giving a definite impetus to industrial expansion, even allowing for the narrowness of domestic markets, by fostering a spirit of national solidarity, by encouraging agrarian reform and an increasingly sound co-operative movement, despite the disproportion between the size of the peasant population and the area of land available, and by attracting foreign aid which, being temporary, would not be incompatible with national prestige. The experiments undertaken in the past ten years would seem to indicate the need for this approach to development.

Employment Problems and Policies in the Ivory Coast

Louis ROUSSEL [1]

WITH 4½ MILLION INHABITANTS and an area of some 125,000 square miles, more or less equally divided between bush and forest, the Ivory Coast is one of the medium-sized newer African States. Still essentially an agricultural country, beset with problems of modernisation and equipment but maintaining privileged economic relations with the ex-metropolitan country, it is subject to the same constraints and imperatives as most other former colonial territories. In fact, the Ivory Coast was even less well off than they were in certain respects upon the granting of independence. School attendance levels had remained very low, with the result that " leadership material " was in even shorter supply than in certain neighbouring countries. After eleven years of independence, however, the Ivory Coast appears as something of a miracle. Its gross domestic product has been growing at a steady 8 per cent per annum, an up-to-date infrastructure has been created, the proportion of children going to school has doubled [2], local industry is steadily developing, while agricultural output has increased not only in volume but also in variety.

As far as employment is concerned, the Ivory Coast started from a relatively advantageous position. Whereas independence found other African countries suffering from acute unemployment, the Ivory Coast was providing jobs not only for its own nationals but also for steadily increasing numbers of immigrants (especially from Upper Volta). In 1961 the Abidjan Employment Service recorded a greater number of job vacancies than of applications.[3] Younger workers, whether literate or

---

[1] Research Director, Institut national d'études démographiques, Paris; Assistant Professor, Faculté des lettres et sciences humaines de l'Université de Paris.

[2] Some 60 per cent of all children, as against 30 per cent prior to independence, now go to school. Since the proportion of girls is lower, it is probable that about 75 per cent of all boys now attend school.

[3] *Statistiques de l'Office de la main-d'œuvre de Côte d'Ivoire* (Abidjan, 1961).

not, experienced no great difficulty in finding the sort of jobs they were looking for.

It was in 1965, or thereabouts, that the problem of unemployment began to make itself felt, especially in Abidjan. Although the economy was booming, the situation gradually deteriorated until at the end of 1969 the Government decided to see just how bad it was by taking a census of the unemployed. In the towns (that is to say, in Abidjan and in towns with more than 10,000 inhabitants), some 44,000 people were found to be unemployed. This figure may well have been an underestimate; today it is probable that at least 50,000 people are out of work.

This is a strange situation—the unemployed are multiplying fast at the same time as the economy continues to flourish. I intend first to analyse the nature and causes of this seeming paradox, and consider how the position is likely to evolve in the medium term. In the second part of the article, I shall describe the policies adopted by the Government with a view to stemming and if possible reducing unemployment.

Present employment problems

Between 1950 and 1960 the only problem was the shortage of available manpower, especially in agriculture producing for export. Accordingly, an attempt was made to recruit extra labour, especially in Upper Volta.[1] We shall shortly see that this problem still subsists. First, however, it is necessary to investigate the position in the towns.

Employment in the towns

In or around 1960 there were some 105,000 urban wage earners (including civil servants and public employees) and an insignificant number of unemployed.[2] Ten years later it was estimated that there were 225,000 urban wage earners for between 45,000 and 50,000 unemployed. Thus unemployment took a hold, and got worse, at a time when urban employment was increasing by an average of 8 per cent per year. The unemployment rate works out at roughly 12 per cent of the 430,000 urban inhabitants of working age.

This figure is alarming enough, but for young job-seekers the position is in fact even worse. The census showed that no more than 10,000 out of the total 50,000 unemployed were former wage earners. All the others

---

[1] See, for instance, Raymond Desclers: *Le problème de la main-d'œuvre en Côte-d'Ivoire* (Abidjan, 1956).

[2] *Statistiques de l'Office de la main-d'œuvre de Côte-d'Ivoire* (Abidjan, 1960). The 20,000 or so persons employed by the State have been added to the 83,000 wage earners employed by private enterprise and semi-public concerns. The ILO *Year book of labour statistics* gives the number of unemployed at this time as only a few hundred, while estimating that there were nearly 12,000 unemployed in neighbouring Ghana.

TABLE I. DISTRIBUTION OF WAGE EARNERS IN THE MODERN SECTOR BY NATIONAL ORIGIN, 1968
(%)

Sector	Ivory Coast nationals	Other Africans	Non-Africans
Private	**47.5**	**46.2**	**6.3**
Primary	19.2	78.5	2.3
Secondary	51.6	43.3	5.1
Tertiary	56.3	34.2	9.5
Public	**75.0**	**17.7**	**7.3**

Source: Ministère du Plan de Côte-d'Ivoire, Direction des études de développement: *Deuxieme esquisse du Plan quinquennal de développement 1971-1975*, p. 329.

were young people looking for their first job. It may well be, therefore, that as many as 25 per cent, or even more, of the entire labour force between the ages of 15 and 29 are without work.[1] Hence unemployment is not something which affects all age groups to the same degree. It is obvious that we have here a state of affairs in which unemployment is produced not by the laying-off of redundant workers but by saturation of the employment market, with the result that newcomers have very little chance of finding work.

Up to now two things have prevented matters from becoming really critical. Solidarity amongst members of the same family is very powerful, and hospitality is often extended for lengthy periods to quite distant relatives.[2] This makes it possible for a young person to stay for several years in town waiting for a suitable job to turn up, with the result that amongst young people up to the age of 20 or even more the consequences of unemployment are not so serious as they might otherwise be.

Moreover, an economy of the traditional kind still exists and absorbs a good deal of labour; this it can do because productivity is so low. Hence if a man cannot find wage-earning employment in the modern sector, he can often fall back on some activity of this kind; it will not be well paid, but it will at least keep body and soul together.

There is one other feature of the employment picture which deserves mention, namely the impressively high proportion of the wage-earning labour force constituted by Africans from outside the Ivory Coast, despite the steady increase in unemployment (see table I).

[1] There are about 220,000 young men in this age group, of whom 50,000 are still at school or college (Ministère du Plan: *Côte-d'Ivoire 1965: Emploi* (Abidjan, 1968), p. 167).

[2] In Abidjan alone there were, in 1965 or thereabouts, some 15,000 young people aged over 20 who were supported in this way.

TABLE II. DISTRIBUTION OF WAGE EARNERS IN THE PRIVATE AND SEMI-PUBLIC MODERN SECTOR BY SKILLS AND NATIONAL ORIGIN, 1965 (%)

Skill level	Ivory Coast nationals	Other Africans	Europeans
All levels	**47**	**46**	**7**
Managerial staff	12	3	85
Senior staff and technicians	17	2	81
Foremen	29	13	58
Senior white-collar employees	55	16	29
Junior white-collar employees	70	27	3
Skilled manual workers	72	26	2
Semi-skilled workers	69	30	1
Labourers	35	65	0

Source: *Côte-d'Ivoire 1965: Emploi*, op. cit., p. 89.

Here, then, is a country in which more than half the wage earners in the modern private sector are foreigners. Table II, giving a breakdown by skills and national origin, is even more instructive.[1]

Ivory Coast nationals are to be found in considerable numbers in the intermediate grades, as well as in administrative posts (in both the private and the public sectors).[2] But in 1965, at any rate, more than 80 per cent of managers and senior staff were Europeans. Such nationals of the Ivory Coast as there were at this level tended to have jobs involving administrative rather than technical responsibilities.

At the other end of the scale more recent figures are to hand.[3] Whereas in 1961 Ivory Coast nationals formed 41 per cent of ordinary labourers, by 1968 this figure had shrunk to 31 per cent; their numbers had declined in absolute terms too. So at a time when the clouds of unemployment were gathering and the number of labourers had increased by 30 per cent, nationals of the Ivory Coast were abandoning to foreigners some of the jobs they had held shortly after independence.

Thus we have the curious state of affairs today that, in the towns alone, 50,000 people are out of work in an employment market providing jobs for at least 70,000 foreigners.[4]

---

[1] See also table A in the Appendix.

[2] See *Côte-d'Ivoire 1965: Emploi*, op. cit., pp. 104 ff.

[3] Ministère du Plan: *Eléments pour une politique de l'emploi en Côte-d'Ivoire* (Abidjan and Paris, SETEF, 1971), pp. 4 and 5.

[4] Probably an underestimate. The estimate for 1966 (*Côte-d'Ivoire 1965: Emploi*, op. cit., p. 88) was that there were 63,000 foreign wage earners, including Europeans.

The reasons

All this obviously requires some explanation. How is it that an economic boom can go hand in hand with worsening unemployment, and how is it that, despite unemployment, so many foreigners have jobs?

The first of these anomalies can be explained by the heavy migration of men and women (mostly young) from the countryside to the towns.[1] This phenomenon is not of course by any means confined to the Ivory Coast—it occurs in every country where industrialisation is taking place—but it has, undoubtedly, led to considerable urban unemployment. One puzzling feature about the situation in the Ivory Coast is that the drift to the towns appears to be unimpeded by a serious shortage of rural manpower, at least in the forest areas. Another strange thing is that the drift from the richer forest areas is just as marked as that from the poorer bush districts. There is no malnutrition in the villages, and in the forest areas a peasant farmer enjoys a standard of living at least as high as, and sometimes higher than, that of a town labourer, and a man can always be sure of finding work. All this notwithstanding, young people are leaving the countryside in huge numbers.

Information on the extent to which these movements vary with school attendance and educational levels can be found elsewhere.[2] But this does not really explain anything. The real question is why better education should systematically lead young people to abandon the countryside. The basic reason is that these youngsters are desperately keen to get on in the world, and are convinced that this is only possible in the towns. Of course, even the most innocent do not really imagine that they have only to go to Abidjan to find their dream-job dropping into their lap; all, however, believe that the only way to succeed is to " escape " from their native village. For such youngsters, rural society is the epitome of the archaic and the antithesis of progress. To remain within it is equivalent to turning one's back on the new world, in which everything is possible (though perhaps not easy). Equipped with their rudimentary primary school education, these young people can conceive of their future only in terms of city life.

This in itself, however, does not satisfy them. They see no attraction in certain kinds of job. What future is there for a common labourer? Does not acceptance of such work mean that a man renounces the promised land once and for all, and puts behind him those dreams which induced him to quit his native village? What is the point of fleeing

---

[1] In *Côte-d'Ivoire 1965: Population*, it was estimated that between 1965 and 1969 some 160,000 persons left the countryside. Roughly half of these were women (p. 175).

[2] *Côte-d'Ivoire 1965: Emploi*, op. cit., p. 151. See, too, the report by an ILO-UNICEF mission which visited the Ivory Coast in 1968, and Louis Roussel: " Measuring rural-urban drift in developing countries: a suggested method ", in *International Labour Review*, Vol. 101, No. 3, Mar. 1970, pp. 229-246.

village constraints, if the end is just another dead-end job in different surroundings? Hence these youngsters settle down to live with a relative or friend and wait for their lucky number to come up in the form of skilled employment or an administrative job.

Here lies the explanation of the second anomaly pointed out above, i.e. the presence of so many Africans from other countries in low-level jobs despite considerable unemployment. These people have poured in to do the kind of work which nationals of the Ivory Coast are more and more reluctant to undertake—a phenomenon which can be observed in industrialised countries as well.

At the top of the scale, among managers and senior staff, Ivory Coast nationals are also poorly represented. This is partly a legacy from colonial times and partly a result of economic growth having outstripped training capacity. During economic take-off, a phase of this kind is nothing out of the ordinary. The progressive elimination of the phenomenon is nevertheless a matter to which the Government is giving high priority, and I shall have more to say about this later.

In brief, then, the existing disequilibrium of the employment market is due not so much to there being an over-all shortage of jobs available compared with the number of job applicants as to the temporary inadequacy of training facilities for nationals, and to the latter's reluctance to accept unskilled jobs, especially in agriculture. The result is that foreigners take the jobs which Ivory Coast nationals are not yet qualified to accept, or refuse to consider.

This is the position today. Hitherto, thanks to the boom, unemployment has remained of tolerable proportions. But the balance is precarious; can it last?

Prospects for the future

In considering probable future trends in supply and demand on the employment market, we shall not go beyond the year 1980.

The demand for urban jobs will vary with the number of townsmen of working age. To begin with, bearing in mind the position as it is at present, we shall assume that all candidates for urban jobs will be males. We shall also assume, as a further working hypothesis, that working age extends from the age of 15 to 60.

Even if we limit ourselves to the next ten years, our estimates of population, and especially of the economically active population, become uncertain as soon as we abandon the hypothesis of a closed population (unaffected by external migrations) and try to carry out a rural-urban breakdown. But since it would clearly be absurd to consider the Ivory Coast as a closed demographic system, it is essential, if we wish to analyse the employment situation, to attempt just such a breakdown of the economically active population.

TABLE III. ESTIMATES OF MALE LABOUR FORCE IN URBAN AND RURAL AREAS, 1970-80

(In thousands)

Area	Position in 1970	Growth 1970-75	Position in 1975	Growth 1975-80	Position in 1980
Urban	**425**	**190**	**615**	**190**	**805**
Natural increase	—	50	—	65	—
Drift from countryside	—	75	—	60	—
Immigration from abroad	—	65	—	65	—
Rural	**840**	**30**	**870**	**40**	**910**
Natural increase	—	65	—	60	—
Drift from countryside	—	−75	—	−60	—
Immigration from abroad	—	40	—	40	—

Table III gives estimates of the male labour force in urban and rural areas. They are virtually identical with the estimates given in the Ministry of Planning document [1] already quoted, to which the reader should refer for detailed explanations. The main assumption on which they are based is that the trends observed over the past ten years will continue as regards both natural increase (fertility less death rates) and movements of population (the drift to the towns and immigration from abroad).

Natural increase, the drift from the countryside, and immigration from abroad—these three factors will, it is reckoned, lead to an extra 380,000 persons looking for work in the urban areas over the next ten years (the increase being spread more or less regularly over the period in question). In other words, the number of males of working age will almost double. It will be observed that during the first five-year period it is the drift from the countryside which contributes most to this increase. During the second period each of the three factors makes a roughly equal contribution. The rural population, it is thought, will increase much less—by some 70,000 males of working age over ten years. This represents an increase of only 8 per cent for the whole period which will probably not suffice [2] either to meet the manpower requirements arising from the Government's agricultural production schemes, or to cope with the towns' increased demand for foodstuffs.[3] This being so,

[1] *Côte-d'Ivoire 1965: Emploi*, op. cit., p. 116. The discrepancies between the two sets of figures are insignificant (less than 1 per cent).

[2] Even if allowance is made for a measure of farm mechanisation and for extra labour supplied by women.

[3] The urban population is expected to rise from about 1.4 million in 1970 to 2.6 million in 1980.

TABLE IV. WAGE EARNERS IN THE MODERN URBAN SECTOR, 1970-80

Source of employment	Position in 1970	Growth 1970-75	Position in 1975	Growth 1975-80	Position in 1980
A. Job creation	**206 900**	**87 500**	**294 400**	**109 000**	**403 400**
Primary sector:					
Urban jobs [1]	1 500	300	1 800	200	2 000
Secondary sector [2]:					
Industry	40 800	26 000	66 800	34 600	101 400
Building and public works	42 000	18 000	60 000	17 000	77 000
Tertiary sector:					
Transport	35 000	12 000	47 000	14 000	61 000
Rent and services	17 600	6 200	23 800	10 200	34 000
Commerce	25 000	10 000	35 000	15 000	50 000
Public administration	45 000	15 000	60 000	18 000	78 000
B. Replacement [3]	—	**28 000**	—	**40 000**	—
C. Total (A+B)	—	**115 500**	—	**149 000**	—

[1] Essentially office jobs in companies with headquarters in Abidjan. The forecasts are very approximate. [2] Source: *Deuxième esquisse du Plan quinquennal de développement 1971-1975*, op. cit. [3] Number of wage earners needed to replace those vacating jobs by reason of death or retirement. The working documents of the Ministry of Planning estimate the rate of renewal, per five-year period, at 13.5 per cent. See, for instance, *Les besoins en main-d'œuvre de l'économie ivoirienne.*

it will prove necessary to have recourse on an even greater scale to seasonal workers or more permanent immigrants from abroad.

But if the demand for labour is likely to outstrip supply in the countryside the position in the towns will be very different. True, it is even harder to estimate urban employment requirements than it is to forecast the size of the population of working age. There are so many imponderable factors that can upset existing trends. In this connection reference may be made to the working documents issued by the Ministry of Planning, and especially to the second draft of the 1971-75 five-year development plan *(Deuxième esquisse du Plan quinquennal de développement 1971-1975)* already quoted. This draft provides forecasts of manpower needs for different industries and occupations for the years 1971 to 1980, based essentially on private and public investment projects that have already been decided or are just probable. From this it will be seen that while a nucleus of reliable data is available (especially for the first five-year period), these forecasts should be accepted with some circumspection. Table IV summarises the chief estimates.

These forecasts anticipate a considerable increase in employment: over-all, a doubling of the number of jobs available, and in certain sectors (industry), a growth of very nearly 150 per cent. Is such a document guilty of lack of realism? To this the authorities could well retort that the growth envisaged is about the same as that obtained during the preceding ten-year period, and that the assumed annual growth in employment (8 per cent per annum on the average) is no higher than the increase in gross national product achieved over a long period of years. Let us, then, accept these estimates as valid, at least in the aggregate, and see how the employment supply is likely to compare with the population of working age.

It is at once obvious that, compared with the over-all figures for the increase in the number of men of working age, there are tremendous shortfalls in the number of jobs available: 75,000 for the first five years, 40,000 for the second. But other factors have to be taken into account. Firstly, quite a number of young people between 15 and 19 years of age continue their studies. However, this reduction in labour supply is to some extent offset by the arrival on the market of students who prolonged *their* studies but have now completed them. Hence we shall simply have to make allowance for the increase from one period to the next in the number of young townspeople who continue their schooling after the age of 15. Let us assume that in relation to 1965-69 this growth is 15,000 for the period 1970-74, and 20,000 for the following five years.

Secondly, the modern sector does not represent the whole of the employment market in the towns. Activities of the traditional kind may also provide an opening, at least for young people who are illiterate or have little education. Here again, let us be optimists and assume that in this sector, during each five-year period, work can be found for 20,000 people.[1] We may then draw up the following balance-sheet for the urban employment market:

Source of supply and demand	1970-74	1975-80
Additional urban jobs required	**175 000**	**170 000**
Increase in the urban male population of working age	190 000	190 000
Less increase in number of students over 15	−15 000	−20 000
Additional urban jobs available	**135 000**	**165 000**
Modern sector	115 000	145 000
Traditional sector	20 000	20 000
Excess of demand over jobs available	**40 000**	**5 000**

[1] Even if non-wage-earning employment is included, this figure is probably over-optimistic for two reasons: firstly, some young people have such a strong preference for employment in the modern sector that they will rather remain unemployed than take a job of the traditional kind; and secondly, it seems most likely that the traditional sector, far from expanding, will gradually be ousted by the modern one.

Truly an alarming state of affairs since by 1975 unemployment will, on these calculations reach 90,000 [1], remaining more or less at that level between 1975 and 1980. However, this is not the whole picture, quantitatively or qualitatively.

Firstly, for simplicity's sake we have taken into account only the demand for male labour. True, in 1965, the number of females working in the modern sector was no more than 6,000 [2] or so out of 180,000 wage earners, or a little over 3 per cent. But between 1955 and 1963 the female participation rate in the capital had increased from 6 to 13 per cent, while in Accra, no great distance away, it reached 55 per cent in 1965.[3] It is as certain as anything can be that changes in modes of life, plus the fact that girls are going to school in ever greater numbers, will quickly boost the female participation rate. The 6,000 women working in the modern sector in 1965 had become at least 10,000 by 1970, and their number may triple by 1980.

Qualitatively, there is a further consideration of capital importance. With the spread of education, and especially with greater access to secondary education, there is a strong probability that job aspirations are going to be set even higher. Having attended a secondary school, even if for no more than two or three years, young people are not going to settle for anything less than an office job. This being so, Ivory Coast nationals will be the first to suffer from unemployment, since foreigners are not shy of working as labourers; in any event they can always go home should they be without work for any length of time.

Lastly, it may be of interest to provide some information about probable trends in the demand for manpower with different levels of skills. The figures given in table V are, generally speaking, in line with those appearing in table IV. The primary sector is not included. If replacement is taken into account, the data given in all the sources quoted are reasonably concordant.

Clearly, such estimates can serve to give us no more than a general idea, and will have to be adjusted in the light of what actually happens. This having been said, it remains highly probable that more than half of the jobs that come on to the market will be labouring ones. Should the people of the Ivory Coast continue to shun work of this kind and occupy no more than their present small percentage of such jobs, then another 100,000 or so labourers [4] will have to be brought in from abroad.

As regards highly qualified staff, the imbalance by 1980 will be very serious indeed. Some 7,000 such persons will be needed by that time, yet at

[1] The 40,000 new unemployed plus the 50,000 of 1970. These figures would be in accordance with an assumption sometimes made to the effect that by 1975 there will be 50,000 unemployed in Abidjan alone, if present trends continue.

[2] *Côte-d'Ivoire 1965: Emploi*, op. cit., pp. 98-99.

[3] *Etude socio-économique de la zone urbaine d'Abidjan*, Report No. 8 (SEMA, 1964).

[4] That is, two-thirds of the 163,500 extra labourers required.

TABLE V. MANPOWER REQUIREMENTS BY LEVEL OF SKILLS

Period	Managerial staff	Medium-level staff	Skilled workers	Labourers	Total
1971-75	3 200	10 800	32 000	66 800	112 800
1976-80	3 900	11 500	37 000	96 700	149 100
Total	7 100	22 300	69 000	163 500	261 900

Source: *Les besoins en main-d'œuvre de l'économie ivoirienne*, op. cit., "Secteur moderne", p. 22.

present no more than a few hundred graduates are turned out each year. Here again, foreign assistance will be temporarily required if this shortfall is to be overcome.

The rate of growth expected between now and 1980 means that some 6,000 skilled workers per year will be needed. In 1968, 400 graduated from technical training colleges [1], and while some progress has of course been made since then, a tremendous amount of leeway has to be made up if output is to match demand.

Our preliminary balance-sheet appears a good deal more sombre when these factors are taken into account. The imminent arrival of more and more women to swell the labour force, the growing army of literate unemployed, the employment of foreign wage earners while young nationals remain without work—the Government by no means underestimates the gravity of all these things and in fact is now giving priority to the problem of employment. In the next part of this article we shall look at some of the plans being made to solve it.

Employment policies

The analysis undertaken above showed that the swift growth of unemployment has been due, not to some momentary downturn in the economic cycle, but to permanent imbalances between town and countryside, the high hopes entertained by the young, the structure of urban employment, and the inability of training facilities for national managerial and senior staff (technicians in particular) to keep up with the rapid pace of economic development.

Should the Ivory Coast try to deal with unemployment by stopgap measures without removing its fundamental causes, the respite would be but brief. The employment position would in fact quickly deteriorate

[1] M. A. Achio: *Ressources humaines et perspectives d'emploi. Côte-d'Ivoire 1968-1975* (Abidjan, Ministère du Plan), p. 301.

again, since mere palliatives would be bound to aggravate matters in the long run. Hence the Government's primary aim is to restore and consolidate the equilibrium of the employment market by a programme of real structural change. Before we turn to this general policy, it might be well to consider the Government's attitude towards certain traditional methods used to combat unemployment or to make life more bearable for its victims.

Short-term action

The Government's first concern is that the employment market should operate smoothly. This is chiefly the responsibility of the Employment Service, the funds available to which have recently been increased. A few figures will suffice to show the growing importance of the Service's role:

APPLICATIONS FOR EMPLOYMENT AND VACANCIES HANDLED BY THE ABIDJAN EMPLOYMENT SERVICE

Year	Job applications	Job vacancies
1958	6 200	3 200
1962	8 000	4 500
1969	46 900	27 900

Source: *Statistiques de l'Office de la main-d'œuvre d'Abidjan.*

Every day, news of vacancies that have to be filled quickly is given over the radio—a procedure which has produced excellent results.

A number of other measures that have sometimes been taken in Africa or elsewhere have doubtless been contemplated by the Government of the Ivory Coast. So far, however, no use has been made of them either because they were considered ineffective or because it was felt that they ran counter to the basic principles on which national policy is based. For instance, the Government feels that the forcible removal from Abidjan of even some of the numerous unemployed youths would in all likelihood prove useless, and would certainly be incompatible with the preference for voluntary procedures which characterises official policy.[1]

Similarly, it is considered that to abruptly put an end to immigration from abroad would be not only unrealistic but also contrary to the co-operation for which the countries of the *Entente* [2] are striving. Even today, the presence of workers from other African countries is considered

[1] The introduction of a compulsory work permit has, however, been envisaged.

[2] Ivory Coast, Dahomey, Niger, Togo and Upper Volta.

to be " a mainstay of the national development policy ".[1] This liberal attitude ought, however, to go hand in hand with stricter application of the existing labour legislation. I do not wish to give the point more importance than it deserves but it may well be that foreign workers are exploited by some small concerns, and if so this could lead to improper competition between national and other African workers.

An even more delicate question than this, perhaps, was whether or not encouragement should be given to labour-intensive industrial techniques. The Government declined to opt wholeheartedly for this, for two reasons. Firstly, it was felt that because Ivory Coast nationals are at present so reluctant to take labouring jobs, labour-intensive methods would lead to a further increase in the percentage of foreign labour employed. Secondly, the maintenance or adoption of obsolete techniques would run counter to the official decision to create modern industries capable of competing in international markets.

This being so, and pending such time as the medium-term measures produce results, ought the workless to be offered substantial assistance in the form of a daily unemployment benefit? The Government, not without reason, has refused to consider this. Of course, the official attitude might well have been different if unemployment primarily affected adult workers without means of subsistence. In the case in question, however, most of the unemployed are young (and able to return to their native villages), or else foreigners who can always go home. Had unemployment benefit been provided in circumstances such as these (giving a new fillip to the drift from the land and to foreign immigration alike), the position would very quickly have become even worse.

On the other hand, it does seem as though the Government is beginning to favour the idea of setting up large work sites close to the towns. No problem of accommodation would arise because the unemployed finding work there could travel to the site each day. This should assuage the fears of a population that would react with particular vehemence to any suggestion of workers being " deported " for " forced labour ". But here too, quite apart from any financial considerations, there are certain pitfalls to be avoided. The projects undertaken would have to be economically worth while, for there is no point in putting men to work on tasks that are of no benefit to the national economy. The question of remuneration would also require very careful consideration. While the wage offered should not be too low, it should not be as high as that of an ordinary wage earner; otherwise it would encourage even more young people from the countryside to migrate to the towns, secure in the knowledge that these work sites would guarantee them a standard of living equivalent to that of the urban population.[2]

---

[1] Quoted in *Eléments pour une politique de l'emploi en Côte-d'Ivoire*, op. cit., p. 14.

[2] See Ministère du Plan: *Le problème du chômage et du sous-emploi* (Abidjan, 1970).

Be that as it may, the scheme has not yet got off the drawing-board. Its importance lies in the fact that if the unemployment problem were to grow much more acute, the Government would doubtless try this approach before taking other action.

The above account may give the impression that official circles have been rather timid, or even passive, in their attitude towards unemployment. Against this it may be argued that the Government was surely wise to pass up expedients which, when applied elsewhere, have proved costly, ineffective, and sometimes downright harmful.

Long-term action

Unemployment is fed, above all else, by an excessive drift from countryside to town, and the Government's first concern is to stem this exodus. For how can the employment market ever be stabilised if more and more young people keep streaming in from the countryside (which is already short of labour) to swell the ranks (which are already overfull) of the urban labour force, or rather the urban unemployed?

As we have already seen, the Government believes that in the long run compulsion is no answer. On the other hand, it is perfectly well aware that not much is gained, either, by simply exhorting the young country-dweller not to leave his village. There is, then, but one way out, namely so to change things that young people have every inducement to stay where they are. Logically, the most effective way of combating unemployment is to improve conditions in the villages. True, modernisation had to begin in the towns, since it was there that the work of administering, controlling and "commercialising" the development effort had to be centred. The result has undoubtedly been to put the townsman in a privileged position, which is precisely why it is now a matter of urgency to extend the benefits of development to the countryside.

In the first place, this means that peasants' incomes will have to be increased.[1] Much has already been done with this in view. Output has been substantially increased, thanks to the technical assistance and advice provided. Farmers now enjoy greater income security thanks to crop diversification, a policy that will certainly be maintained because, apart from anything else, it offers the only chance of raising the tonnage of agricultural exports to the much higher levels called for by the Five-Year Plan. Moreover, the growth of towns will lead to a considerable extension

[1] It is by no means easy to compare a townsman's income with a peasant's. As a very rough guide, an urban wage earner in the modern sector is paid, on the average, 20,000 CFA francs a month. The guaranteed minimum wage or SMIG (fixed at 58.30 CFA an hour in 1969) corresponds to a monthly wage of over 11,000 CFA. The law provides for leave at the rate of a day-and-a-half per month worked, and seven public holidays a year. Clearly, no young peasant, be he independent or working for his family, has much chance of enjoying such advantages.

of market gardening, thus making its own contribution to improving rural standards of living.

Taken all together, will the various measures described above suffice to secure the desired result? It seems unlikely. On the bigger farms and plantations of the traditional kind [1] wage earners already enjoy the same advantages as in modern industry. But the proportion of indigenous labour among the ordinary workers on such farms does not exceed 20 per cent. It follows that if young nationals are to be induced to seek work in agriculture, the certainty of earning a wage equivalent to that of an urban worker is a necessary, though by no means a sufficient, pre-condition.

The second draft of the Five-Year Plan provides for the establishment of permanent bodies to carry out an overhaul of existing rural structures. The modernisation programme will have three main emphases:

(1) The creation of regional rural development funds to ensure that the countryside is satisfactorily equipped. Programmes will be drawn up by the responsible authorities in the region concerned. The money required will come jointly from state subsidies and local contributions. The provision of modern housing has already led to vast changes in the living standards of many peasants, and the development of the rural infrastructure should further narrow the gap between urban and rural ways of life.[2]

(2) A rural development agency will be responsible for handling all the problems involved. It will be in charge of devising development programmes and training men capable of putting them into effect. One interesting feature is the proposed creation of small " zones " (each containing some 5,000 people on the average) radiating around a central village; these zones will constitute the basic units from which the modernisation drive will start.[3]

(3) In the villages elementary schooling will be better adapted to rural needs. Post-school training, resembling agricultural or craft apprenticeship, will also be made available.[4] This will take the form of practical work rather than theoretical instruction and should give young people a useful grounding in the technical and economic aspects of rural life.[5]

Finally, all sorts of things have been done, or are envisaged, with a view to making it easier for the young farmer to set himself up:

[1] Such as the SODEPALM oil-palm plantations, which employ several thousand workers.

[2] *Deuxième esquisse du Plan quinquennal de développement 1971-1975*, op. cit., pp. 183-184.

[3] Ibid., p. 179.

[4] Ibid., pp. 341 ff.

[5] The new training bodies would not, at any rate for the time being, mean abolition of the *service consigne*, the object of which is to train young farmers in modern farming skills. It would be unfair to say that the service in question has been a failure; certainly, however, it has proved somewhat disappointing.

overhaul of the traditional rules governing inheritance [1], reform of the land tenure system, and the allocation of especially profitable plantations (palm-oil plantations, for instance) to young farmers.

Generally speaking, the projects outlined above accord quite closely with the conclusions of an ILO memorandum submitted to the Ivory Coast Government on the exodus of young people from the rural areas.[2] The memorandum urged a speedy and substantial increase in investment credits destined for the rural infrastructure. But above all it recommended that the educational and training system be thoroughly overhauled to ensure that the achievement of universal education in the countryside does not necessarily lead to a universal exodus to the towns.[3] Only if this be done can the country be endowed with modern-minded farmers and craftsmen quick to take advantage of the changes now under way. For without these people, the effort made to modernise the infrastructure and improve conditions of life will inevitably be barren. Hence, priority to the countryside, and at the same time, investments in materials and human resources.[4]

Although the drift to the towns is the main cause of unemployment, a major contributory factor is the repugnance evinced by Ivory Coast nationals for any form of manual labour, even in the towns. How is unemployment ever to be overcome if this attitude persists? To create more labouring jobs would simply mean speeding up the rate of immigration from abroad. Nevertheless, work done in preparation for the Five-Year Plan provides for a higher proportion of nationals in ordinary manual jobs (an increase from 31 per cent in 1968 to 50 per cent in 1975, the primary sector included).[5] Present trends, therefore, have to be reversed, and very soon too.

An appropriate wages policy could obviously contribute to this result. In 1969 wages and salaries rose by an average of more than 20 per cent [6], but the gap between highest and lowest remunerations hardly narrowed at all. The humblest clerk in a government department or private firm earns more than a navvy. The free play of supply and demand

[1] Under the matrilineal system, which is still widespread in the Ivory Coast, the nephew could inherit instead of the son, even though the latter had helped to work his father's farm. Vigorous action by the Government is now tending to modify this custom.

[2] ILO: *Mémorandum au gouvernement de la République de Côte-d'Ivoire concernant l'exode des jeunes ruraux et les actions préconisées pour améliorer leurs conditions de vie et leurs possibilités d'emploi* (Geneva, 1969).

[3] For the detailed proposals the reader is referred to the memorandum itself.

[4] Although a policy of this sort is very much in the peasants' interests, they should be asked to air their views before it is applied. Consultation regarding the measures to be taken on their behalf is a prerequisite for raising the status of the farmer or cultivator to that of the townsman. In this respect, the rural development agency will constitute one of the channels through which it is hoped to promote a constant exchange of views between the Government and the peasants.

[5] *Eléments pour une politique de l'emploi en Côte d'Ivoire*, op. cit., p. 11.

[6] The guaranteed minimum wage, for instance, went up from 44 to 56 CFA.

cannot in itself lead to an adjustment in the wage scale, since foreigners are always there to oust local workers in jobs otherwise difficult to fill. Hence a deliberate wages policy is needed to restore the balance.[1]

An overhaul of the existing scale would not, incidentally, suffice to change things very much. As was explained above, young people fight shy of unskilled jobs for the same reason as they do not want to stay on the land. They are convinced that there are today two entirely different worlds: in the first a man can hope to make his way and satisfy the legitimate aspirations of a " modern " citizen, while in the second he has to resign himself once and for all (or so they believe) to a degradingly low and archaic standard of living. Hence what young people want above all is to live and work in an environment where they have a chance to make their way up the ladder of success.

If young people, especially those who can read and write, are to be induced to accept manual work, it is essential that the upward mobility be genuine and to some extent " institutionalised "; moreover, they must be clearly told that such opportunities for advancement exist. Action must be taken to ensure that ordinary labourers, if they have the requisite skill and determination, can gradually improve their qualifications, without necessarily having to pass through secondary schools and technical training colleges. This, however, brings us face to face with the problem of education and training, which will have to be dealt with at rather greater length in discussing the third aim to be pursued, namely the replacement of foreign managerial staff and technicians by nationals of the Ivory Coast.

It is in the logic both of political independence and of economic development that this should be done with all possible speed, as long as production does not suffer in the process. The rate of expansion provided for will in any event require increasing numbers of non-African " assistants " between now and 1980. This is an additional reason why the whole problem of training deserves reconsideration, with a view to reducing to a minimum the period during which the country is technically dependent on foreigners. The aim pursued will accordingly not be properly attained by a hasty and ill-considered transfer of responsibilities; the only practical way is to speed up the training of qualified indigenous staff. But this brings us once more face to face with the problem of education and training.

The President of the Republic has recently given striking proof (by himself taking over the portfolio of national education) that the Government attaches the very highest priority to an overhaul of the educational system. Although the efforts made in this direction since 1958 have been considerable, the educational authorities are only too well aware of the present system's defects and shortcomings. True, the system existing

[1] As regards wage structures, see tables B and C in the Appendix.

before independence has been substantially enlarged. But it has not been radically changed, with the result that, as experience has shown, it is ill-adapted to the needs of an economy growing at the rate of 8 per cent per annum. The fact that the Head of State should have decided to take personal responsibility clearly heralds far-reaching reforms. Whatever shape these take, it is to be hoped that, throughout the system, there will be fewer drop-outs, fewer cases of pupils having to repeat a class, and a reduction in unit costs.

Academic standards would doubtless be improved if scholarships were meted out somewhat less generously than at present. They could be distributed liberally enough to pupils entering the first form, but thereafter should continue only if the beneficiaries work satisfactorily throughout the school year.

Another innovation was the establishment in 1970 of the Ministry of Technical Education and Vocational Training. Joint committees, composed of officials and managers of undertakings, will meet under its auspices and devise policies to ensure that the content and form of training correspond to the needs of the economy.

These discussions will very likely show up the need to provide more channels of advancement other than a university education. Senior staff will, as is the case already, normally be persons with a secondary school and university background. But the times are not normal, and in a period of economic take-off exceptional measures are called for. Retraining courses, advanced training, in-plant training—all these things are needed to create the vertical mobility which is so urgently required.

In a free enterprise economy such as the Ivory Coast's it is important that personal merit, rather than social background, should be the key to success. It is essential for the health of society, but it is also indispensable if the nation is to lose no time in procuring the skilled personnel its development requires. In this fashion, real vertical mobility would be assured, and the excessive gulf between town and countryside, between skilled and unskilled urban worker, would be overcome. In brief, the solution of the Ivory Coast's employment problems lies in substituting harmonious economic development for the somewhat anarchic growth of the past.

It is in recognition of this fact that the Ivory Coast has made no attempt to alleviate the long-term employment problem by encouraging a reduction in the birth rate. The country is as yet comparatively thinly populated (39 inhabitants to the square mile) [1], and there is still plenty of room. All in all, the Government takes the view that an increase in population—even a rapid one—is to be welcomed rather than feared.

---

[1] The annual rate of population growth is roughly 3 per cent (including the balance of migration). If this percentage is maintained, the population should easily exceed 6 million by 1980 and be approaching 9 million by 1990.

Conclusion

As we have seen, the employment situation in the Ivory Coast is a curious one. Rising unemployment goes hand in hand with steady economic development, which by itself will clearly never provide a real solution to the employment problem. In the not-too-distant future, many more women will be seeking work in the modern sector; this will be a valuable addition to the country's labour force, but will also create a risk (difficult to assess with any accuracy) of further unemployment. This latter factor is perhaps the one that will have the greatest impact in the decade to come. Little time remains before these newcomers appear on the employment markets, so studies will have to be carried out and action taken as a matter of urgency to ensure their smooth absorption.

For a country at grips with employment problems as formidable as these, the Ivory Coast would seem to have chosen the only conceivable course, at any rate in the long run. Modernisation of the rural environment, measures to encourage vertical mobility, and the priority given to training should bring the drift to the towns under control, change young people's attitudes towards unskilled jobs, and equip Ivory Coast nationals to take over managerial and technical responsibilities.

Splendid as these principles are, the policy embodying them remains somewhat nebulous. Most of the bodies responsible for rural modernisation as yet exist in name only. Not a great deal has been done so far, especially in the countryside, to reform the educational system, and vertical mobility is still a very distant goal.

True, the Five-Year Development Plan does define the aims and describes the means whereby they are to be attained. But though the Plan has force of law, it consists more of an array of feasible projects than of an inventory of measures on which definite and binding decisions have been taken. It would be unfair to blame the authors of the Plan for not having given priority to full employment, since they take the view that this can be achieved only through rapid economic development and rural modernisation. But it is a little worrying to observe that the various reform measures seem to be lagging behind the factors which cause imbalances on the employment market. It is often believed—wrongly—that a medium-term programme will not lose a great deal if its implementation is delayed. The Ivory Coast authorities are perfectly aware that reform is urgent; however, it will require no little tenacity and political courage to see it through. Only by setting in motion the whole machinery of State will it be possible to bring about the requisite changes.

APPENDIX

The following three tables are taken from Ministère du Plan: *Dossiers pour l'exploration du long terme—Consommation et mode de vie* (Abidjan and Paris, SETEF, 1971), pp. 24 and 26.

TABLE A. DISTRIBUTION OF WAGE EARNERS IN THE SECONDARY SECTOR BY SKILLS AND NATIONAL ORIGIN, 1968-69
(%)

Skill level	Ivory Coast nationals	Other Africans	Total Africans	Non-Africans
All levels	**56.0**	**39.1**	**95.1**	**4.9**
Managerial and senior staff	5.6	0.8	6.4	93.6
Foremen	29.6	8.5	38.1	61.9
Skilled workers	65.2	31.0	96.2	3.8
Unskilled workers	56.9	43.0	99.9	0.1

TABLE B. DISTRIBUTION OF WORKFORCE AND WAGES IN THE SECONDARY SECTOR BY SKILLS AND ORIGIN, 1968-69

Category	% of total labour force	% of total wages paid
Skill level:		
Managerial and senior staff	1.6	18.2
Foremen	4.5	21.4
Skilled workers	14.5	18.4
Unskilled workers	79.4	42.0
Total	100.0	100.0
Origin:		
Africans	95.1	64.3
Non-Africans	4.9	35.7
Total	100.0	100.0

TABLE C. DISTRIBUTION OF AFRICAN WAGE EARNERS BY LEVEL OF WAGES AND SECTOR OF EMPLOYMENT, 1967

(%)

Monthly wage (CFA francs)	Modern secondary sector			Modern trade in Abidjan	Government
	Ivory Coast nationals	Other Africans	Total		
5 000- 9 999	7.1	29.7	18.4	18.0	—
10 000-14 999	37.9	38.2	38.1	28.0	2.1
15 000-19 999	19.6	15.5	17.5	14.0	8.0
20 000-24 999	13.1	5.5	9.3	13.0	9.5
25 000-29 999	7.6	4.1	5.8	8.0	11.6
30 000-34 999	4.4	2.7	3.6	5.0	10.8
35 000-39 999	3.1	1.3	2.2	3.0	17.4
40 000-44 999	2.1	0.8	1.5	2.0	15.4
45 000-49 999	0.9	0.6	0.7	3.0	9.6
50 000-59 999	1.2	0.8	1.0	2.0	2.0
60 000-69 999	1.3	0.3	0.8	1.5	4.2
70 000+	1.7	0.5	1.1	2.5	9.4
Total	100.0	100.0	100.0	100.0	100.0

Mass Emigration from Upper Volta: the Facts and Implications

Ambroise SONGRE [1]

EMIGRATION from Upper Volta is one of the most striking social features, not only of Upper Volta itself, but of West Africa in general and, as such, deserves a special place in any research covering this part of the African continent. An unusually large number of people are involved, and if the movement could be analysed in detail and its various implications and fundamental causes found, a considerable step forward would undoubtedly have been made towards discovering solutions that would benefit not only Upper Volta but also other countries facing similar difficulties.

This article does not in any way claim to reflect the official attitude on the matter, and its sole purpose is to make an objective contribution to the solution of what constitutes a serious social and economic problem for Upper Volta. It views the population drift in the light of the country's over-all economic situation, and successively describes the historical background, assesses its impact on society and suggests possible approaches whereby the country's manpower potential could be efficiently employed in developing the national economy rather than the economies of other countries.

I. Historical background

Seeking new frontiers has long been a characteristic of the peoples of Upper Volta; even the way the country came to be settled, and especially the colonial system and its various forms of exploitation, have had a decisive influence in arousing this urge to go abroad. Other factors have

[1] Regional labour inspector at Bobo-Dioulasso (Upper Volta). Responsibility for the opinions expressed in this article rests solely with the author.

played a part since independence: economic imbalances between various sectors, regions and nations, and between the developed and developing countries, coupled with the stagnation of the economy of Upper Volta, have been instrumental in perpetuating the country's reputation as a pool of labour, to be drawn upon by others when in need.

The history of emigration from Upper Volta can be divided into two parts, the first covering the colonial period down to independence, and the second running from independence to the present day.

The colonial era

A backward glance at how the country came to be inhabited shows that most of the ethnic groups at present living there came from other areas of Africa, as a result partly of fortuitous migration and partly of conquests that led to the emergence of vast empires, such as the kingdoms of the Mossi.

Colonisation, however, with its various forms of exploitation, did more than anything else to induce large sections of the population to emigrate: the forced labour system, the operation of major concessions by private companies, large-scale development projects undertaken by the colonial authorities, conscription (mainly during the two World Wars), the " voluntary " labour system and, last but not least, financial considerations led people to emigrate in large numbers to virtually all the countries of West Africa—Mali, Senegal, Ghana (formerly the Gold Coast) and the Ivory Coast. Particularly noteworthy, however, because of their scale, were the movements to Ghana and the Ivory Coast.

EMIGRATION TO GHANA

As long ago as 1919, the French administration reported that people were leaving Upper Volta for the Gold Coast. At that time the main causes were the famine of 1914 and the recruitment of men for the armed forces during the First World War, but more and more people joined the movement to avoid the system of forced labour instituted by the colonial authorities for their development projects, such as the building of harbours, bridges, roads and the Abidjan-Niger and Bamako-Thiès railways.

The number of migrants involved is known to have been large, but it is virtually impossible to give even approximate figures. In 1929, however, an official British source estimated that more than 60,000 people had entered the Gold Coast from Upper Volta in 1928. In 1931 another British source reported a total of 287,483 persons entering the Gold Coast between 1921 and 1931, but it is impossible to say how many of them came from Upper Volta. According to yet another British source 34,400 people from Upper Volta came to the Gold Coast in 1934, despite the fact that the country was in the throes of an economic crisis. In 1937 the French consulate at Accra quoted a figure of between 80,000 and 100,000 for the number of migrants from the French colonies then living in the Gold Coast.

Very little statistical information is available for population movements during the Second World War. In 1944 it was estimated that about 200,000 persons from the French colonies were working in the Gold Coast, and that half of them were permanently settled there.

EMIGRATION TO THE IVORY COAST

Over the years, however, an even larger number of migrants made their way to the Ivory Coast. Whereas emigration to the Gold Coast had always been on a purely voluntary basis, people moving to the Ivory Coast did so, in the initial stages, under duress. In this context, therefore, the changes of population could more appropriately be described as transfers of conscripted labour than as emigration.

It was mentioned earlier in this article that Upper Volta has traditionally been regarded as an ideal source from which labour could be drawn, and this view was taken both by the colonial administration and by the private companies running concessions in the Ivory Coast whenever they needed to round up labour for their projects. The mass recruitment that this involved was only occasionally checked by the outbreak of one of the major endemic diseases, such as sleeping sickness.

In 1936 European companies operating in the Ivory Coast employed about 20,000 workers from Upper Volta, half of whom had been brought over by recruiting officers and half of whom could be described as " volunteers ". Both halves, in any event, suffered the same fate of semi-slavery. Consequently, when social reforms were introduced by the French authorities in 1936 and the system of conscripted labour was abolished (at least on paper), vast numbers of people left their jobs on the various worksites and plantations. Even so, the number of " voluntary " workers steadily increased, because a flow of " volunteers " was pumped into the country by the colonial administration and the local chiefs.

During the Second World War, moreover, recruitment for the armed forces was resumed under the vigorous direction of Governor-General Cayla. A few figures will suffice to convey an impression of the scale of the operation: whereas in 1940 there were 6,228 recruited workers and 3,021 volunteers, the corresponding figures for 1941 were 14,897 and 24,668, rising to 36,300 and 70,860 in 1942. For the years 1943 and 1944 the only statistics available relate to recruited workers, the numbers being 55,000 and 58,555, respectively.

A further factor was the colonisation of the lands administered by the Office of the Niger in the French Sudan (now known as Mali), which began at the same time. To quote one authority on the subject: " The Béline Mission (1919-22) had a grandiose project for resettling 1.5 million Mossi in the area covered by the Office of the Niger. In 1937 there was talk of resettling 800,000, but on the eve of the Second World War a series of recruiting drives had yielded a meagre 8,000." [1]

Forced labour was effectively abolished in 1946, and the workers' first reaction to this measure was to desert the worksites in the Ivory Coast. After the Territory of Upper Volta was reconstituted in 1947, there was a radical change in the pattern of migration, any movements that occurred being individual and spontaneous. The inflow of labour in this way did not suffice to cover all the manpower needs of the Ivory Coast plantations, and in 1951 the employers there were obliged to set up an industry-wide association to arrange for the supply of labour. This association, which received a subsidy from the territorial budget, arranged for workers to be recruited locally in Upper Volta for subsequent employment on plantations in the Ivory Coast.

According to the annual statistics published by the Ministry of Labour of Upper Volta, the number of workers recruited and transported to the Ivory Coast by the association ranged from 30,941 (in 1952) to 15,710 (in 1957). In 1959, which was the association's last full year of operation, the figure stood at 18,143.

Independence and after

Over the 12 years since independence, the pattern of emigration from Upper Volta has not been essentially different from that followed in the later years of the country's colonial history, except that financial considerations have come to play a greater part than other reasons in influencing the migrants' decision to leave. As in the past, the great majority of people continue to emigrate to Ghana and the Ivory Coast; only a very small minority of businessmen and professional people go to other African countries, such as Niger and Mali.

EMIGRATION TO GHANA

The number of migrants admitted to Ghana from neighbouring Upper Volta is impossible to estimate, in the absence of any manpower agreement between the two countries or any statistical check at the frontier posts. Even so, there is evidence enough that far fewer people are involved than during the colonial era. This is due to the fact that the two countries belong to different currency areas, to the competition between Ghana and the Ivory Coast (which operates in favour of the latter), to the economic difficulties that Ghana has been facing for some time and, more recently, to Ghana's policy towards aliens.

According to the 1960 census, persons born abroad then represented 8 per cent of the Ghanaian population, or 538,000 out of a total of 6,730,000 inhabitants. Of these persons, 194,590, or 36 per cent, came

[1] J. Suret Canale: ***Afrique noire, l'ère coloniale*** (Paris, Editions sociales, 1964), p. 319.

from Upper Volta, which consequently accounted for the highest proportion of Ghana inhabitants born abroad after Togo, with Nigeria ranking third. However, a census taken in 1970 by the United Nations Economic Commission for Africa showed that by then the largest group of Ghana inhabitants born abroad consisted of Nigerians.

There is no way of making even an approximate estimate of the number of people migrating to Ghana per year.

EMIGRATION TO THE IVORY COAST

It is quite impossible to make any statistical assessment of the scale of emigration from Upper Volta to the Ivory Coast, partly because the methods of enumeration leave much to be desired and partly because there is no real check on the movement itself.

Even so, most of the emigrants from Upper Volta undoubtedly go to the Ivory Coast. There are several reasons why this should be so: in the first place, a manpower agreement has been concluded between the two countries; secondly, they belong to the same currency area; and lastly, the economy of the Ivory Coast has been expanding rapidly over the past ten years, with the result that, economically, it is the stronger country of the two.

As was mentioned earlier, the recruitment of workers from Upper Volta for employment on the plantations in the Ivory Coast was dealt with for some years after 1951 by an industry-wide association. In 1960, however, the Government of Upper Volta prohibited the association from continuing its work because of certain undesirable practices in which it had engaged (it had, in fact, quite blatantly resorted to some types of forced labour). By its action the Government made it abundantly clear that it intended to defend the interests of its nationals abroad, and even to organise and control migration. This, to some extent, it achieved by concluding an agreement with the Ivory Coast on 9 March 1960 governing the recruitment and conditions of employment of workers from Upper Volta in the Ivory Coast.

Under this agreement planters in the Ivory Coast have to notify the national Manpower Office of their labour requirements, and the Office forwards the information to the labour services in Upper Volta, whose manpower centres then endeavour to find volunteers for employment in the Ivory Coast. Each migrant is recruited on a six-month contract, which is renewable, and is guaranteed, at least in theory, food, wages and accommodation. The authorities in the Ivory Coast pay the Government of Upper Volta a very modest fee to cover its outlay on the lodging, maintenance, medical examination and vaccination of the volunteers in the manpower centres.[1]

---

[1] An ad hoc national committee has recently been set up to revise the 1960 agreement.

TABLE 1. PROPORTION OF THE TOTAL POPULATION AWAY FROM HOME DURING THE 1960-61 POPULATION SURVEY IN UPPER VOLTA

Sex	In Upper Volta	Abroad	Residence unknown	Total
Males	5.4	6.2	0.2	11.8
Females	5.0	0.9	0.2	6.1
Total	10.4	7.1	0.4	17.9

Information is readily available on the officially recognised forms of emigration, i.e. those covered by the agreement. Over the past ten years, the competent authorities in Upper Volta have sent a certain number of workers to the Ivory Coast each year, ranging from a minimum of 2,117 in 1962 to a maximum of 5,783 in 1968. In 1970 and 1971 the figures were 5,409 and 4,747, respectively.[1]

By contrast, there is no direct statistical information on unofficial migrants, which is obviously what the very great majority of people are. For anyone trying to make an over-all assessment of the scale of movements of this kind, the only sources available are the population survey carried out in Upper Volta in 1960-61 and various documents and studies relating in one way or another to migration from the country.

The 1960-61 population survey was carried out by sampling techniques covering the country as a whole, with the exception of the two main cities of Ouagadougou and Bobo-Dioulasso.

The survey involved a 1 in 10 sample of the population of 12 towns of secondary importance and a 1 in 50 sample of the remaining 7,055 inhabited localities. Information on migratory movements was prepared on the basis of the registration of persons away from home at the time the survey was conducted.

As may be seen from table 1, population movements within the country and abroad, respectively, affected 10.4 and 7.1 per cent of the total population. On the assumption that these rates remained stable, out of a total population of 5,470,500, there were 388,400 persons absent from Upper Volta and 568,900 persons away from home but still within the country during 1971.

In table 2 the absentees are classified by length of absence at the time the survey was conducted.

Absences of one, or even of one to five months' duration are not particularly significant, but it is reasonable to assume that absences of between 6 and 11 months' duration reflect seasonal movements of the

[1] République de Haute-Volta, ministère du Travail et de la Fonction publique, Direction du travail, de la main-d'œuvre et de la formation professionnelle: *Statistiques* (annual reports).

TABLE 2. PROPORTION OF THE TOTAL POPULATION AWAY FROM HOME DURING THE 1960-61 POPULATION SURVEY IN UPPER VOLTA, BY LENGTH OF ABSENCE

Length of absence	Males	Females
1 month	23.3	40.2
1-5 months	26 7	23.7
6-11 months	6.7	6.1
1 year	14.3	10.4
2-3 years	22.0	15.4
4 years or more	7.0	4.2

Upper Volta peasantry, linked to the cultivation of various crops from May to October. People who are away for more than a year can be regarded as temporary or permanent migrants, according to the case.

An analysis of the information by marital status (table 3) shows that single men are away from home more often and for longer periods than married men and that divorcees come next in order. The lowest rate of absence is recorded among polygamous husbands, which bears out the contention that people with the least family responsibilities are the most likely to migrate.

This, in brief, is what the 1960-61 population survey shows as far as migratory movements are concerned. The next question that arises is whether the findings are confirmed by the other relevant documents and studies.

Some idea of the present number of persons from Upper Volta living in the Ivory Coast can be derived from the research carried out by

TABLE 3. PROPORTION OF THE TOTAL POPULATION OVER 14 YEARS OF AGE AWAY FROM HOME DURING THE 1960-61 POPULATION SURVEY IN UPPER VOLTA, BY MARITAL STATUS

Marital status	Males		Females	
	Away from home	Absent for over six months	Away from home	Absent for over six months
Single	29.8	18.3	6.4	2.8
Widowed	6.6	2.9	6.3	2.1
Divorced	17.2	7.3	2.7	0.7
Married	9.5	3.5	4.1	1.3
Monogamous	11.3	4.3	.	.
Polygamous	5.8	1.9	.	.
Over-all	16.4	8.6	5.9	1.9

Samir Amin [1], by the African Development Bank [2], and by various participants attending the international African seminar organised jointly by the African Institute for Economic Development and Planning (IDEP) and the International African Institute (IAI) in Dakar in the spring of 1972 on the subject of contemporary migration in West Africa [3], as well as from the unpublished research on the population and the activities of African aliens in the Ivory Coast, carried out by G. Remy, of the French Overseas Scientific and Technical Research Office, on the basis of various documents from the Ivory Coast.

This research has shown that there were 700,000 foreign residents in the Ivory Coast in 1965 (the term " foreign residents " being defined as aliens who have been living in a rural area for more than five years or in an urban area for more than six months), i.e. 17 per cent of the country's population; this figure does not include some 300,000 aliens who had been living in country districts on a " temporary " basis (i.e. for less than five years). Of this total of 700,000 persons, 300,000 were living in the countryside and 400,000 in the towns; immigrants from Upper Volta accounted for 300,000 of them (165,000 in the countryside and 135,000 in the towns). However, if allowance is made for all the peasants and their dependants who had been living for less than five years in country districts, there were probably at least half a million persons from Upper Volta living in the Ivory Coast in 1965, and this estimate does not include the very many seasonal migrant workers, whose number can be tentatively assessed on the basis of the 1960-61 population survey carried out in Upper Volta. According to the statistics drawn up at that time, seasonal migrants represented about 30 per cent of the total number of persons who had gone abroad, which would give a figure of 116,500 for 1971. It would therefore seem reasonable to assume that the present scale of seasonal migration from Upper Volta is in the region of 120,000-150,000 persons a year.

II. Causes and effects of emigration from Upper Volta

This historical survey of emigration from Upper Volta has conveyed some idea of the present number of persons involved, but it provides no answer to the fundamental question of why the movements have occurred, and still occur, on such a scale.

---

[1] Samir Amin: *Le développement du capitalisme en Côte-d'Ivoire* (Paris, Editions de Minuit, 1967), and *l'Afrique de l'Ouest bloquée* (Paris, Editions de Minuit, 1971).

[2] African Development Bank: *Etude des possibilités de coopération entre le Ghana, la Côte-d'Ivoire, la Haute-Volta, le Niger, le Dahomey et le Togo* (Abidjan, 1969; mimeographed).

[3] Peter Cornelisse: " An economic view of migration in Western Africa (a two-country study) "; Songre and Sawadogo: " Les effets de l'émigration massive des Voltaïques dans le contexte de l'Afrique occidentale "; Papers submitted to the IDEP-IAI seminar, Dakar, spring 1972.

There are two avenues that might be explored in search of an answer: first, the phenomenon seems to be explainable in terms of the country's position on the outer fringes of the developing world and, secondly, there is a general feeling that emigration is a necessary evil, since it does at present have a beneficial influence on the country's economic growth and that of the other countries in this part of Africa.

Economic stagnation

Since colonial times, as already mentioned, Upper Volta has been reduced to playing the part of a supplier of labour for the development of the countries along the coast of the Gulf of Guinea, and particularly the Ivory Coast. In 1932 it was decided that the territory was not economically strong enough to stand on its own feet and it was split up into three parts, one joining the Ivory Coast, one the French Sudan (now known as Mali) and the third Niger. Subsequently, pressures from various quarters resulted in its reconstitution in 1947. It is consequently a perfect example of an outback territory that never benefited in any way from colonial development; on the other hand, with its plentiful supply of labour, it has provided the primary economies of the coastal areas (the Ivory Coast and Ghana) with a fair proportion of their labour force. While workers from Upper Volta made a major contribution, for example, to what has come to be known as the " miracle of the Ivory Coast ", Upper Volta, for its part, paid the price in terms of prolonged economic stagnation, as may be seen from an analysis of its subsistence economy and the pattern followed by its modern sector.

SUBSISTENCE ECONOMY

One of the main features of the economy of Upper Volta is that it has very little contact with the markets of the world. The accounts for 1964 show that the gross domestic product (GDP) was 56,500 million francs CFA, of which 68 per cent, or 38,400 million, came from the traditional economy, i.e. agriculture and stockbreeding (32,300 million) and handicrafts, construction and traditional services (6,100 million). Agricultural production is almost entirely devoted to covering subsistence needs. Despite minor improvements in productivity achieved through agricultural development schemes (which have been limited in time and space), Upper Volta suffers from periodic shortages of certain basic foodstuffs. In 1970 the value of production derived from traditional activities reportedly increased to 42,400 million francs CFA, which is 10.4 per cent more than in 1964 and represents an annual growth rate of 1.7 per cent.

THE MODERN SECTOR

In 1964, value added at factor cost is reported to have been 11,700 million francs CFA for the modern sector, of which 50 per cent

TABLE 4. ECONOMIC TRENDS IN UPPER VOLTA, 1964-70

	1964	1970	Absolute increase	Percentage increase	
				Total	Annual average
GDP [1]	56.5	71.5	+ 15	26.5	4.4
Traditional sector [1]	*38.4*	*42.4*	+ *4*	*10.4*	*1.7*
Modern sector [1]	*18.1*	*29.1*	+ *11*	*60.7*	*10.1*
Total population	4 760 000	5 363 000	603 000	12.6	2.1
Product per head of population [2]	12 000	13 400	1 400	11.6	1.9

[1] In thousands of millions of francs CFA (1 franc CFA=0.02 French francs). [2] In francs CFA.

was attributable to commerce, 11 per cent to industry, 14 per cent to building and construction, 15 per cent to transport and 10 per cent to miscellaneous services. The total product at factor cost for the modern sector, including government and domestic service (6,400 million) was 18,100 million in 1964. In 1970 the corresponding figure was 29,100 million, an increase of 60.7 per cent (or 10.1 per cent per year) over 1964. Industry's contribution to GDP in 1970 is estimated to have been about 5 per cent, or 3,575 million francs CFA.

Economic trends in Upper Volta between 1964 and 1970 are summarised in table 4. Given the country's continuing economic backwardness since the days of the colonial administration and also the increase in its population, there has been hardly any real economic progress, as may be seen from the virtually unchanged product per head of population.

The employment problem

The economic situation has produced a serious employment problem in both the traditional and the modern sectors.

EMPLOYMENT IN THE TRADITIONAL SECTOR

An analysis of the economically active population by social group and occupation shows that over 98 per cent consist of non-wage earning peasants, artisans and family workers engaged in primary activities.

Farming is relatively unproductive, and consequently unremunerative, for a variety of reasons: the limited duration of the crop cycle, which means that the peasant population is underemployed for seven or eight months of the year; the use of very elementary methods or methods that have little intrinsic capacity for development; and the absence of progressive and efficient leadership. This explains why output in the traditional sector has improved so little and, at the same time, why income per head has remained virtually unchanged. Since the standard of living of the rural population has hardly changed for the better, and may even have fallen if allowance is made for rising prices, part of the active population is obliged to emigrate in search of better-paid employment.

The fact that the implementation of various rural development projects and schemes for the improvement of handicrafts by making them more productive, with a consequent increase in earnings, has begun to limit the drift of population away from Upper Volta bears out the assumption that financial considerations are the most important factor in the decision to migrate.

EMPLOYMENT IN THE MODERN SECTOR

Employment in the modern sector accounts for a bare 1.5 per cent of the country's active population, 6 per cent engaging in primary, 18 per cent in secondary and 76 per cent in tertiary activities.

These characteristic distortions and the lack of balance between the two sectors which is a feature of developing countries reflect how far workers in the modern sector are crowded into virtually dead-end jobs in public and private service; industry consists entirely of small firms specialising in import substitution and catering for the very limited demands of the domestic market.

Statistics for wage-earning employment over the past ten years reveal how marginal and relatively stagnant the " modern " economy really is. In 1961 statistical surveys carried out by the Ministry of Labour revealed that there were 23,217 persons holding permanent wage-paid jobs; in 1970 the figure had only risen to 32,034. The implications for development, and hence the expansion of employment, are disquieting, to say the least.

The figures are particularly disturbing when it is remembered that the population is expanding rapidly and that between 3 and 4 per cent of the total population, i.e. not less than 150,000-200,000 persons a year, are youngsters reaching working age.

Another disquieting factor is the increase in the number of people receiving primary, secondary or higher education, because employment opportunities are not being created at anything like the rate needed to absorb the number of school leavers. The acute unemployment prevailing among so many educated young people casts doubts on the suitability of school curricula and indeed on the educational system as a whole, and at the same time has precipitated a serious social crisis for the country. For a small proportion of these young people, emigration may offer an immediate and short-term solution to their difficulties, but the fact remains that the training of the younger generation and their employment in the interests of the national economy is a pressing problem calling for basic reforms and a national employment programme coupled with rigorous economic planning.

Economic and social effects of emigration

Consequently, while it would be wrong to underestimate the other psychological and sociological factors at work, the stagnation so typical of the traditional and modern sectors of the national economy has led the active population to resort to large-scale emigration, whose economic and social implications need to be assessed objectively.

The first reaction of anyone faced with such a task would be to try to draw up a balance sheet, with the advantages on one side and the disadvantages on the other, but he would soon find that the job was difficult, if not impossible, because of the lack of accurate information and the existence of various intangible factors of psychological, sociological or physical origin.

EFFECTS FOR THE HOST COUNTRIES

In the context of the national economies of Ghana and the Ivory Coast it is difficult to assess what proportion of their respective product is attributable to immigrants from Upper Volta and accordingly to deduce how much the two countries gain from their presence. As far as the Ivory Coast is concerned, however, it has been recognised that " national development over the past 15 years has been and still is to all intents and purposes based exclusively on foreign labour ". As an illustration, " in what can be regarded as the real plantation areas, aliens account for between half and two-thirds of the labour force ".[1] Similarly, according to one source [2], the percentage of nationals employed in the modern sector is 47.5, while that of other Africans is 46.6.

Since the host countries cover none of the social costs of training foreign workers, the latter's countries of origin in fact help to finance the development of their countries of employment. Furthermore, the study made by the African Development Bank, to which reference has been made above, shows that planters make a considerable profit by employing wage-paid labour: " Since a labourer is paid between 60 and 80 cents a day, the planter makes a net profit of between $1.2 and $2.3 on each day's work." [3] Hence, by employing 100,000 labourers from Upper Volta for 275 days a year, planters in the Ivory Coast make a net profit of between 8,200 and 15,700 million francs CFA.

This brief outline gives some indication of the scale of the advantages offered by arrangements of this kind to countries whose development largely depends on foreign migrant labour.

---

[1] Amin, op. cit., pp. 43 and 44.

[2] *Mémento de l'économie africaine* (Paris, Ediafric, 7th ed., 1972), p. 95.

[3] *Etude des possibilités de coopération entre le Ghana, la Côte-d'Ivoire, la Haute-Volta, le Niger, le Dahomey et le Togo*, op. cit., p. 16.

EFFECTS FOR UPPER VOLTA

The effects of emigration can be analysed in either a micro- or a macro-economic context.

A person contemplating the possibility of emigration on financial grounds weighs up what he stands to gain from it and what personal advantages he might derive from his activities abroad, without regard for any implications it may have for his native country from the standpoint of the economy in general. The potential benefits are primarily financial: the earnings from a job will enable him to cover his own social and financial needs and, furthermore, to maintain any members of his family he has left behind, so that they can pay their taxes and living expenses generally. In actual fact, a person emigrating from Upper Volta will be employed at a very low level of skill and consequently earn a very modest wage of the order of 60 to 80 cents (150 to 200 francs CFA) a day on a plantation in Ghana or the Ivory Coast. A further point to note in this connection is that few migrants enjoy any social security coverage.

In the macro-economic context, it is very difficult to assess the amount of money and goods remitted by migrants to their homes in Upper Volta, and no method has yet been devised to give satisfactory results. It is not even possible by using postal cheque accounts to ascertain how much of the money transferred belongs to emigrants from Upper Volta. The only really effective way would have been to require all migrants to comply strictly with Article 13 of the agreement of 9 March 1960, which states that " if a worker so requests on signing his contract of employment, part of his wages, subject to a maximum of 1,000 francs a month, shall be paid by his employer at monthly intervals into an account opened in his name with the Savings Bank of the Republic of Upper Volta. The Manpower Office of the Republic of Upper Volta shall satisfy itself that such payments are made regularly." Since this provision has remained a dead letter, there is no possibility of using it to determine how much of the migrants' savings have been remitted to their homes.

There is virtually no point in trying to assess the flow of money from Ghana, but one possible approach in the case of the Ivory Coast would be to compare the balance-of-payments position of the two countries. According to an as yet unofficial study made by the Central Bank of West African States, Upper Volta's balance of payments has shown a surplus over recent years which is not explainable in terms of the circulation of banknotes issued by the various States. The sum involved amounted to 3,200 million francs CFA in 1968, 3,900 million in 1969 and 5,000 million in 1970. According to the Central Bank, this surplus in all probability corresponds to the remittances made by Upper Volta migrants working in the Ivory Coast. This explanation may or may not be plausible, but there can be no doubt that considerable sums of money are transferred from the Ivory Coast to Upper Volta, even though the actual amount

TABLE 5. MAIN TYPES OF JOBS OBTAINED BY UPPER VOLTA NATIONALS ABROAD (%)

Type of job	Before 1923	1924-32	1933-39	1940-45	1946-50	1951-55	1956-60	Total
Plantation labourer	15.1	21.8	23.7	40.4	51.0	61.2	70.1	51.8
Industrial labourer	14.9	14.8	22.5	27.6	27.9	28.2	21.1	23.9
Policeman, soldier, etc.	67.4	59.0	49.5	26.5	12.5	4.8	2.8	18.4
Total [1]	97.4	95.6	95.7	94.5	91.4	94.2	94.0	94.1

[1] Since the table covers only the main types of jobs, not all emigrants are accounted for; hence the totals fall short of 100 per cent.

remains a mystery. For the time being, as was mentioned earlier, there is no reliable way of finding out.

Apart from these advantages to emigration, there are certain disadvantages, which can be summarised as follows:

(1) The potential earnings forfeited by Upper Volta through the absence of so large a fraction of its active population are enormous; many country districts have been drained of their young blood and only the children and the old people have been left behind to try to farm the land.

(2) There is a distinct possibility that the emigrants' remittances cause a certain amount of inflation and rising prices in Upper Volta, because they are directly used for immediate consumption and not for savings or investment.

(3) The introduction of new ways of thinking and new scales of values into Upper Volta have an inhibiting effect on national development, for they are not invariably constructive. What happens is that the emigrants, most of whom are young, come back with a spendthrift attitude rather than a development-conscious one, based on a knowledge of production and management techniques. There is thus a vicious circle in which the flow of migrants is maintained and strengthened by the very fact of migration.

(4) Finally, judging by the kinds of jobs the migrants do, there are very few of them who learn a skill which could qualify them for higher-level and better-paid employment after their return to Upper Volta. Table 5 provides some figures on the kind of jobs obtained by Upper Volta nationals abroad, based on the findings of the 1960-61 population survey.

As a result, the emigrants' level of " skill " has steadily declined over the years and most of them are now employed as labourers either in industry or, more commonly, in agriculture. A few are also working in domestic service.

III. Possible solutions

Emigration both reflects and aggravates the social problems facing Upper Volta and is increasingly regarded as a deep-rooted evil having a detrimental influence on the nation as a whole, by reason of its scope, the persons it involves and the meagre benefit it yields. Even so, it is for the time being a necessary evil and should as far as possible be so organised as to contribute to development. Ways and means must therefore be devised to make migratory movements more productive and to employ the active population more efficiently within the country.

Emigration for development

If the emigration problem is viewed in the over-all context of population movements, it is clear that the first task is to draw up a development strategy based on the best possible population distribution, not only between one country and another or one region and another but throughout the whole of Africa.

While internal migration, whether spontaneous or otherwise, does not give rise to any conflict of interests between States, external migration inevitably creates friction and it is essential to safeguard the interests of the countries concerned as far as possible by proper co-ordination.

In the first place some thought has to be given to the economic and social changes that the organisation of migration on a multinational basis is hoped to produce. In this connection it may be mentioned that a functional analysis of the reasons for emigration is of no assistance in understanding the economic implications at the national or multinational level. In the second place (and this observation follows from the first) a decision must be taken concerning the population distribution required for achieving the proposed economic and social changes.

It follows from these two premises that migration would need to be strictly controlled by means of bilateral or multilateral agreements clearly specifying the obligations of the contracting parties. Every entry into or exit from a country would have to be recorded. In this way the host country would not find itself obliged to take in undesirable elements or to resort to large-scale expulsion; at the same time the migrants' country of origin could protect its interests and offset to some extent the loss of earnings represented by the departure of its nationals.

Some place would have to be found within the system of such agreements for the necessary safeguards not only for the migrants themselves but also for their countries of origin. The former would need to be covered by labour and social security legislation in the same way as the workers belonging to the host country and to be able to send home all or part of their savings and belongings; the countries of origin, for their part, could set up development funds financed from the savings remitted by their nationals abroad.

On this basis migration would not only act as a regulating mechanism in relation to population growth but would also contribute to the economic progress of the countries and regions concerned.

Rational use of human resources

It would certainly be most desirable if all the various States responded positively to the attempts that have been made to achieve some form of economic integration for West Africa, but nations nowadays are all too aware of their individual identities and tend to build up defence mechanisms that are hardly conducive to any integration of this kind.[1] This process whereby each small nation gradually turns in upon itself, however foolish it may seem, is none the less a fact, and it means that each country has to try to make efficient use of its human resources potential within its own frontiers. If in fact economic imbalances are at the root of population movements, causing workers to emigrate in an endeavour to escape the hardships of unemployment and underemployment—and there seems to be ample evidence that this is so—any policy concerning emigration will clearly have to be linked with an employment programme which, in turn, is formulated within the framework of an over-all national plan based on the implementation of an investment and incomes policy and the expansion of industrial and rural employment.

To this end, each government department responsible for economic affairs or planning will have to set up a human resources division responsible for preparing a national programme for achieving an over-all balance on the employment market, in the light of the manpower foreseeably required by economic growth. To achieve this balance, the human resources division, acting in co-operation with the other departments concerned, will have to prepare an inventory of the present state of the employment market, make forecasts and projections of labour supply and demand, and carry out any necessary adjustments in consultation with training centres and educational establishments. As part of this process, an assessment could be made of the manpower requirements of the modern sector, while determining the number of workers it would be desirable to have in the agricultural sector. For instance projects such as that for the development of the Volta river valleys call for genuine planning of the

[1] See Pierre Fougeyrollas: " La question nationale et les phénomènes migratoires en Afrique de l'Ouest "; Paper submitted to the IDEP-IAI seminar, Dakar, spring 1972.

human resources available in rural areas, concurrently with the establishment of the necessary infrastructure for the resettlement of the population displaced in this connection.

A proper control over migratory movements is a *sine qua non* of any development policy for West Africa. The aim of full employment, as set by the World Employment Programme, will certainly involve population movements at the national and regional levels, and even at the continental level, but whether such movements are spontaneous or otherwise, they will have to offer a prospect of genuine development for the African countries through the achievement of greater economic independence; the attainment of this objective is, in turn, the real task facing those responsible for the destinies of the nations of Africa.

Out-of-School Education and Training for Primary-School Leavers in Rural Kenya: a Proposal

Walter ELKAN [1]

The school leaver problem

A MAJOR PROBLEM facing Kenya is that for a great majority of those who leave primary school there is no further education of any kind. It is estimated that some 150,000 leave primary school each year, of whom probably not more than 30,000 go on to secondary school or receive some other form of further education. This is a problem for two reasons. First, because it is perpetuating the shortage of people with intermediate skills in a wide range of occupations extending from, say, farm mechanics to catering staff. Secondly, when education ceases completely after only seven years of school, there is a danger that what was so painfully learnt will shortly be forgotten. This danger is the greater in the relatively unsophisticated environment of countries like Kenya because there may be only sporadic opportunities to use what one has learnt at school.

The first of these problems might be called the " manpower problem " and this article will have little to say about it. I am concerned here primarily with the second problem, the lack of provision for topping up and extending what has been learnt at primary school. Why does this constitute a problem? Partly because it is a waste of scarce resources to give people a primary education unless what has been taught is retained, and it almost certainly will not be unless steps are taken to ensure that it is. There is a second reason why the lack of provision for further education is a problem. Kenya is anxious to see the economy of its countryside transformed and what, for want of a better word, is often

---

[1] Professor of Economics, University of Durham.

spoken of as " modernised ". But such transformation and modernisation require the wide dissemination of aptitudes, both intellectual and manual, for which seven years of school, often in rather primitive conditions, cannot have done more than lay the foundations.

It ought perhaps to be said at once that the modernisation of the countryside is not simply, or even primarily, to be achieved through education or training. No amount or kind of education will, by itself, make Kenya's agriculture as productive as, for instance, Denmark's. That requires a great many other inputs apart from education, and it also requires the pursuit of economic policies which provide the right incentives and which recognise and overcome the barriers to action.

But it is fairly clear that one such barrier is the fact that the great majority who live in the countryside lack the basic endowments needed for faster progress. Consequently, progress is too slow to satisfy young people and their one ambition in life is to find a job in town. Very few succeed. The number of vacancies that occur in the course of a year is small, partly because total employment is expanding very slowly and partly because, in contrast with the position only a few years ago, those who are lucky enough to have jobs tend to hang on to them so that there are few vacancies for newcomers from the rural areas.[1]

It is likely that the prospects of finding a wage job will be a little better in the coming years than it was during the 1960s when employment virtually stagnated and in some years was below the number it had reached towards the end of the previous decade. The development plan for 1970-74 [2] aims to increase wage employment by 5.1 per cent a year; this means that between 1968 and 1974 the number of wage earners is expected to increase by 375,000 from just over 1 million in 1968. Of this increase 200,000 jobs are " planned " to be outside agriculture. But even this modest increase is thought by one competent observer to " look highly ambitious in relation to both past performance and to experience in other countries ".[3]

Even if the employment objectives of the plan are attained, it will still only be a minority who find jobs in the towns because, given Kenya's population increase of over 3 per cent a year, these additional employment opportunities are not even sufficient to provide urban wage jobs for all who enter the labour force for the first time each year. The current

---

[1] See Walter Elkan: " Urban unemployment in East Africa ", in *International Affairs* (London), Vol. 46, No. 3, July 1970.

[2] Republic of Kenya: *Development Plan 1970-1974* (Nairobi, Government Printing Office, 1969).

[3] Dharam P. Ghai: " Employment performance, prospects and policies in Kenya ", a background paper submitted to the University of Cambridge Overseas Studies Committee Conference, September 1970 (mimeographed); to be published. For a recent view of the employment aspects of the development plan see Eric S. Clayton: " Agrarian reform, agricultural planning and employment in Kenya ", in *International Labour Review*, Vol. 102, No. 5, Nov. 1970, especially pp. 446 ff.

rate of population growth is adding 126,000 persons to the labour force each year. Indeed the plan estimates that during the period 1970-74 the numbers leaving school at the end of a primary education will have been over half a million and in addition 138,000 will have left secondary school. It estimates that less than half the secondary-school leavers will have found urban wage jobs and that virtually all the primary-school leavers will have to find their livelihood in rural areas, and only a few of them in wage employment.

What are the implications of this? First, since wage employment is so keenly sought after and so scarce, further education and training are universally regarded as the way to fulfil one's ambition. Places in secondary schools or on training courses are eagerly sought after because when employers have a vacancy they tend to fill it, in the absence of better criteria of selection, with whoever can produce the most certificates. This emphasis on formal qualifications or certificates then also leads to the erroneous but widespread belief that it is only the lack of the cherished certificate which is responsible for continued unemployment.

Secondly, all post-primary education and training is either focused on wage employment, or tends sooner or later to be diverted in that direction. If only the focus were explicit and really sharp, it might at least go some way towards solving the " manpower problem " referred to earlier, but in practice the educational system at present oversupplies youngsters with a purely academic " arts " education, whilst shortages of people with more specialised training, and especially with certain manual skills, persist. But an even greater shortcoming is that post-primary education and training at present make little contribution to rural development although this is one of the major objectives of the development plan and of government policy to bring about a transformation of the countryside.

Such a transformation requires educational inputs of two kinds. First, it will need proper training for the next generation of small-scale farmers as envisaged in the development plan. There will also be a need for properly trained rural craftsmen, tractor drivers, maintenance mechanics and so forth. This type of training can necessarily be provided for only a minority except perhaps for short courses at Farm Training Centres. But rural transformation also requires a lifting of the general level of competence in the countryside, and this means that it may be equally important to make some provision for the great majority who will never obtain specific vocational training. This provision for the majority should have two principal ingredients: first, the maintenance of skills acquired in primary school—literacy, and the ability to calculate; and secondly, the teaching of rudimentary manual skills of the kind that are found almost universally in the countries of Western Europe for example, irrespective of people's occupation—the use of simple tools and the maintenance of simple equipment such as bicycles.

An educational strategy for primary-school leavers

In arriving at a strategy for providing further education for those primary-school leavers for whom there is no opportunity of going on to secondary school or receiving pre-vocational training, certain constraints are overriding. First, the development plan makes it clear that *rural* development is to be given overriding emphasis. I shall therefore confine myself to proposals for rural areas. Secondly, expenditure on education is already very high, in relation both to government expenditure and to the gross domestic product. Expenditure on formal education has been estimated to be about 7 per cent of GDP and 20 per cent of the combined recurrent expenditure on central and local government.[1] No proposal is therefore likely to be practicable which is costly to implement. As the intention is to make provision for large numbers—all those who have no opportunity for full-time further education—low cost in terms of both finance and trained staff is the only hope of rapid progress.

Within these constraints what kind of post-primary education should one provide? As was argued earlier, it needs to do two things: first, to " top up " what was learnt at school, and secondly, to add manual skills by providing the opportunity to use simple hand tools like hammers, saws, screwdrivers and sewing-machines. To make this kind of provision for large numbers at low cost implies acceptance of two conditions: the education can be provided only on a part-time, non-residential basis, and there will have to be, broadly speaking, as many establishments in an area as there are primary schools, given that the number of primary schools is determined by the length of the daily journey to and from school. Finally, it will be advisable, if possible, not to create new institutions, but rather to reform existing ones or to graft new functions on to existing institutions.

Village Polytechnics

One proposal that has been widely canvassed is the setting up of Village Polytechnics. This was originally proposed in the report of a working party established by the National Christian Council of Kenya [2], and some twenty such institutions have since come into existence with an average enrolment of thirty each.[3] Their aim is education for self-employment, or to teach young people skills with which they could earn a

---

[1] See Kyale Mwendwa: " Constraint and strategy in planning education ", in James R. Sheffield (ed.): *Education, employment and rural development* (Nairobi, East African Publishing House, 1967), p. 273.

[2] National Christian Council of Kenya: *After school what? A report on the further education, training and employment of primary-school leavers* (Nairobi, 1966).

[3] John Anderson: *The Village Polytechnic Movement* (Institute of Development Studies, University of Nairobi, 1970) (mimeographed).

livelihood in the countryside. The skills range from bee-keeping to tanning hides or building houses, and the idea is that each Polytechnic should make an assessment of opportunities in its locality and then train people to take advantage of them. In practice there is a heavy concentration on carpentry, bricklaying, tailoring and leather work, although bicycle and watch repairing are also taught. The courses last two years, although many of the students leave earlier if they find an opportunity of earning money before they have completed the course; some reappear later to receive further training.

The Village Polytechnics so far established have all been the result of initiatives taken by one or other Christian mission. The local churches have mostly provided land and initial equipment and the missions are bearing a major part of the cost. They have also in some instances provided the instructors, whilst in other cases young volunteers from overseas have played a leading role.[1] There is great diversity in almost every respect, and the annual recurrent cost of running these institutions varies accordingly between K£11 and K£51 per student with typical figures of K£25 to K£30 per student.[2] This compares with an average of K£8 per pupil in primary schools and K£45 to K£50 per pupil in rural secondary schools.[3]

Whilst it is to be hoped and anticipated that Village Polytechnics will spread and prosper, it has also to be recognised that they face a number of problems. First, they have so far been very dependent on Christian missions and overseas volunteers, and this dependence must inevitably limit their spread. Secondly, whilst there may be a great *need* for rural craftsmen the *effective demand* for them can be easily exaggerated. So long as the Village Polytechnics only produce a small number of craftsmen there is not much danger of a glut, especially if some of them combine practising their craft with farming and other ways of earning a livelihood. But many market centres in Kenya already have bicycle mechanics and watch repairers, not to mention contracting carpenters and masons, and if this is true, then, to quote John Anderson's careful study of the Village Polytechnics, " the new faith in practical skill training that has developed amongst parents and students must be treated very cautiously ".[4] Thirdly, the idea that after two years in a Village Polytechnic a youngster is equipped to start up his own business is surely a little naïve. Even if he is given some elementary introduction to book-keeping and associated arts it is surely rather unrealistic to imagine that this is all he needs to make him a successful businessman. This, if nothing else, explains why, despite all the talk of " education for self-employ-

[1] Anderson, op. cit., pp. 27-28.

[2] K£1 = US$2.80 or £1.17.

[3] Anderson, op. cit., pp. 24-25.

[4] Ibid., p. 13.

ment ", the Village Polytechnics are still seen primarily as helping their students to find paid wage employment. Finally, in terms of the criteria adopted above, the cost per pupil of providing a place in a Village Polytechnic must rule this out as a way of providing further education for the majority of primary-school leavers.

Out-of-school education and Youth Centres

Village Polytechnics are still essentially part of the " formal " or " school " structure of education. But if low cost is to be a crucial criterion, then it almost inevitably points to the desirability of making provision for primary-school leavers on the basis of " out-of-school " education. This term is used to comprise multifarious activities ranging from literacy classes, via instruction given at Youth Centres, to part-time courses at Polytechnics or evening classes, agricultural extension work, correspondence courses and perhaps even instruction in family planning. The term " non-formal " education is also sometimes used interchangeably, and, in Great Britain, " adult education ".

Out-of-school education has an important contribution to make to development, and in the short to medium run, its contribution may be greater than that of formal school education. But this assertion is at present impossible to substantiate. Whilst formal education is reasonably well documented, there are no comparable figures for out-of-school education. Thus in the case of formal education we know that between 1958 and 1967 the number of pupils in primary schools increased from 650,000 to 1,000,000 and in secondary schools, from 15,000 to 80,000. For out-of-school education there are no comparable figures of numbers receiving instruction or for expenditure. This is hardly surprising in view of the heterogeneity of out-of-school education and the fact that whilst formal education is largely the business of one ministry—the Ministry of Education—out-of-school education, as we shall see, is not.

I argued earlier that the need to keep costs to a minimum meant that one had to think of some way of providing further education on a part-time and non-residential basis, preferably by building on existing institutions. It seems to me that the best way to achieve these aims is to graft what is proposed on to the existing Youth Centres.[1] The fact that the role of these Centres has already changed somewhat over the years is an indication that it may be made to evolve still further. Originally started by the British Administration during the Mau-Mau emergency, they were intended to provide young people with something to do that would remove the temptation to join Mau-Mau for lack of alternative

[1] For an account of the origins and work of these Centres see G. W. Griffin: " The development of Youth Centres in Kenya ", in *International Labour Review*, Vol. LXXXVIII, No. 1, July 1963, pp. 52-65.

occupation. Later, they were recast to provide exactly the kind of topping-up of primary education that is proposed here, but for a younger age group, in the days when most children had only four years of primary education.

Today there are some 170 Youth Centres attended by an estimated 13,000 young people aged 7 to 20, of whom rather more are boys than girls. They are the responsibility of the County Councils, which provide their buildings, staff and equipment, though some of the buildings have been put up by villagers themselves under self-help schemes—or " harambee " as they are known. They are supervised by Community Development Assistants—employees of the County Councils—and, more remotely, by the District Community Development Officers—employees of the Central Government. The latter are ultimately responsible to the Director of Social Services in the Ministry of Co-operatives and Social Services, who has a Youth Officer on his staff. The Youth Officer also acts as Secretary to the Kenya Association of Youth Centres, which is a co-ordinating body.[1]

Their object and function are not very well defined and indeed a salient characteristic of the Youth Centres is their extreme diversity. At their best they provide just the kind of further post-primary education I am advocating—a mixture of conventional reading, writing and arithmetic, some of it in English, and an equal amount of time spent on practising the use of simple tools. But this latter and most important part of the whole is also most often in abeyance, usually for lack of finance. One can practise the use of tools only if there are tools and materials on which to practise them, but few County Councils seem able or willing to keep the Centres supplied. The only well-equipped Centres seem to be those which had received their tools as gifts from UNICEF, the Dulverton Trust (an English foundation specialising in social welfare projects) or the Save the Children Fund. One County Council—and perhaps there were others—supplied timber and other materials from a revolving fund, created by the sale of the youngsters' work. Because they depend so much on charities for equipment, it tends to be only the newest Centres which are well equipped. Eventually equipment wears out, is lost or stolen, and then this side of the Centres' work atrophies.

There is also great diversity in the ages and previous experience of those who attend them. Some are small children, whilst others are in their early twenties. Most commonly, their real role seems to be that of providing a kind of primary schooling for those who for one reason or another are not attending, or have not attended, primary school. These are mostly of two kinds. First, those who have not been able to get into a primary school since the maximum age of entry was reduced. Having failed to gain admission at the age of 5 or 6, their only hope of obtaining

---

[1] *Development Plan 1970-1974*, op. cit., p. 539.

a Kenya Preliminary Examination Certificate, i.e. the certificate awarded on completing primary school, is to attend a Youth Centre. Secondly, there are those whose parents prefer the lower fees of the Youth Centres. Although the Youth Centres are not supposed to accept children who are eligible to go to primary school, there is little doubt that some of them do. But as quasi-primary schools the Youth Centres are poor substitutes. Their staffs are less well paid and therefore less well qualified. They lack the guidance and supervision of the Ministry of Education as well as the textbooks and other materials which schools get from the Government. It would therefore be very good if the Youth Centres could be so reconstituted that they can perform a distinct role and do so properly. Indeed the Government has quite recently begun to do just that by designating some of them as Senior Youth Centres and confining them to genuine primary-school leavers.

What kind of changes are needed? With regard to the existing Youth Centres, the aim should be to bring the less effective ones up to the standards of the best. This will almost invariably involve two processes. First, to ensure an adequate supply of tools and materials, and secondly, to alter the teaching of the academic subjects so that it continues where primary schools left off, so that there is no risk that the education provided by Youth Centres will duplicate that given in the primary schools. To ensure that there is an adequate supply of tools and materials is a financial and administrative problem. A Youth Centre at Watuka, near Nyeri, Central Province, opened in 1967-68, was equipped by UNICEF, at a cost of K£80, and this figure is likely to be fairly typical. The running costs are more difficult to estimate but assuming that the Centres can be staffed mostly by part-time instructors, since they need only operate for part of each day, and can perhaps draw on local school-teachers and craftsmen glad to have the opportunity to supplement their regular earnings, it is reasonable to estimate that cost per pupil will be a great deal less than even in primary schools.

The administrative structure of out-of-school education

The administrative structure of out-of-school education is described in a paper by Paul Fordham and James R. Sheffield, entitled " Continuing education for youth and adults " in the Kericho Conference report.[1] They explain that responsibility for different *kinds* of out-of-school education resides in different ministries and that, in addition, some is provided by voluntary agencies, or " non-governmental organisations ", to use the United Nations term. Thus health education is provided through the Ministry of Health; the National Youth Service, which also in a sense provides out-of-school education comes under the Ministry of Labour, as

[1] Sheffield, op. cit., pp. 366-389.

does artisan training. The Ministry of Agriculture and Animal Husbandry run some 850 " 4-K Clubs ", which teach about 25,000 schoolboys and school leavers modern methods of farming for profit. Finally, the Ministry of Co-operatives and Social Services is responsible for Youth Centres and also, since 1967, for that part of adult education which is to be provided under the Board of Adult Education Act of 1966. The Board of Adult Education created by the Act was intended to co-ordinate the diverse activities of government departments and voluntary agencies and has a membership of not more than twenty-seven representing all facets of adult education, defined as " full-time or part-time education or instruction of any kind provided for any person over the age of 16 who is not in full-time attendance at any . . . school or . . . university ". At the same time the Government allocated K£20,000 specifically for the launching of an adult literacy campaign; this allocation has been steadily increased and is expected to rise to K£156,000 in 1973-74.[1]

An Adult Section was established in the Ministry of Education in 1966 and transferred to the Ministry of Co-operatives and Social Services, the following year. In 1966-67 a start was made with the literacy campaign in ten Districts where Assistant Education Officers were appointed specifically to look after adult education. Each of the chosen Districts was expected to establish fifty centres in whatever premises happened to be available—school buildings, community centres or church halls. In 1967-68 twelve more Districts were added and the remaining Districts were covered by 1970. This programme of adult literacy teaching, organised by Assistant Education Officers appointed by the Ministry of Co-operatives and Social Services, has been the main outcome so far of the Board of Adult Education Act. By 1969 over 140,000 students had been enrolled for four-year courses, and by 1974 enrolment is expected to have risen to some 800,000. The development plan envisages the elimination of illiteracy in less than twenty years. The main emphasis is on literacy, but literacy is being used as the tool for instruction in matters relating to the students' work, e.g. how to improve farming techniques and livestock. This is called " functional literacy ". The literacy teaching is done by school-teachers in their spare time (for which they are paid extra) and agricultural officers, veterinarians and other professional people are brought in to help with the other aspects of the programme.

At present the activities resulting from the passing of the Board of Adult Education Act of 1966 are thus mainly concerned with adult literacy. It is arguable that the reconstituted Youth Centres ought to be administered under the same aegis. Since the Youth Centres are intended to provide further part-time education (in the widest sense) they ought to be administered by whatever body is responsible for all forms of after-school education.

---

[1] *Development Plan 1970-1974*, op. cit., p. 533.

One may go further and question whether the Ministry of Co-operatives and Social Services is really the appropriate ministry for activities of this kind. If responsibility for Youth Centres were transferred to the Adult Education Section and if this section were moved back to an enlarged Ministry of Education, this would go some way towards reducing the danger that Youth Centres will overlap the education provided by primary schools. But these are matters on which no outsider can pronounce with certainty after only the most cursory examination of the issues involved.

One further question calls for an answer: how many Youth Centres would be needed if the proposal in this article were fully implemented? Given that they must be non-residential, the numbers required must be approximately the same as the number of primary schools, which is now just over 6,000. As we saw earlier there are at present only about 170 in existence and most of these are in need of overhaul. The task of creating such large numbers of Youth Centres may therefore seem daunting. But the buildings may well be provided by local self-help or the Centres could be housed in existing buildings, including schools; the major capital cost is the provision of an initial stock of tools and materials at a cost not exceeding K£100 per Centre, or a total of K£600,000. The more serious problem is posed by the recurrent costs, however modest, since the numbers who at present receive no further instruction after they leave primary school are very large.

It has unfortunately not proved possible to make convincing estimates of recurrent costs. Assuming that two-thirds of school leavers continued to attend for, say, the equivalent of one day a week for three or four years, each Centre would probably need two or three full-time staff members—all of whom should be capable of helping with the teaching of reading, writing and arithmetic, so as to allow maximum flexibility in the allocation of teaching loads. They should also be capable of teaching at least one craft each at this pre-vocational level and would be responsible for bringing in other instructors in the area on a part-time basis. Assuming that the full-time staff members were capable of doing all the " literary " teaching, the part-timers to be brought in would be local artisans—government employees or others—and would be used to supplement the craft teaching. As we saw earlier, there is a precedent in the field of adult literacy for using people with regular jobs on a part-time basis, but those to be recruited by the Youth Centres would be different people, so as to avoid competing with the organisers of adult literacy classes.

Finding the part-timers will probably be easier than finding, say, 12,000 full-time instructors, and it will almost certainly be necessary to phase the development of Youth Centres over a period of three or four years. It may also be necessary to set up a training institution, or convert an existing one, for the training of instructors. Short courses of a few weeks' duration should be quite sufficient since the object cannot be to teach prospective instructors either the literary or the manual skills. Candidates must already have acquired these elsewhere and the purpose of the institution should rather be to make sure that the objectives of the reconstituted Youth Centres are properly understood and to provide some initiation into teaching methods at this level.

The recurrent costs of all this are difficult to estimate realistically, but on the assumption that instructors are paid about the same as untrained primary school-teachers, the total annual recurrent cost when 6,000 centres have come into existence is not likely to exceed K£3 million a year. If they cater for, say, 300,000 school leavers, this would mean a recurrent cost of K£10 per person enrolled. This should be regarded as an outside estimate, and is in any case intended to give no more than a rough order of magnitude for when all the centres have come into operation in three or four years' time. Initially the cost would be a great deal less. The estimate assumes that any materials required will be paid for by the users; this is best done by charging everyone a small fee intended to cover the cost of materials and maintenance of the stock of tools and other equipment.

Summary and conclusion

It is wasteful to invest heavily in primary education in a predominantly rural society like Kenya unless steps are taken to make sure that what is learnt in seven years at school continues to be topped up. It needs also to be extended to manual skills. Schools must necessarily concentrate on their proper function, which is to teach their pupils to read, write and calculate with a modicum of proficiency, and they cannot easily take on the task of teaching them manual skills. Yet topping up literacy and extending education into manual skills are essential if the investment in primary education is to yield returns in the form of faster rural development. The alchemy of rural development must of course contain many other ingredients, not least the gradual extension of secondary education and vocational training of all kinds. But this is an expensive process and it will be a long time before it can cater for more than a minority. A solution for the majority must be based on less costly processes. It must also be in a form in which it will not be seen as a form of training for urban jobs, because urban employment opportunities cannot increase fast enough to provide jobs for all those reaching manhood. For the great majority the prime need is that they should be able to lead a more effective and lucrative life in the rural areas.

One solution that has been widely canvassed is the setting up of Village Polytechnics. They may indeed make a valuable contribution to the training of rural craftsmen. There is, however, a risk that they will once again be seen as providing vocational training leading to unrealisable job expectations. It is also doubtful if enough Village Polytechnics can be established to provide for the very large numbers involved.

As an alternative or supplement it may be better to use the existing Youth Centres as places where what was learnt at primary school is topped up and extended to include basic training in the use of tools. Many of the Youth Centres now operate as " poor men's primary schools ". The advantage claimed for the proposal is that the service to be provided will be exactly what is needed in the rural areas and that, because they will be cheap to establish and to run, it will be quite feasible to create them in very large numbers without adding too greatly to government expenditure.

Some may contend that a proposal such as that advanced in this article should have been justified specifically in relation to " manpower requirements ". One overriding manpower requirement for the 92 per cent of Kenya's people who live in the countryside is a gradual raising of the standards of literacy and manual competence without which rural progress will be continuously retarded. This is not a question of specific skills for the performance of specific jobs, but rather a raising of the general level of competence. It is not easy to demonstrate that a widespread ability to use a hammer and nails efficiently will have specific effects on the growth of rural incomes but it must be intuitively obvious that *not* to be able to do so, and not to be able to read and understand farmers' magazines or printed manuals for a new piece of equipment, is bound to hold back progress. It is, however, quite possible that the need for institutional arrangements to impart these skills will decline. In the advanced industrial countries these skills are normally passed on by parents to their children, but first there has to be a generation of parents who have acquired them.

IV. Methodological study

African Manpower Plans: an Evaluation

Richard JOLLY and
Christopher COLCLOUGH [1]

THIS ARTICLE SURVEYS over thirty manpower studies prepared in more than twenty countries of Africa during the past twelve years.[2] It also examines briefly ten rate-of-return studies which followed a very different methodology but which also tried to quantify the economic priorities for educational expansion.[2] Much of the article is concerned with the central but narrow question: " How adequate were the attempts of the various studies to estimate the future economic demand for educated manpower? " This is, of course, only one of the many questions that need to be answered in order to assess the relevance of manpower surveys to policy formulation and their usefulness to policy-makers. A few of these wider issues are considered in the last part of the article, which attempts to summarise conclusions for future work in this field.

The article begins with a general introduction indicating the main features of the manpower situation in Africa and giving the historical background of the recent manpower surveys. The second part provides a broad description of the manpower surveys made in Africa from 1959 through 1970: their objectives, the methods used and the sources of data. The third and central part concerns the problem of projecting the

---

[1] Respectively Fellow, Institute of Development Studies at the University of Sussex, and Manpower Economist, Government of Botswana. This article is the forerunner of a more extensive study initiated by Professor Jolly, to be published as a separate monograph. Mr. Lawrence Lockhart also assisted with the research, which has been supported by a grant from the Overseas Development Administration of the United Kingdom Government. The authors are grateful to the many individuals—especially some of those mainly responsible for the preparation of the plans surveyed—who contributed through personal interviews, letters or their original work. They are also grateful for detailed comments on an earlier draft by John Anderson, Ron Dore, Gerry Helleiner, Gordon MacKerron, Krishna Patel, George Psacharopoulos, Emil Rado, Sven Erik-Rastad and Clive Smee. Dudley Seers commented extensively but with a warning lest the heavy emphasis on a narrow range of technical aspects divert attention from even more fundamental issues of education policy and employment. The authors themselves are solely responsible for the views expressed in this article.

[2] See appendix I.

demand for and supply of skilled and educated manpower (SEMP) in the formal sector. This part begins with a brief summary of the theoretical issues involved in manpower forecasting, and the actual techniques used in manpower surveys are then related to this theoretical framework. The fourth part evaluates ten African cost-benefit studies of education, with particular reference to the assumptions embodied in them. The fifth part briefly introduces the question of training and shows one method of taking account of the trade-off between education and training in manpower planning. The final part draws conclusions for improving future manpower surveys and discusses future trends in the employment and unemployment of educated manpower in African countries in the light of the surveys analysed in the article.

In some respects the article is primarily of historical interest. The manpower plans considered were almost all prepared in a period of acute manpower shortage—when the main concerns of policy were how to expand essentially colonial educational systems to meet the demands of independence, and in particular, the urgent need of localising high-level posts predominantly held by expatriates.

Now in most of Africa, with the exception of a few countries south of the Zambezi, the problems are rapidly changing. Almost all the top government posts and a high proportion of the top posts in the rest of the public sector and in the private sector are held by nationals. Shortages of manpower are giving way to surpluses among secondary-school leavers in East Africa and often among university graduates in West Africa.

Most important—and more significant—there are stirrings of a more critical awareness of the deficiencies of the educational systems and thus of a new and broader approach to educational planning. It is now realised that the qualitative weaknesses of these systems are just as serious as the quantitative weaknesses and probably more difficult to remedy. Moreover, whatever its overt purpose, education is now seen to have actually played a very different role in development in Africa and outside it. Instead of providing training which prepares people for high-level work, education sometimes has served as little more than a means of rationing the certificates needed to enter the best jobs. The expansion of university places, instead of increasing educational opportunity, has often interacted with colonial salary scales to create an educated élite.

More fundamental still, disillusionment with many aspects of the formal educational system is going hand in hand with a re-discovery of the possible values of informal education. What is learnt outside school—on the farm, in the village, in apprenticeship, on the job, in the home and in a multitude of other ways not conventionally thought of as formal education—may add up to a more significant range of knowledge and level of intellectual development than are acquired in the classroom. This shift of focus not only directs attention to a whole lot of different types of informal education but also suggests that measures to develop formal education may in effect often have acted to retard and distort informal education.

All these changes will call in question much of what has previously been done in the name of manpower planning. Reconstruction will be necessary, though in our view many of the earlier building blocks will remain. But first one must ascertain what has been done—and how reasonable it was in its context. That is the primary purpose of this article. In the conclusions we attempt to indicate some of the changes that will need to be made if manpower planning is to become more relevant to the problems ahead.

Much of the article is concerned with the methodology of forecasting, and in this connection a warning may be useful, lest we be misunderstood. Forecasting needs for educated manpower was and is, in our view, useful and important. Nevertheless, manpower forecasting is only one of a number of technical exercises required for improving the formulation of policy in the fields of education, training, localisation, wages and any of the other major fields with which manpower planners are or ought to be concerned. Indeed, in our experience the manpower planners employed in full-time government positions (as opposed to those on short-term technical assistance assignments for the specific purpose of producing a manpower survey and projection) typically spent a relatively small proportion of their working time on the manpower survey and plan and perhaps rather less than 10 per cent on forecasting demand. The rest was spent on many other planning issues, committee work, lobbying, and direct liaison with planning and operational staff in various government posts and in the private sector. This round of additional activity, though often neglected in technical discussions, was a vital link in the whole process and, indeed, usually determined whether the manpower planner made any impact at all on policy formulation and implementation.

Our concentration on the task of surveying and forecasting manpower needs should not, therefore, be taken as indicating that this is mainly what manpower planners have done or ought to do. It is simply the particular aspect of their work on which we have chosen to focus most of this review—though in our conclusions we attempt to evaluate the manpower surveys and forecasts within a wider perspective.

I. Introduction

Unquestionably, throughout the 1960s, the people of Africa were the most under-educated in the underdeveloped world. Even today there are in Africa fewer persons with secondary or higher education in relation to the total population than in Latin America, Asia or the Middle East. In spite of a large and rapid expansion of education during the period since

TABLE I. EXPATRIATE EMPLOYMENT AS A PERCENTAGE OF TOTAL EMPLOYMENT AT DIFFERENT LEVELS OF SKILLED AND EDUCATED MANPOWER

Country	Year of survey	Educational level [1]				Total
		A	B	C	D	
Botswana	1967	94		81	19	42
Ivory Coast	1962	79	61	.	.	.
Kenya	1964	77 [2]	25 [2]	54 [2]	18 [2]	48 [2]
	1969	58	48	36	.	41
Malawi	1966	64	10	14	.	18
Nigeria	1964	39	5	.	.	13
Somalia	1970	7	2	20	2	2
Sudan	1967-68	12	6	2	0	3
Swaziland	1970	80	74	57	23	35
Tanzania	1965	82	23	31	9	31
	1969	66	20	12	6	18
Uganda	1967	66	32	16	11	21
Zambia	1965-66	96	92	88	41	62

[1] A = university degree or equivalent; B = " A " levels (higher secondary school examination generally taken after six or even seven years of secondary schooling) or " O " levels (examination taken after four or sometimes five years of secondary schooling) plus one to two years of formal training; C = " O " levels or secondary school, form II, plus two to four years of formal training; D = secondary school, form II, or primary schooling plus one to four years of formal training. For simplicity, the educational classifications used in all the manpower plans analysed in this article have been converted into the above four categories.

[2] All non-Africans.

Source: calculated from the manpower surveys.

independence (or from shortly before that date), most countries of East and Central Africa, and many of West Africa, are still heavily dependent on expatriate manpower and are far from self-sufficient in terms of their own graduate or even second-level manpower. Most African economies have had considerable experience of the inefficiencies and the constraints on development arising from inadequate supplies of skilled personnel in relation to other economic resources.

School enrolment ratios at primary, secondary and higher education levels were and are well below those in other continents. In terms of outputs, the annual number of graduates per 100,000 of the population in Africa was between 1 and 10 compared with the 30 to 150 which is typical of countries in Latin America or Asia.[1] Moreover, the dependence on expatriate manpower even five to ten years after independence was still extreme. Figures are given in table I for certain African countries. The counterpart of this dependence on expatriates was the high

[1] UNESCO: *Statistical Yearbook 1969* (Paris, 1970), table 2.16.

proportion of manpower aid going to African countries. For example in 1968, 84 per cent of all British publicly financed personnel working overseas were in Africa; of these, roughly two-fifths were in East Africa and two-fifths in Central Africa.

On the demand side, the needs at independence for educated manpower were swollen by ambitious development plans, the desire to accelerate rates of economic growth and the necessity to embark upon a range of new activities (for instance the additional responsibilities of the civil service in regard to foreign affairs). More than any other sector, education itself generated an enormous demand for additional skilled manpower (to become students at the higher levels, as well as for teachers). In the years to come the expansion of education which occurred during the 1960s will dramatically improve the manpower situation, but its initial effect was to add enormously to the short-term problem.

With supply and demand far out of balance, it is hardly surprising that the number of vacant posts at graduate level was often equivalent to well over 10 per cent of total employment at that level. Nor is it surprising that in almost all countries of middle Africa, government plans, company reports and technical assistance documents so often referred to the shortage of skilled, educated and experienced manpower—particularly for managerial posts—as being a major, if not the major, impediment to economic growth. In many countries this position is now rapidly changing, particularly as regards persons with formal middle-level qualifications and increasingly also for those with relevant job experience or higher formal qualifications. Nevertheless, a general situation of widespread and widely recognised shortage was the typical context in which African manpower plans were first conceived. This is important, since it distinguishes the manpower surveys in Africa from those in other continents, where the economic and manpower situation was often very different.

The widespread awareness of the scarcity of skilled and educated workers in Africa was largely responsible for the spate of manpower surveys covering over twenty countries, mainly English-speaking, which are analysed in this paper. In most of these countries they were the result of a common-sense appreciation of obvious problems. They were not the creation of academic planners.

The context has affected the approach to African manpower planning in two important ways. First, it was generally assumed that the educational systems needed major, not marginal, adjustment to meet manpower needs after independence. This assumption proved to be justified: secondary school enrolments have expanded by more than 15 per cent per annum on average in middle Africa over the past ten years—a rate of expansion in many cases five or ten times greater than that in more developed countries. Second, the very number of expatriates employed provided a minimum measure of future needs. Given the goal of localisation, calculation of the demand for educated local persons to replace expatriates was in the first place a matter of simple arithmetic. This is not to deny that some subtle economic issues were involved. But the subtleties were of little importance compared with the obvious dimensions of the basic problem. Since it was evident that the replacement of expatriates accounted for the major proportion of the total estimated demand for educated manpower, manpower planning was readily accepted by practical policy-makers, who in different circumstances might have needed more persuasion to move towards measures of formal economic planning.

II. The manpower surveys

Objectives

Although a central objective of most of the manpower plans was to identify current shortages (not to deal with possible surpluses) and to forecast the demand for skilled and educated manpower, certain other objectives were almost always involved. These included the provision of guidelines for educational expansion; the examination of priorities and prospects for localising skilled jobs, particularly in the civil service; the formulation of recruitment and immigration policy in respect of skilled expatriate manpower; and the establishment of priorities for training schemes of various sorts. A few of the plans also directed their findings to other economic objectives—recommendations on population policy, for instance—though these were generally not a central feature, nor were they integrated quantitatively with the rest of the forecasts.

The most notable omission of the manpower surveys concerned general policies respecting employment, both in urban and rural areas. Most of the manpower plans concentrated on skill requirements in wage-earning employment, giving only limited attention to wage- and self-employment in general, or to work opportunities or needs in the informal sector, urban as well as rural. This omission need not necessarily have been a weakness, since if the skilled manpower surveys had been supported by other studies of the general employment situation, it would have been simply a matter of focus. But in fact there has been a notable lack of general studies on employment in government publications.

The second major omission concerned incomes policy, especially with regard to the structure of incentives and future trends in the earnings of skilled and educated persons. This is particularly serious, since the existing wage structure is often sharply at variance with what would be required to ensure that those given specialist training generally seek work in jobs related to their training.

The third omission concerned the whole question of the allocation of the labour force, within sectors, occupations and geographical regions. It is true that a number of the manpower surveys mentioned these problems and suggested general policy approaches to deal with them. But the data, analyses and policy proposals were in general extremely thin, particularly when compared with the work on projections of skilled manpower demand.

Besides the overt economic objectives, or possibly underlying them, there were others [1] more directly related to the domestic and international contexts in which the plans were prepared. Domestically, the manpower surveys served—and have been used—to document the government's record, particularly in localisation, and thus to defend its achievements since independence. To some extent this was a helpful influence, giving the manpower survey publicity and providing support for the work involved in preparing it. In some respects, however, this political dimension may have compromised the clarity of the survey and its recommendations by making it tend to play up past successes, minimise certain problems and even obscure some of the more unpleasant facts of the situation. There have, of course, been notable exceptions, of which the annual manpower report of the President of Tanzania is a good example.

Internationally, the manpower surveys served some of the same objectives as national plans with respect to international aid. Donor agencies demanded such surveys to identify priorities for technical assistance and educational aid. Abroad and at home, various groups with an interest in educational expansion found it useful to associate themselves with the notion of a manpower survey in the expectation that it would provide " scientific " evidence of the need for further educational expansion. Some international donors and private foundations initially found it useful to adopt the same approach, in the belief that their support for a survey calling for educational expansion would help their relations with the new government. Of all the various interest groups, some of the professional educators have been perhaps the most shameless—anxious to invoke the approach of the manpower analyst as long as his answers supported their programmes of expansion, equally willing to denounce him for " neglecting the wider purposes of education " immediately his projections suggested that educational expansion should be slowed.

In a few cases academic pressures and individual ambitions have entered into manpower planning—particularly by influencing the presentation of the results, often favouring techniques and forms of publication that might make an impression in the developed countries and further the careers of those responsible for producing the document. Given the rudimentary state of manpower planning, such academic concerns could

[1] Borrowing from sociological terminology, one might refer to the latent—as opposed to the manifest—objectives of the surveys.

in principle have offered genuine advantages in the sense of improving analyses and the methodology used in projections, or of stimulating the interest required for long-run improvement. But academic bias also carried dangers, particularly in situations where the analyst was an expatriate on a limited contract, whose personal career concerns were not closely aligned with the long-term interests of the country, yet whose position gave him disproportionate control over the focus and balance of the survey work—often undertaken at the expense of less sophisticated work more closely related to urgent policy matters.

Statistical base

Appendix II shows the data available on the stocks of skilled and educated manpower for the purposes of the surveys we have analysed. In many cases this information was collected from a survey of establishments specially organised by those responsible for the manpower studies. Usually this meant that the data were obtained outside the framework of the regular organisation of the national statistical offices, either by units attached to the planning office or by a unit of the Ministry of Labour. Census information has so far rarely been used, though it may soon become available as a result of the 1970 round of censuses.

The data were generally compiled on the basis of interviews with senior management executives or the personnel officers of government departments or the larger firms and with the owner or manager of the smaller concerns being surveyed. Thus the information was based on the employer's records or personal knowledge of the occupational structure, nationality, educational qualifications, etc., of his labour force. In only a few cases were individual skilled workers themselves interviewed to ascertain their personal characteristics and qualifications.

It can be seen from appendix II that often only the most basic tabulations of the skilled labour force are available. Usually these include occupation, " normal " educational requirements, race and vacancies. But only the minority of countries tabulated this information separately by economic sectors. Nor is information generally available on the age, sex, training, experience or earnings of the skilled and educated labour force. Only two plans inquired about the education that went with each occupation in the base year. This is a formidable list of omissions for those concerned with analysing the basic characteristics of the skilled labour force, let alone with making projections. And the omissions were particularly unfortunate in that many were unnecessary. Often the data required had been collected but never tabulated or published.

Some important conclusions can be drawn from this experience of collection and tabulation of data on the skilled labour force. First, although the allocation of responsibility for the collection of data outside the central statistical offices may have had short-run advantages (and may, indeed, have been essential if the surveys were to get under way), this procedure was unfortunate in the long run. It often caused manpower information to be collected on a one-shot basis, instead of along with other economic information, with which it should have been integrated. Moreover, the statistical definitions used in many of the surveys, for instance of economic sectors or occupations, were often different from those used by the central statistical office or established by international convention. In a few cases there may have been good reason for adopting this procedure, but in most cases it would have been possible both to follow international practice and to adapt the definitions to local conditions.

About half of the surveys investigated recommended that special institutional machinery, separate from the central statistical offices, should be established on a permanent basis to deal with manpower planning and undertake administrative functions. Often this seemed to imply that the new machinery would also have responsibility for data collection. A number of manpower planners certainly see value in having the manpower planning function separate from the main stream of data collection by the government. Although it is impossible to pass judgment without reference to particular circumstances, there is a real danger of planners building mini-statistical empires related more closely to their own interests as manpower planners than the wider statistical interests of the country. In principle the relative merits of alternative institutional arrangements with respect to (1) data collection, (2) data processing and preparation of a report and (3) implementation of policy conclusions ought to be examined—for example the trade-off between autonomy and isolation in the case of a separate body with complete control and the trade-off between lack of power or influence and contact with other government activities and priorities where the workload is shared between different government groups. One important danger involved in a division of responsibility for the above-mentioned functions is that the process may break down due to lack of communications, administrative liaison or co-ordination of work priorities between the manpower planning body, the central statistical establishment, the ministries of labour and education (and other ministries involved) and any Cabinet manpower committees.

With regard to the resources and effort put into the manpower surveys, the statistical techniques used were often extremely inadequate. This is particularly true of the sampling techniques, even allowing for the fact that the population that was to form the basis of the sample was typically unknown. None of the surveys to our knowledge provided any estimates of the statistical margins of error implied by the sampling fractions it used. Indeed, the sampling methods used were generally extremely casual and unscientific rather than statistically professional. Similarly, the processes used for grossing-up the data were weak, particularly in the private sector. This lack of rigour in the collection of basic statistical data was extremely unfortunate given the time and effort spent on the surveys.

It is true, of course, that the number of skilled and educated persons employed at all levels in most of the countries surveyed was really quite small, and to some extent this accounted for the casual statistical techniques employed. The impression was easily obtained that, given so few people, a complete listing of individuals was possible and satisfactory. In fact, the limited numbers involved should have made the problem of surveying easier, but they hardly justified the casual approach usually adopted.

III. Projecting manpower supply and demand

Theoretical issues

As mentioned earlier, a major purpose of most of the manpower surveys was to project the demand for skilled and educated manpower. In those cases where the target date of the projections has been passed and where data are available on the situation at that date, it is possible to compare the projected situation with the outcome and so to evaluate the original projections. Unfortunately only one such case exists so far in Africa, that of Tanzania, where the 1964-65 five-year projections can be compared with the actual situation in 1968-69 as revealed by the data given in the 1968-69 manpower survey.[1] In all other cases the period of the projections has yet to run its full course or the target date has been reached but no comparable data are available by which to judge the accuracy of the original projections.

Because of this, only an indirect evaluation can be made by considering *(a)* the methodology used for the projections, and *(b)* the accuracy and basis of the key parameters and variables assumed in the projections. Even if direct comparisons were possible, it would still be necessary to adopt the above approach in order to investigate the reasons for a projection's accuracy or inaccuracy and to improve projection methodology in the future.

It is only possible to evaluate the methodology used for projections by reference to some general system which specifies the determinants of the future demand for skilled and educated manpower, preferably with a listing of each determinant in order of its importance. This is a difficult task, particularly because of the weaknesses of the social sciences when it comes to appreciating the relations between education, skilled manpower

---

[1] Government of Tanzania: *Tanzania Second Five-year Plan for Economic and Social Development, 1 July 1969-30 June 1974* (Dar es Salaam, Government Printer, 1969); Vol. IV: *Survey of the high- and middle-level manpower requirements and resources.*

and development. Indeed the particular area of manpower forecasts and educational planning is unusually subject to controversial views.

Almost all of the manpower plans related their projections to growth and structural change in the economy, but with more emphasis on growth. Methodologically they assumed that manpower was an essential input for production and calculated what level of skilled manpower was thus required to make possible a projected increase in output. Sometimes these assumptions were explicit, sometimes implicit, in projections built up from estimates by employers or by government departments of their future demand.

In general two main criticisms can be raised to this approach. In the first place, by concentrating solely on the economic demand for skilled and educated manpower for the skilled jobs that have to be performed at a specified level of production, it ignores the additional manpower involved in the actual process of reaching that level or structure of production (not to speak of that required to man the investment goods industries or for regular administration). Second, the simple production approach almost entirely neglects the wider effects of higher education on, for example, family structure, student attitudes (unrest), fertility and population growth, job aspirations, work attitudes, income distribution, etc.—all of which may in turn have repercussions on the development of the economy. In principle, the only justification for neglecting these wider economic and social relationships would be that their impact was secondary compared with the direct impact of skilled and educated manpower at the level of production. But there is scarcely a manpower report and few research projects which have paid even passing attention to these possible broader effects, let alone attempted to investigate them.[1]

It is important at this point to distinguish " needs " from " demand ". Needs are defined in terms of the requirements for meeting certain objectives, economic, social or whatever. Demand refers to effective market demand in terms of willingness and capacity to hire and employ. Many needs are never supported by the economic and other resources that would enable them to be met. This is not an argument for necessarily accepting market valuations, but a reminder that, in order to achieve objectives, needs must be translated into demand.

It is possible to set out the projection problem in tabular form, and this is how it appears in many of the African manpower plans. In this case the table in question takes the form of a typical statistical layout summarising the base year manpower situation in a particular country. The table as a whole shows the numbers of skilled and educated persons (or posts for such persons if vacancies are included) in employment in the country, cross-classified by occupation and level of education (actual or normally required). It also includes for the base year some basic

[1] Nor have rate-of-return studies been significantly better in this regard.

DIAGRAM 1. DEMAND AND SUPPLY SCHEDULES FOR SKILLED AND EDUCATED MANPOWER AT TWO PERIODS *(hypothetical)*

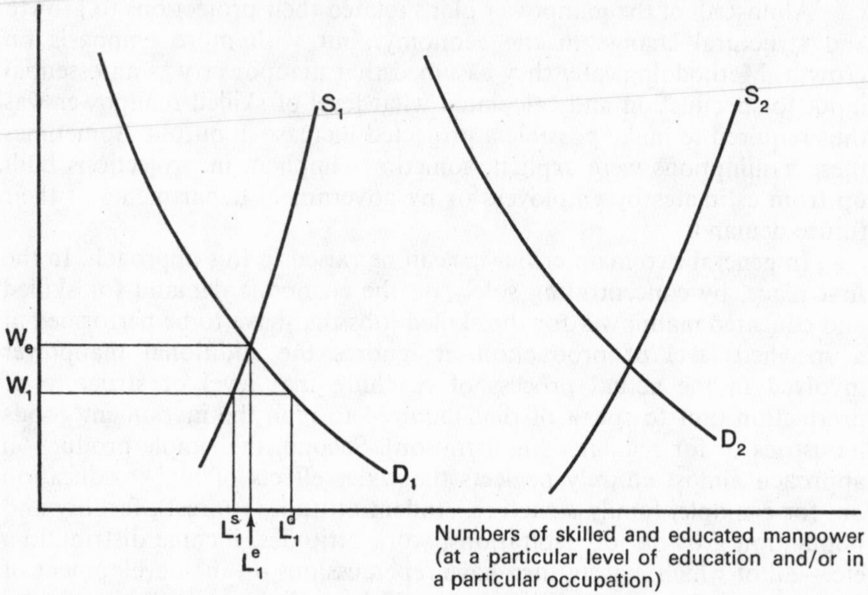

Note: subscripts 1 and 2 refer to the respective time periods.

indicators of economic output, shown—typically—as GDP. In a few of the African manpower plans the classification of base year manpower and economic indicators are available separately by economic sector, but this is the exception rather than the rule.

The problem then is to produce a second similar table showing the manpower demand at a future target date (or dates), broken down to a level of detail comparable with (though probably more aggregated than) the first table. This constitutes a conditional projection, calculated as a necessary condition for achieving some specified objectives or projected change in the level of GDP or other economic indicators (particularly for the government sector).

The projection problem may also be illustrated graphically, as in diagram 1. This shows the short-run demand and supply curves for a particular category of educated manpower—say, for all graduates or all graduate engineers—at the initial point of time, t_1, and at a future time, t_2. The horizontal axis measures the quantity of the particular category of manpower under investigation; the vertical axis indicates the wage rate, either per hour worked or per person employed. If there are substantial vacancies, the base period position is likely to be as shown in the diagram, with the actual quantity of manpower in demand being L_1^d and the quantity employed L_1^s.[1]

The process of making a projection of demand at a future date (say, time period t_2) involves projecting—on various assumptions related to the growth of output and to changes in the structure of production as well as, in principle, in institutions, technology, the use of capital, unskilled labour, etc.—(i) the outward shift in the demand curve, from D_1 to D_2, and (ii) the point on this demand curve where the future short-run supply curve should ideally intersect it.

This presentation of the projection problem is simply the graphical counterpart of the arithmetical presentation that can be made in tabular form, except that variations due to changes in the level of wages can now be shown. But in whatever form the projection problem is presented, it involves in one way or another the key steps and assumptions set out in table II.

Each of the points enumerated in table II will now be taken up, both to describe how they were dealt with in the different manpower surveys and to see whether this mode of treatment is likely to have introduced any biases in the projections made.

Demand projections

ADJUSTMENTS TO CORRECT FOR SUB-OPTIMALITY IN BASE YEAR EMPLOYMENT

All the manpower surveys that were studied used actual or estimated data on the existing level of employment of skilled and educated manpower as a base for their projections. As is indicated in appendix II, this base was usually broken down by occupation, often by actual or required level of education, and sometimes in addition by economic sector. In some of the surveys [2] the base was normally the occupational distribution of the labour force divided into four categories (A, B, C and D [3]) corresponding to the level of education required for entry into the occupations concerned; but it is not always clear how the required levels of education were estimated—whether by the actual qualifications of persons in these occupations, employers' current minimum recruitment standards, or some ideal entry standard at which the country should aim.

The manpower surveys for the French-speaking African countries generally followed a different classification system for skilled and educated manpower, based on a few very broad occupational categories

[1] There are many reasons why wages do not adjust to bring market supply and demand into balance and eliminate vacancies, and they are well documented in the literature on African labour markets.

[2] These included Kenya (1965), Mauritius (1969), the Sudan (1967), and Tanzania (1965 and 1969).

[3] See table I, note 1.

TABLE II. KEY STEPS AND ASSUMPTIONS IN MACRO-PROJECTIONS OF THE DEMAND FOR AND SUPPLY OF SKILLED AND EDUCATED MANPOWER

1. *Demand projections*
   - 1.1 Establish base year data on employment of skilled and educated manpower (including an evaluation of reliability and coverage).
   - 1.2 Make adjustments to correct for sub-optimality in base year employment.
     - 1.2.1 Assess the relevance of vacancies (or over-manning).
     - 1.2.2 Assess the relevance of structural imbalances (e.g. shortage of middle-level in relation to high-level manpower).
     - 1.2.3 Assess the relevance of qualitative weaknesses in education, training or job experience.
   - 1.3 Project growth in demand.
     - 1.3.1 Evaluate growth and structural change in the economy.
     - 1.3.2 Evaluate assumed elasticity of growth of demand with respect to changes in output and structural change.
     - 1.3.3 Evaluate changes in wage levels of educated manpower.
     - 1.3.4 Evaluate assumed demand elasticity with respect to changes in wages.

2. *Supply projections*
   - 2.1 Estimate base year data on employment of skilled and educated manpower.
   - 2.2 Estimate gross additions from education, training, upgrading on the job, etc.
   - 2.3 Estimate wastage from death and migration (possibly also from retirement).
   - 2.4 Estimate labour force participation rates.
   - 2.5 Adjust for assumed changes in hours and intensity of work.
   - 2.6 Estimate supply of non-citizens (or target proportions of requirements to be met by citizen manpower).

3. *Balance, costs and sensitivity*
   - 3.1 Adjust supply and demand to achieve balance of stocks in target year (i.e. balance of total quantity in demand and supply at target date).
   - 3.2 Adjust supply and demand to achieve flow balance (i.e. balance of annual net additions to demand and supply at target dates).
   - 3.3 Minimise costs of implied education and training programme.
   - 3.4 Apply sensitivity analysis showing sensitivity of policy conclusions to variations in key assumptions.

each identified with a unique level of required qualification. For example, the highest-level categories were management (*personnel de direction, cadres supérieurs*) and administrators and technicians (*cadres et techniciens*), requiring thirteen and eleven years of education respectively. The rest of the labour force was divided into a further six or so categories. The disadvantage of this approach is that it fails to provide the occupational detail needed to assess the most appropriate type of education at each level. Moreover, in the absence of such occupational detail there is hardly any evidence on which to judge the reliability of even the estimated breakdown of the labour force by level of education.

A much better procedure is that followed in the Zambian manpower survey, in which data on the current labour force were collected and tabulated both by occupation (according to ISCO categories [1]) and level of education actually attained. Moreover, data on the level of education normally required for each post were also collected, enabling a comparison to be made between the actual and desired levels of qualification in the base year.

With a few exceptions, most of the African manpower plans projected demand by some simple expansion of the existing number of posts in each sector or in the whole economy, making no allowance for changes in the occupational or educational structure, at least as regards the skilled and educated members of the labour force. The two major exceptions were the surveys for Zambia (1966) and Uganda (1967). In the Zambian manpower survey projections were based on the required minimum level of education of each post as estimated by the employers, rather than on the actual levels of education in the base year. This in effect allowed for a modest amount of upgrading of qualifications over the projection period.[2]

The Uganda manpower survey explicitly planned for a change in the structure of different levels of jobs within each occupation, envisaging that during the fifteen years covered by the projection there would be increases of 30 and 45 per cent respectively in the proportion of persons in posts at the middle and lower skill levels relative to the number of those in posts at the highest skill level.[3] This change was in line with the balance of current opinion, which at that time identified the largest relative shortages as being in middle-level occupations.

TREATMENT OF VACANCIES

A general problem for all manpower surveys has been whether to include or exclude existing vacancies in establishing the base line for projections. When vacancies have been included, the main argument used is that the sum of existing employment and vacancies equals the total labour force which employers evidently consider optimal in the current situation. This assumes that vacancies have been strictly defined, usually

---

[1] ILO: *International Standard Classification of Occupations* (Geneva, 1959).

[2] For non-Africans actual education was normally distributed around required education. For Africans in the survey actual education was normally distributed but with a mean somewhat below required education.

[3] In the Uganda survey it was assumed that the rate of substitution between middle- and high-level workers would be in proportion to their relative wages at the base year. For a detailed evaluation of the Uganda method see Emil Rado: " Manpower planning in East Africa ", in *Journal of Development Studies*, 1967.

by employers' estimates of the current additional numbers they would employ at going wage rates in each occupation and at each skill level, provided that potential recruits existed. The main argument against including vacancies is that the existing level of production has evidently been achieved with the existing employed labour force, despite the vacancies. Moreover, particularly in the public sector, the number of vacancies after independence often reached staggering proportions, to an extent where it seems difficult to believe that the governments would really have been prepared to fill all vacant posts even if sufficient qualified applicants had been available.[1]

As diagram 1 makes clear, economic theory would suggest that the " optimal " base line position lies somewhere between the extremes of including or excluding all vacancies. In the diagram the optimal quantity of skilled and educated manpower, at point L_1^e, lies between points L_1^s and L_1^d, its exact distance between the two depending on the relative elasticities of the demand and supply curves. This suggests that a better procedure for the treatment of vacancies in manpower surveys would be to estimate the base line position somewhere between the extremes, perhaps as a rough assumption at the midway point.[2]

In summary, it seems likely that the African manpower surveys in general may somewhat have underestimated the base line by excluding vacancies. The few surveys that included vacancies are likely to have overestimated the base line. More significant, but a point on which evidence for evaluation is lacking, is the failure of almost all the surveys to deal with any change in the structure of the present labour force by accepting the existing structure as an adequate base line. In the absence of evidence it is difficult to see whether this led to future needs being underestimated or overestimated.

GROWTH OF DEMAND

At a minimum, four crucial steps are involved in projecting the growth in the number of skilled and educated persons needed in the labour force at some future date. One needs an evaluation of the rate of economic growth and change in economic structure, of the assumed or implied elasticity linking outward shifts in the demand curve to economic growth and structural change, of the assumed elasticity of the

[1] The increase in established posts arises in part from competitive bargaining among ministries at the time of preparing annual changes in establishments, often as part of the budgetary process. Since ministries of finance realised there was little likelihood of filling many of the new posts during the manpower shortages of the 1960s, they often reacted leniently to inflated claims, achieving a financial balance by subtracting from the over-all total of estimated salaries an item for unfilled posts. Thus estimates of vacancies in the public sector are often less reliable than those for the private sector. It is for this reason that a number of the manpower plans excluded entirely vacancies in the public sector.

[2] This of course would imply that the elasticities (with respect to changes in wages) of the demand for and supply of educated manpower are equal—in fact, it seems likely that the former is greater.

future demand curve with respect to changes in wages, and of future wage changes.

This is of course a highly aggregated account of the process and ideally what is required is a much more disaggregated approach, giving greater emphasis to the particular manpower needs of particular sectors, sub-sectors or even particular activities—say education, or the work of individual ministries or even of a line of production in a particular major industry. A number of the African manpower plans in fact adopted a somewhat more disaggregated approach in making short-run projections; but for the longer term, most of the plans, for better or for worse, followed techniques that are highly aggregative in their approach. To evaluate their methodology it is necessary to consider step by step the assumptions they made. Moreover, it should be borne in mind that for long-term projections disaggregation soon becomes statistically impossible because of a lack both of the data required for this purpose and of knowledge of the relationships involved in the long run. Finally, work in other countries suggests that the over-all growth rate and the elasticity of demand for skilled manpower with respect to growth are quantitatively the most important factors in long-run manpower projections, being considerably more significant than changes in economic structure.[1] There is thus an appropriate basis for contrasting the assumptions made.

Nevertheless, either for making or for evaluating long-run projections, completely aggregative projection methods have serious deficiencies. Some disaggregation by main sectors is essential in order to pinpoint at least the broader aspects of structural change. Moreover, within key sectors—education, health and government services being notable examples—it is essential to make sub-sectoral projections that can take more account of sectoral programmes and detail than is possible in an aggregative projection.[2] It is lack of data alone that explains why, in the evaluation which follows, we have concerned ourselves solely with total GDP rather than sectoral disaggregation.

ECONOMIC GROWTH

Table III[3] compares the rates of economic growth explicitly or implicitly assumed in eighteen of the African manpower surveys with the

[1] See R. G. Hollister: *A technical evaluation of the Mediterranean Regional Project* (Paris, OECD, 1966).

[2] The 1966 Zambian manpower survey not only made projections of government needs at a disaggregated level but also related long-run requirements to certain physical indications of expansion rather than to GDP (which for employment projections in the government sector is largely tautological). The physical indicators included population, urban population, government employment and employment or output of various sectors or government departments.

[3] Where the projection period has yet to be completed, the comparisons in table III are based on the actual and estimated rates of growth over the first few years of the period concerned. We have excluded plans where data on achieved growth are available for less than half of the projection period.

TABLE III. ASSUMED GDP GROWTH RATES IN MANPOWER SURVEYS COMPARED WITH OBSERVED RATES UP TO 1969

Country	Projection period	Average annual increase in GDP at constant prices (%)	
		Assumed	Observed up to 1969
Botswana	1967-72	5.2	3.0
Egypt	1965-70	7.2	1.5
Ghana	1960-65	5.0	2.6
	1963-70	5.5	1.5
Ivory Coast	1963-70	7.2	7.5
Kenya	1961-66	1.9	7.0
	1964-70	5.7	6.1
Nigeria	1960-70	4.0	1.3
	1963-70	4.0	−0.2
Rhodesia	1961-70	4.1	4.5
Sudan	1967/68-71/72	6.1	11.1
Tanzania	1961-66	1.9	5.7
	1962-67	5.0	5.5
	1964-69	8.5	5.2
Uganda	1961-66	1.9	5.7
	1967-71	6.3	6.5
Zambia	1961-70	4.2	7.8
	1965/66-70	11.0	6.6

Source: calculated from the manpower surveys. Observed GDP, from unpublished Economic Commission for Africa (ECA) national accounts data.

rates actually achieved. In most cases the growth rates assumed were those projected in national development plans, not a separate projection. In this respect the manpower demand forecasts were essentially tied to the achievement of national plan targets.

Although there is an obvious logic in tackling the problem in this way, it must be recognised that the procedure is methodologically justifiable only in situations where the manpower constraint is a relatively minor one (and thus likely to have only minor repercussions on the achievement of the over-all target) or where the manpower projection is merely the first round in a larger iterative calculation that takes account of the effect of projected shortfalls in manpower on the achievement of the original GDP projection.

A more serious question must be raised at this point concerning the reliability of the data on growth rates, both projected and actual. Apart from all the usual limitations, the African projections, during the period studied, suffered from particular weaknesses. They were nearly all among the first attempts at long-run projections and were prepared by a small, hard-pressed and often inexperienced planning staff. The data base was almost always seriously deficient in several respects: only limited data on past trends were available, especially in the case of series at constant prices. Without going into detail it may be stated that allowance must be made for large margins of error in all the GDP projections.

Unfortunately, the above-mentioned problems affect almost equally the data on actual GDP growth rates. There is a spurious precision in the national accounts of most African countries that makes it difficult to consider the statistics on growth rates at constant prices as much more than an order of magnitude.[1]

With these qualifications in mind, let us compare the rates of growth under the manpower projections with the outcome.

A majority (some 60 per cent) of the surveys appear to have been pessimistic about future rates of economic growth, though the median survey underestimated by only about 5 per cent. But the important feature of table III is the large discrepancy between actual and projected growth rates in most cases. The less optimistic manpower surveys, as indicated by the lower quartile, underestimated growth rates by as much as 50 per cent while the more optimistic ones overestimated by as much as 70 per cent. These are considerable errors, affecting one of the most sensitive assumptions of the whole projection. Allowing for statistical errors in the data increases the extent of the possible divergence between forecasts and reality.

SHIFT OF THE DEMAND CURVE WITH RESPECT TO GROWTH RATES

Table IV shows the elasticities implicitly or explicitly assumed for the growth of different levels of educated manpower in relation to the growth of output. These elasticities can be somewhat misleading, since they are calculated according to aggregated rates of economic growth and neglect structural change, even though some of the surveys calculated manpower requirements on a sectoral basis. In general it can be seen from the table that most of the surveys assumed that skilled manpower requirements, at least for the top three educational categories, would develop at a considerably faster rate than the projected rate of economic growth. This is true whether teachers are included or excluded for purposes of the comparison. Moreover, the upper quartile survey assumes an elasticity which is almost twice the rate of growth of output.

To assess the realism of these elasticities, factual information is needed on the relationship between economic growth and the expansion of high-level employment. Even if such information were available, considerable conceptual problems would be involved in isolating and interpreting the relationship. But unfortunately, as yet, the only informa-

[1] See B. Van Arkadie and C. Frank: *National accounting and economic planning* (Oxford University Press) for a good description of the strengths and weaknesses of African national accounts statistics.

TABLE IV. ASSUMED ELASTICITIES OF THE EXPANSION OF SEMP WITH RESPECT TO GDP GROWTH [1]

Surveys (ranked by size of elasticities)	Educational category [2] A	B	C	D	Total
Highest	2.34	3.24	1.57	2.07	2.59
Upper quartile	1.92	2.54	1.19	1.36	1.99
Median	1.25	1.74	1.09	0.97	1.22
Lower quartile	1.00	1.09	1.02	0.83	1.02
Lowest	0.59	0.81	0.74	0.20	0.46
Number of observations	(22)	(22)	(16)	(13)	(22)

[1] The object of this table is to contrast the assumptions made in different plans and not in different projections within the same plan. Thus mean assumptions were used in all cases. The following points should be noted:

(a) where projections were given for both a short and a longer period, the elasticity assumptions for the latter were used (five plans);

(b) where projections were given on the basis of two different assumptions, i.e. for the growth of SEMP with respect to a given growth rate of GDP or vice versa, the means of the two sets of elasticities were used (four plans);

(c) the 1962 surveys for Kenya, Tanzania and Uganda gave projections for different pairs of assumed growth rates for two consecutive time periods. The mean assumptions for the first time period, 1961-66, for each of the countries were used in the above table;

(d) in all cases vacancies were excluded from the base year;

(e) in most cases teachers were excluded, though this was not possible for four of the surveys.

[2] See table I, note 1.

Source: calculated from the manpower surveys.

tion available for any reasonable number of countries concerns the present cross-sectional relationship between stocks of educated manpower and the level of national output per head. Although this relationship has been investigated and yielded statistically significant results, it must be emphasised that it reflects the existing situation and does not constitute a time series relationship.

Table V summarises the results of regressions using cross-sectional data produced by two of the most comprehensive international studies that have been made.[1] Too much should not be made of the similarity of the results, since they are largely, though not entirely, based on the same data. In general Layard and Saigal have taken the most trouble to standardise the data used for their regressions, while the OECD data cover the largest number of countries, in several cases as many as forty-four, of which over half are developing countries.

The general picture that emerges from the cross-sectional regression studies is that elasticities of educated manpower in employment and

[1] P. R. G. Layard and J. C. Saigal: "Educational and occupational characteristics of manpower: an international comparison", in *British Journal of Industrial Relations*, Vol. IV, No. 2, July 1966, pp. 222-266; OECD: *Occupational and educational structures of the labour force and levels of economic development* (Paris, 1970).

TABLE V. ELASTICITIES IMPLIED BY REGRESSIONS USING CROSS-SECTIONAL DATA ON EDUCATED MANPOWER IN EMPLOYMENT AND GDP IN VARIOUS COUNTRIES

Educational level	High growth [a]	Low growth [b]	No. of countries covered	R^2
		OECD regressions		
Degree level or above	0.84	0.93	25	0.42 [c]
Completed secondary schooling or above	0.89	0.94	21	0.56 [c]
Matriculation level or above	0.87	0.94	17	0.71 [c]
Completed middle schooling or above	.	.	.	.
		Layard and Saigal regressions		
Degree level or above	0.96	0.93	15	0.66 [d]
Completed secondary schooling or above	0.97	0.94	21	0.47 [d]
Matriculation level or above	1.03	1.05	19	0.64 [d]
Completed middle schooling or above	0.92	0.85	16	0.35 [d]

[a] Assumes GDP grows at the rate of 8 per cent and employment at the rate of 5 per cent per year.

[b] Assumes GDP grows at the rate of 3 per cent and employment at the rate of 1 per cent per year.

[c] Significant at 5 per cent level.

[d] Significant at 1 per cent level.

Source: OECD: *Occupational and educational structures of the labour force . . .*, op. cit.; Layard and Saigal, op. cit. These sources should be referred to for definitions, details and qualifications.

GDP tend to range around 0.9 to 1, rather than higher or lower. Of course very considerable assumptions are involved if these values are used as an indication of a future time series relationship within any particular country. The assumptions are somewhat reduced if one uses the range to indicate an order of magnitude of the maximum likely elasticity.[1] In this case estimated maximum " true elasticity " of no more than unity suggests that most of the manpower surveys (i.e. all those

[1] This point is both important and controversial, and as such deserves some elaboration. Most projections depend on the assumption that certain parameters or relationships observed in the past or at present will continue unchanged in the future. This assumption is also involved when using cross-sectional relationships of skilled and educated manpower as a basis for estimating future requirements. But, in addition, three further difficulties arise:

(1) The observed cross-sectional relationships show the result of the interaction between the supply of and demand for skilled and educated manpower in a variety of countries at different levels of income per head. A serious identification problem occurs when these data are used to determine demand relationships. Indeed, the above-mentioned OECD study concluded that the data were dominated by supply effects rather than by demand effects.

(Footnote continued overleaf)

TABLE VI. SEMP EXPANSION ELASTICITIES WITH RESPECT TO ACTUAL GROWTH RATES [1]

Surveys (ranked by size of elasticities)	Educational categories [2]				Total
	A	B	C	D	
Upper quartile	1.97	2.28	2.46	1.98	1.95
Median	1.32	1.68	1.51	1.63	1.37
Lower quartile	0.81	0.94	0.80	1.06	0.97
Number of observations	(18)	(18)	(13)	(11)	(13)

[1] These are in fact the SEMP expansion elasticities from table IV multiplied by the assumed growth rates and divided by actual growth rates.
See table IV, note 1, points *(a)* to *(e)*. However, as regards point *(a)*, for the above table short period projections (ten years) were used, since the expiry date of the longer projections is too recent for reliable comparisons with " actual " growth rates to be made. As regards points *(b)* and *(c)*, for the above table the findings of the surveys relating to Uganda (1965), Kenya (1969) and Tanzania (1969) were excluded. In the first of these no short period projections were made, while for the others growth rate statistics are not yet available. These factors account for the differences in the number of observations indicated in the two tables.
[2] See table I, note 1.
Sources: calculated from the manpower surveys and unpublished ECA national accounts data.

above the lower quartile as shown in table IV) overestimated the increase in the employment of educated manpower in relation to economic growth by a margin which in most instances more than offset their underestimates of the rate of economic growth itself.

This can be clearly seen in table VI, which summarises the effect of combining the elasticity and growth rate assumptions for eighteen plans. The median survey, for each of the categories of educated manpower, considerably overestimated the rate at which employment at these educational levels should increase. And the more *pessimistic* surveys, as indicated by the upper quartile, overestimated future skilled manpower requirements by a factor in excess of 100 per cent.

(2) Since the relationships are only between skilled manpower and output, the effects of technology, capital and other factors are ignored. In this respect the same drawbacks affect the use of cross-sectional relationships of SEMP for projecting manpower requirements and of capital output ratios for projecting capital requirements in macro-planning.
(3) In spite of the fact that R^2 is shown as being comparatively high in the relationships, there is a considerable dispersion of observations around the regression line. Thus if a country starts below the line, should one project its requirements so that the regression line is reached in the future or simply so that they increase parallel with the regression line? The latter is the assumption implied by using the elasticity given by the slope of the regression rather than the regression line itself as a basis for future estimates.

These are serious problems and they must be taken into account if one is to make estimates of how the skilled manpower demand curves shift over time. Obviously much more work is required in this field. But in the meantime the elasticity implied by past regression studies is the best aggregative estimate we have of the *maximum* rate of outward shift of demand curves.

CHANGES IN WAGES

None of the African manpower surveys assessed in quantitative terms the effects of changes in the future structure of wages on the demand for educated manpower. In general the implicit assumption appears to have been either that real wages (relative to other production costs) would not change or that the demand for skilled manpower would not be affected by the level of wages—the latter assumption being based too much, one suspects, on experience in manufacturing. In fact the elasticity of labour demand with respect to wages is likely to be significantly different from zero. Unfortunately, no adequate evidence is available on this point, but as an order of magnitude, it would seem that the elasticity could be as high as 0.6 to 0.8 in many countries [1], primarily because the major proportion of educated manpower is employed in the government, education and services sectors, where the number of persons that the government can afford to employ is inversely related to the level of wages.

The effect of assuming non-zero elasticity of demand with respect to wages will depend, of course, on the amount by which wage levels change. For reasons made clear at the end of this article, which projects a general surplus in the supply of educated persons relative to demand at present wage levels, one can expect an increasing downward pressure on the remuneration structure of more educated persons in Africa. This is likely to be offset by increasing upward pressures related to the international market and the skilled labour market in developed countries. If the downward pressures win out, as on balance seems probable for most occupations, demand will be further increased, the extent depending on the elasticity and the size of the fall in wages. In other words, over the long run, one can expect the demand for and the supply of skilled manpower to move more nearly into balance by some adjustment of the wage structure. Although in our opinion there are definite limits to the speed at which this can happen and to the extent to which it can totally clear the market, we have little doubt that some adjustment will take place.

Some indication of the extent to which real wages of the educated groups might fall is given in table VII. This shows average earnings by level of education in Uganda and India, both in absolute terms and as a multiple of income per head. Although comparisons between countries involve a number of difficulties, the large margin by which Indian wages

[1] This estimate is a weighted average of sectoral estimates of the elasticity of the demand for skilled and educated manpower with respect to changes in wages within each of the four sectors shown in appendix III. The assumptions were that the elasticity of demand with respect to wages was 1.0 in education, 0.9 in the public sector, 0.1 in manufacturing and 0.5 in services. The weighted average for the total elasticity of demand will naturally vary according to the proportion of skilled manpower employed in each sector, but 0.6 to 0.8 is the main range implied by the above figures.

TABLE VII. AVERAGE YEARLY SALARIES BY LEVEL OF EDUCATION IN UGANDA AND INDIA
(£)

Educational level	Uganda (1965)	India (1960-61)
Junior secondary/middle	209	131
School certificate/secondary	556	185
Higher certificate/Indian graduate	852	311
Ugandan graduate	1 373	.
Income per head	28	25
Salaries as multiples of income per head		
Junior secondary/middle	7.3	5.4
School certificate/secondary	20.0	7.7
Higher certificate/Indian graduate	30.4	12.4
Ugandan graduate	49.0	

Notes: *(a)* the data refer to average earnings over all age groups;
(b) the data for Uganda refer to civil service earnings and those for India to average urban earnings;
(c) Indian earnings are converted from Rs to £s at the 1961 exchange rate;
(d) under educational level, that for Uganda is shown first, followed by the roughly comparable Indian level.

Sources: (i) Uganda: J. B. Knight: "The determination of wages and salaries in Uganda", in Oxford University Institute of Economics and Statistics: *Bulletin*, Vol. 29, No. 3, Aug. 1967, pp. 233-264.
(ii) India: Mark Blaug, Richard Layard and Maureen Woodhall: *The causes of graduate unemployment in India* (Allen Lane, Penguin Press, 1969), table 7.1.

in the 1960s were below Ugandan wages for any level of education is particularly striking.

Average earnings for graduates in India during the 1950s were not constant but fell by 2 to 3 per cent per annum in real terms. This drop was caused not so much by a reduction in the money earnings of persons already in employment as by the effects of inflation in reducing the real value of wages fixed in money terms and by surpluses of educated manpower in the labour market forcing newcomers to accept jobs below the level of those for which they were formally qualified.

If the Indian experience is accepted as representing the upper limit of the likely reduction in real wages and no change as representing the lower limit, we may calculate the variation that this would imply in the estimates of future demand: a zero change in real wages corresponds to the figures already given in table V; a reduction of up to 3 per cent per annum in real wages could increase future demand each year by around 2 per cent in total.

With this final step, we are now in a position to summarise the combined effect of the four crucial assumptions—the growth of output, the elasticity of the demand for manpower in relation to output growth, the change in real wages, and the elasticity linking the demand for skilled manpower to changes in their wages. The results for the eighteen African manpower plans for which there were sufficient data are summarised in table VIII.

Just under a quarter of the projections were within a range of 10 per cent of those based on more realistic assumptions—though often achieving comparative reliability by means of a series of compensating errors rather than accurate estimates at each stage of the calculations. Of the remaining three-quarters, almost all were within a range of 50 per cent of the projections based on more realistic assumptions, though slightly overestimating future demand rather than underestimating it.[1] This result is also largely dependent on real wages falling fairly rapidly. If they do not, the extent of overestimate would turn out to be considerably greater.

Supply projections

We turn now to the six steps involved in making projections of the supply of skilled and educated manpower. Since the issues here were perhaps better understood and raised fewer methodological problems, our treatment of them will be briefer than in the case of the demand projections. But we would stress that from a policy point of view accuracy is no less important for supply projections than it is for demand projections.

ESTIMATING THE SIZE AND COMPOSITION OF BASE YEAR STOCK OF EDUCATED MANPOWER

In effect, the estimates of base year supply in all the projections were, except as regards vacancies, identical with those of base year demand, each relying on the information obtained from the surveys of high-level manpower. We have already expressed certain criticisms concerning the basic data.[2] These criticisms apply equally to the data used for estimating base year supply and to those used for estimating base year demand. In particular, lack of information about actual educational attainments precluded any estimate of the number of people trained for jobs they were not doing, which might have shown a " surplus " of manpower in some sectors at current wage rates. Given the effort and resources devoted to collecting the basic information, it is

[1] This tendency is more marked among the later plans than among the earlier ones.
[2] See above pp. 214-216.

TABLE VIII. ESTIMATED RANGE OF ACCURACY OF EIGHTEEN AFRICAN MANPOWER PROJECTIONS

Country	Year of survey	Projection dates	Accuracy of projected demand for SEMP [1]	
			Category A [2]	All categories [2]
Zambia	1964	1961-70	0.6-0.8	0.5-0.7
Kenya	1965	1964-70	0.7-0.9	0.6-0.8
Rhodesia	1964	1961-70	0.6-0.9	0.6-0.9
Sudan	1967	1967/68-71/72	1.0-1.2	0.7-0.8
Kenya	1962	1961-66	0.5-0.7	0.7-0.9
Tanzania	1962	1961-66	0.6-0.8	0.8-1.0
Uganda	1962	1961-66	0.6-0.8	0.8-1.0
Tanzania	1963	1962-67	0.9-1.2	0.9-1.2
Egypt	1966	1965-70	2.7-7.0	1.0-2.5
Botswana	1967	1967-72	1.0-1.7	1.1-2.0
Uganda	1967	1967-71	1.2-1.4	1.2-1.5
Tanzania	1965	1964-69	1.5-2.0	1.3-1.9
Ghana	1960	1960-65	1.7-3.2	1.3-2.5
Zambia	1966	1965/66-70	1.1-1.5	1.4-1.9
Ivory Coast	1964	1963-70	1.1-1.4	1.5-2.0
Ghana	1963	1963-70	1.0-2.3	1.5-4.0
Nigeria	1964	1963-70	2.1-∞	2.1-∞
Nigeria	1960	1960-70	2.3-7.0	3.5-8.0

[1] The plan projections of demand are shown as multiples of the estimates based on " more realistic assumptions " given in the text. A multiple of less than 1 implies a plan underestimate and a multiple of more than 1 implies a plan overestimate.

[2] See table I, note 1.

Source: calculated from the manpower surveys.

unfortunate that the sampling techniques, the information gathered, and the classifications used were often so unsatisfactory and fell so far short of what would have been possible.

ESTIMATING ADDITIONS FROM IMMIGRATION, EDUCATION AND TRAINING

This crucial step involved indicating estimated outputs from the school system in relation to the demand for education and skills. In principle, of course, account should have been taken not only of outputs from the educational system but also of those from informal and adult education, from all forms of training and from immigration. In practice, although training was mentioned in many surveys, and a few included some data on it and undertook a quantitative analysis of it, in general the information on it was excluded from the calculations of future supply and, even where included, was not fully incorporated with the main analysis. This was frequently the case also as regards information on persons returning from studies abroad, which was often seriously incomplete.

Perhaps more surprising is the casual and unsophisticated manner in which outputs from the school system were projected. Often only the simplest analysis was undertaken. Usually no allowance was made for repetition within the school system and estimates of outputs were taken largely at their face value. It was the exceptional manpower survey that allowed for changes in rates of progression within (as opposed to between) the main levels of the system. Yet educational expansion during the past decade has brought about considerable changes in this respect and general improvement of continuation rates within the system. By neglecting such improvements, the projected outputs from education often underestimated the likely magnitude of supply.

ESTIMATING WASTAGE DUE TO RETIREMENT, DEATH AND EMIGRATION

In view of the comparative youth of most persons with high-level qualifications in Africa, it is surprising that a number of the manpower surveys estimated wastage rates from base year stock at as much as 4 or 5 per cent per annum. On the face of it these estimates should have seemed implausibly high given that the age profile of the skilled labour force was skewed towards the younger age groups and that the labour force as a whole was growing rapidly. Data compiled in connection with the 1968-69 Tanzanian manpower survey showed that for a sample of high-level manpower in the civil service the rate of wastage from death and retirement over the previous five years had been 1.8 per cent—less than half of 1 per cent per annum.

In the absence of direct evidence, it seems obvious that other manpower surveys should have estimated wastage to be of this order of magnitude. Indeed, the main conclusion to be drawn is that, at least in the short and medium run, wastage due to death and retirement is a comparatively unimportant factor, far outweighed by the margins of error in other more central assumptions.

As regards particular occupation groups, wastage caused by transfer to other occupations (in many cases there was a major shift of teachers from teaching into the civil service or politics) could be quantitatively more serious and of obvious importance. It is not certain, however, that net transfers between occupations should have been incorporated in long-run projections. One could argue that the substantial transfers which occurred were peculiar to the times and that, with a proper adjustment of the incentives structure, large-scale net transfers would be avoided in future, without prejudice to some movement between occupations and industries to allow for individual flexibility.

ESTIMATING THE LABOUR FORCE PARTICIPATION RATE OF THE TOTAL FUTURE STOCK OF SKILLED MANPOWER

This step was ignored by all but a minority of the African manpower surveys.[1] Yet the participation rate of women, and that of men in certain age groups, is usually far less than 100 per cent. By assuming that everyone emerging from the school system would join the active labour force and be employed, most of the African manpower plans considerably overestimated the forthcoming supply of educated manpower. The extent of overestimate depends largely on the age structure and sex composition of the labour force and of the students leaving the educational system. Assuming that a quarter of the students were female, it may have been as much as 15 or 20 per cent over a period of one decade.

This is a suitable moment to draw attention to an alternative and perhaps more accurate method of taking account of wastage and estimating labour force participation. Instead of projecting entry into and retirement from the labour force, it might have been better to have followed the method used in one manpower survey and deal with the matter in two stages. In the first stage the levels of educational attainment of the whole population are projected, allowing for wastage due both to death and migration; in the second stage the labour force participation rates of the total population, grouped in various ways, are estimated. This avoids the difficult problem of estimating retirement separately.

Unfortunately, for projecting stocks of educated manpower in the labour force, it is necessary to know labour force participation rates which are specific with regard to age and education. To the best of our knowledge such information is not yet available for any African country, although more detailed tabulations of census data could provide it in some cases. In the few less developed countries where these data are available, they seem to reveal that age-specific labour force participation rates decline slightly among persons with the lowest and middle levels of education and then rise sharply among those with the highest levels.

ADJUSTMENTS FOR ESTIMATED CHANGES IN HOURS AND INTENSITY OF WORK

In none of the African manpower plans were the calculations of manpower supply adjusted to take account of changes in hours worked or the intensity of work of skilled and educated manpower. Yet it seems difficult to believe that these factors were not potentially and sometimes actually responsible for an increase in the effective supply of skilled man-hours. In many English-speaking countries at the time of independence,

[1] Those for Zambia (1966), Botswana (1969) and Ethiopia (1970).

for instance, the length of the working week was often around 37 hours in the public sector and not much longer in parts of the private sector, in line with the pattern established by the British Colonial Service. Not only were such hours short in comparison with working hours in more developed countries; they were particularly surprising in a situation of extreme shortage of skilled and educated manpower. Since independence, civil service regulations have been adjusted in a number of countries, often so as to increase the standard working week by several hours. In effect this has meant a quantitative increase of around 10 per cent in man-hours worked, a significant increase of flexibility—yet this has been ignored by the manpower planners. As, even today, the formal working week is seldom longer than 42 hours, it seems difficult to believe that the extension of working time would have been more than marginally offset by any fall in output per hour. Moreover, many high-level people work far longer hours than are formally required.

Output per hour raises the more general question of the intensity and productivity of work. Again the manpower plans ignored the effects of changes in this respect. Both casual observation and a number of individual reports and studies suggest that the productivity of skilled labour has in many cases been far lower than it should have been, partly because of the inefficient allocation, use and supervision of skilled manpower and partly because of inadequate incentives. These failings reflect, in turn, the scarcity of qualified personnel who could organise and supervise more effectively the skilled manpower available. Nevertheless, with hindsight, one can see numerous opportunities for such manpower to have been used more productively. These again, therefore, are considerations which manpower planners should attempt to take into account when calculating manpower needs.

LOCALISATION

A crucial factor in estimating total supply is the assumption made concerning the rate of retention of expatriate, non-local manpower over the projection period. This raises the question of localisation policy. Most of the African manpower plans assumed that complete localisation would be achieved by 1980 or possibly 1985. Various intermediate localisation targets were set for intervening dates. Although dealing with localisation in this way meant that it was possible to make simple calculations of the numbers of expatriates remaining in their posts at various dates, it is not certain that this was the best method of approaching or calculating the effects of the policy issues involved. The rate of localisation is not simply an unchangeable policy datum but a policy instrument to be used along with others for achieving the whole range of government objectives. With faster expansion of education and the application of measures to raise labour force participation rates among educated persons or to slow down the expansion of skill-intensive sectors, it could be accelerated or vice versa. It is thus best treated as a policy variable to be considered in the light of what the calculations reveal rather than as a technical element noted at the beginning of the projection period and assumed to remain unchanged throughout.

The same point can be made about a number of other parameters involved in the calculation of the future supply of and demand for educated manpower. The African manpower plans tended to make their projections assuming various values for the key parameters and to deduce that the resulting gap between supply and demand must be closed by expanding the output of the educational system. In principle the gap could be closed by alterations in one or several of the various parameters involved (see table II). From a policy point of view *all* these options should be considered and the necessary adjustments in each weighed in terms of their implications for the full range of government objectives.

Balance, costs and sensitivity

BALANCE OF STOCKS AND FLOW BALANCE

The projections of demand and supply must be brought together through some form of analysis of the levels at which the quantities in supply and in demand at different dates should be balanced. This involves the four steps identified earlier.[1]

The achievement of the first two of these steps (i.e. the adjustment of supply and demand to achieve (i) a balance of stocks in the target year and (ii) a balance of annual net additions to demand and supply at target dates—a " flow " balance) can be illustrated by means of diagram 2, which shows over a period of years the hypothetical growth of the demand for and of the supply of some particular category of skilled and educated manpower.

Thus it can be seen, by reference to the level of supply shown in the diagram, that a balance of future stocks of skilled and educated manpower is achieved at point X, the intersection between the growing supply of citizen manpower, S_LS, and the required demand, DD. Most of the African manpower plans projected for this sort of balance.

Although a balance in terms of stocks will enable a country to achieve its localisation targets at a particular date, diagram 2 makes it clear that a balance in the annual supply and demand increments is also necessary. Otherwise the period of supply deficiency will be followed immediately by a period of excess—and although this seemed a remote possibility when manpower plans were first conceived, it is now a danger even in Africa, in the formal sector. The alternative is to plan for a growth of supply equal to the growth of demand after the target

[1] See table II above.

DIAGRAM 2. GROWTH OF DEMAND FOR AND OF LOCAL SUPPLY OF SKILLED AND EDUCATED MANPOWER, 1965-80 *(hypothetical)*

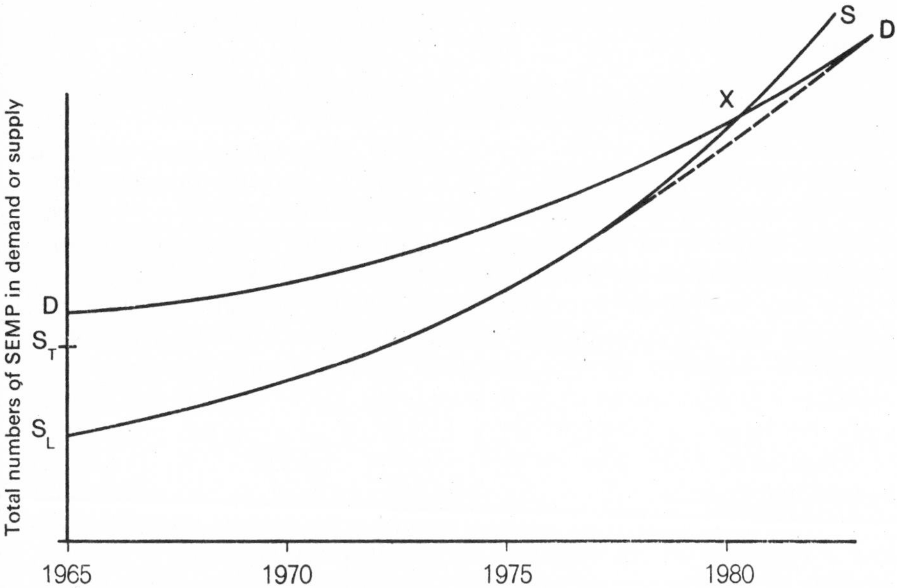

Curve DD = the growth of demand.
Curve S_LS = the growth of local supply.
$0S_L$ = the stock of citizens at the base period.
S_LS_T = the stock of expatriates at the base period.
S_TD = the stock of vacant posts at the base period.

date—equivalent to the achievement of tangency in the supply and demand curves as indicated by the dotted line in diagram 2.

Fundamental as this is to the objectives of manpower planning, it is unfortunately true that only two or three of the African manpower plans used a methodology that provided for achieving this second form of balance. Others were often drafted in such a way as to give the impression that this requirement had been taken into account, but their methodology belied this. Typical was the methodology which divided a fifteen-year planning horizon into three periods of five years, calculating the net increments in demand and supply for each of the periods separately. In principle, if a balance of stocks were achieved in each of the three periods, an approximate flow balance would also be achieved in terms of diagram 2. This would mean achieving a balance of stocks at three points along the DD curve. In fact, however, although calculations were made over three successive periods, most of the plans adopting this methodology achieved a balance between supply and demand only in the final period, differences in the earlier periods being left unresolved. The implication, if stocks are balanced only at the terminal date, is that there is no assurance of any flow balance either at the terminal date or at any other date. Furthermore, these plans ignored all trade-offs with education outside the school system, some of which will be discussed in part V, on training.

MINIMISING THE COSTS OF ACHIEVING A BALANCE

As indicated earlier, in the discussion of methodology, the ideal approach would be for costs to be taken into account simultaneously with the process of achieving a quantitative balance in supply and demand. However, as already indicated, this seems excluded on account of the limitations of the statistics and other information available.

It does not follow that the costs of achieving an increased supply of educated workers have to be entirely neglected (as some critics of manpower planning have suggested). A second-best strategy is to calculate a physical programme of manpower supply based on manpower and other targets and then minimise the cost of achieving this programme of educational expansion. A great deal of evidence shows that most educational systems in Africa are operating at a level of costs which is far above what is feasible and which could be reduced without substantial loss in efficiency and reduction in output. It follows, therefore, that cost minimising is an important and possible part of a manpower plan.

What cost minimising would involve is beyond the scope of the present article. It may, however, be worth mentioning areas which seem to offer immediate scope for major reductions in cost.

Adjustment of the pupil-teacher ratio. At present wide variations in the pupil-teacher ratio exist between different schools, different regions and different countries. A change to a more economic class size in schools with excessively low pupil-teacher ratios and small classes could bring considerable savings in cost. And such changes could be made without affecting at all the largest classes (25 per cent as of now).

Changes in the salary structure of teachers. Without doubt the increases in money and real average earnings of teachers have been the primary cause of the increases in the per pupil cost of education at all levels.[1] At least half of the 15 per cent increase per year in expenditure on education in nine countries of Africa from 1955 to 1965 can be attributed to increases in the average teacher's salary. Part of these increases, perhaps about one-quarter, are the result of upgrading and are a direct consequence of teachers' salaries so often being linked to their educational qualifications rather than to their level of responsibility or work performance. In view of this, all attempts to increase the quality of

[1] The conclusions and data in this paragraph summarise the argument in an earlier paper. See Richard Jolly: " Costs and comparisons in African education: some implications of recent trends ", in idem (ed.): *Education in Africa; research and action* (Nairobi, East African Publishing House, 1969).

education by formal upgrading courses lead to higher salaries and to education becoming ever more expensive. Yet in a situation where scarcity of educated manpower is rapidly giving way to unemployment of such manpower (particularly at the middle levels and even now looming on the horizon for the higher levels) there is no economic case for tying salaries to qualifications, either on grounds of justice or by way of an incentive. As the figures in appendix III suggest, differentials by level of education in Africa (particularly English-speaking Africa) far exceed those in other continents. The reduction of these differentials is a necessary condition for avoiding a growing surplus of unemployed educated manpower. Breaking the link between the formal qualifications and salary level of teachers would thus offer general advantages in addition to being a major step towards reducing the costs of education, and would simultaneously permit an improvement in quality. This is not to suggest that changes in the methods of fixing salaries and in salary levels should apply only to teachers. It would be fairer, more economically sound and probably more acceptable, if the policy were applied to all skilled and educated manpower.

Reducing capital costs per student. The colonial tradition still continues in many African countries in that most primary schools are built simply and cheaply of local materials, but secondary schools and higher education institutions are built expensively and to a standard far above what can generally be provided for the population as a whole—or even for the students themselves after they graduate. The result is that the very style of the school buildings and environment often raises aspirations and strengthens élitist attitudes. To switch to cheaper building methods would not only lessen these tendencies but could greatly reduce the capital costs of education. In Uganda in the early 1960s each secondary-school place had a capital cost amounting to fifty-five times the national income per head—more than the expected lifetime income of the majority of Ugandans. It is not unreasonable to plan for some reduction in these circumstances. There is also a strong case for more intensive utilisation of school buildings at all levels. It is not uncommon for some university buildings to be used only ten or fifteen hours per week and most secondary schools are still operated only on a single-shift basis. Moreover, under-utilisation during term-time is often followed by a virtual shut-down during vacations. A widespread application of the double-shift system in the use of school buildings and a staggering of school vacations would greatly reduce the capital cost of schooling with little if any effect on the quality of education.

However, the possibility of achieving major cost reductions should not be allowed to detract from the importance of increasing expenditure and resources in certain strategic areas of education. Most schools, particularly primary schools, are desperately short of basic teaching materials. Doubling or even quadrupling expenditure on these could do

TABLE IX. DATA AVAILABLE IN AND METHODOLOGY OF AFRICAN RATE-OF-RETURN STUDIES 1960-70

(X = assumption made or available data)

Item	Ghana	Kenya		Nigeria		Rhodesia	Uganda			Zambia
	1969	1968	1969	1967	1969	1960	1963	1967	1968	1966
Characteristics of data in studies										
1. Source of earnings data (civil service salary scales (CSSS), sample survey (SS))	CSSS [1]	CSSS	SS	SS	CSSS [2]	SS	CSSS	CSSS	CSSS	SS
2. Coverage of earnings data										
Sectors (government (G), private (P), mixed (M))	M	G	M	P	M	M	G	G	G	M
Number of educational levels [3]	4	4	6	5	4	4	2	4	4	6
Education (primary (P), secondary (S), higher (H))	S/H	S/H	P/S/H	P/S/H	S/H	P/S [4]	S/H	P/S/H	P/S/H	P
Training		X								
Sex (male (M), female (F), both (B))	M	B	MF	B	M	B	B	B	B	B
Key assumptions in estimation of benefits										
3. Marginal earnings = average earnings	X	X	X	X	X	X	X	X	X	X
4. Future earnings = present earnings	X	X	a.g. [5]	X	X	a.g. [5]	X	X	X	X
5. Social benefits = private earnings before tax	X		X [6]	X	X	X	X	X	X	X
6. Private benefits = private earnings after tax		X	X							
7. Proportion of earnings differentials attributed to education	1	1	<1 [7]	1	1	1	1	1	1	1
Key assumptions in estimation of costs										
8. Marginal costs = average costs	X [8]	X	X	X [8]	X [8]	X	X	X	X	X
9. Opportunity cost of students = average salaries	X	X	X	X	X	X		X	X	X
10. Opportunity cost of teachers = present earnings	X	X	X	X	X	X	X	X	X	X

Controls										
11. Allowance for mortality/participation rates			X	X						
12. Allowance for unemployment	X [9]		X	X	X [9]					
13. Discount rate used				5		6	6½	12	12	12
14. Sensitivity analysis with regard to number of variables indicated	3 [10]	1 [11]	9 [12]		3 [10]	2 [13]				1 [14]
Results										
15. Private benefit/cost ratios [15] for										
Primary education			7 [16]							
Secondary education [17]/school certificate			19 [16]							
Secondary education [18]/higher school certificate		negative [16]	23 [16]							
Higher education		19 [16]	20 [16]							
16. Social benefit/cost ratios [15] for										
Primary education			5 [16]	16.9		3.1	4.1	3.7	1.5	1.4
Secondary education [17]/ school certificate	11.3 [16]		15 [16]	3.5	13 [16]	8.1	3.4	1.7	1.1	
Secondary education [18]/higher school certificate	17.6 [16]		15 [16]	0.3	20 [16]			4.1	2.6	
Higher education	15.4 [16 19]		9 [16]	8.5	16 [16 20]			0.99	0.7	

[1] Except for primary- and middle-school leavers, where a weighted average calculated from the *Quarterly Digest of Statistics* (Ghana, 1967) was used. [2] Except for primary-school leavers, where a weighted average calculated from the *Digest of Statistics* (Nigeria, 1967) was used. [3] i.e. all output points for which cost/benefit calculations were made. [4] Further calculations using hypothetical data were made for two levels of post-secondary schooling. [5] Assumed growth. [6] Except for the public sector, where a downward adjustment was made. [7] Age-earning profiles adjusted for 14 socio-economic variables, using regression analysis. [8] Except for university level, where marginal recurrent costs were calculated. [9] An allowance was also made for failure and drop-out rates within the educational system. [10] Unemployment, drop-out, failure. [11] Costs. [12] Age, mortality, socio-economic background, examination scores, examination certificates, government employment effects, landowning, family size, probability of finding employment. [13] Future costs, future earnings. [14] Seven discount rates. [15] In each case benefit/cost ratios refer to the returns to the level of education shown over the preceding level of education shown. [16] These are rates of return; benefit/cost ratios were not calculated. [17] Form IV output (approximately 11 years' schooling). [18] Form VI output (approximately 13 years' schooling). [19] Three other rates were calculated: middle school over primary school—11.0 per cent; secondary school over middle school—11.3 per cent; university over secondary school, form V—16.0 per cent. [20] Two other rates were calculated; secondary-modern school over primary school—6.0 per cent; university over secondary school, form V—18.25 per cent.

much to raise the quality and morale of schools and accordingly to increase the contribution of education to economic development.

SENSITIVITY ANALYSIS

The inevitable uncertainties concerning many of the assumptions underlying the projections of supply and demand make it unwise to base policy on a single projection. It is therefore necessary to make a number of projections, varying the central assumptions over the range of what seems reasonable and thereby calculating the range of likely outcomes. What really matters is whether the policy conclusions derived from the projections are sensitive to variations in the assumptions underlying them. If they are, they can inspire less confidence and there is a greater need for flexibility in carrying out the policies so as to leave room for adjustments as further evidence becomes available.

Unfortunately sensitivity analysis was undertaken in only a few of the African manpower plans and it is therefore difficult to establish the range of uncertainty attaching to the forecasts.

IV. Rate-of-return analysis

It seems appropriate to mention, even if briefly, an alternative approach to manpower planning much advocated in the economic literature as a guide to educational planning. This is rate-of-return or cost-benefit analysis. In practice, this approach has received most attention from academics and there are relatively few examples of such work being undertaken by planning offices or other operational bodies. In Africa up until 1970, to the best of our knowledge ten rate-of-return calculations had been made, and these are summarised in table IX.

Before turning to the detailed assumptions and results of these studies, it may be useful to indicate the methodology of this approach to educational planning.[1] In brief, the method consists of calculating separately the social and/or private costs of education, estimating the discounted social and/or private benefits of education and comparing the two as a guide to which parts of the educational system should be expanded or contracted.[2] In each case, costs or benefits are in reality a

[1] A good introduction to the literature is Maureen Woodhall: *Cost-benefit analysis in educational planning* (Paris, UNESCO International Institute for Educational Planning, 1970). See also Mark Blaug: *An introduction to the economics of education* (Allen Lane, Penguin Press, 1970).

[2] In fact, the literature on cost-benefit analysis in the education sector is often ambiguous about the focus of the policy conclusions to be drawn from the calculations. In principle, differing rates of return between different levels of education (and investment elsewhere in the economy) could lead to at least three different conclusions: (i) that outputs of the level or type of education showing the highest rate of return should be expanded relative to outputs at other levels; (ii) that the growth in outputs of the level or type of education

stream of expenditures or returns spread over the life of an individual while he is being educated or afterwards when he is working as a contributor to the production of the economy. Rate-of-return calculations initially estimate the costs or earnings over an individual's lifetime and then either discount the stream using conventional discounting techniques to obtain the present value of costs and benefits *or* calculate an internal rate of return, defined as that rate of return for which discounted costs would just equal discounted benefits over the individual's life.

The approach outlined above is of course an ideal. In practice, a number of important assumptions have to be made in order to use the limited data available to produce an estimate of the real rates of return or cost-benefit ratios in any actual situation. Table IX shows the actual data used, and lists the most important assumptions made, in the ten calculations undertaken so far in Africa. Before turning to the results a few comments on the key steps in the calculations are in order.

Data

Of crucial importance for the rate-of-return calculations were data on earnings by age and education level. Such data are rarely available in Africa from the regular statistical surveys of employment and earnings, and the calculations were thus based on two alternative sources of information: specially conducted sample surveys, or estimates of actual earnings derived from government salary scales. In both cases, the main weakness was the neglect of earnings in agriculture, particularly in the subsistence sector. Although this omission may seem similar to the neglect of the subsistence sector in the manpower plans, it was perhaps more important, since the rate-of-return calculations explicitly attempted to calculate the returns of primary education, whereas the manpower plans did not calculate needs at primary level. Table IX shows that most of the rate-of-return calculations collected data relating to all the main levels of education. Only the 1969 Kenya study attempted to collect data on training, in addition. One noteworthy contrast with many rate-of-return calculations made elsewhere is that most of the African calculations included data on earnings for both men and women, rather than for men alone.

---

showing the highest rate of return should be expanded relative to the trend of the growth in output over recent years; (iii) that expenditure on education should be increased relative to expenditure on other investments.

Each of these conclusions involves different assumptions and has quite different implications for policy. Yet the cost-benefit literature often fails to distinguish between them or even to state unambiguously whether the conclusions apply to total enrolments, or to total outputs or to gross (or net) outputs joining the labour force. Only on fairly strict assumptions will a proportional change in one of these be identical to a proportional change in another. These are serious omissions for a methodology whose primary claim to fame is rigour and precision.

Benefits

In principle, rate-of-return methodology requires calculation of benefits as the marginal, future production attributable to education, adjusted to include all additional external effects throughout the economy. In practice, estimates of benefits were made in Africa (as generally elsewhere) from a cross-section of current earnings of a sample of the labour force, grouped by age and education. Table IX shows the key assumptions implied by this approach (items 3 to 7). In the case of both earnings by age and earnings by education marginal earnings were assumed to equal average earnings and, except in two surveys, future earnings were estimated to equal present earnings. Except in the Kenya 1969 study, earnings differentials between persons of different levels of education were attributed totally to education, no part of them being ascribed to differences in social background, or to differences in individual intelligence or to the host of other factors often considered relevant in this respect. To some extent the simplifications were cruder than those introduced in recent rate-of-return calculations in other countries. The net result was almost certainly an overestimate of future benefits. This is obviously the effect of assumptions 3 and 7 and perhaps also of assumption 4 (future earnings will equal present earnings). Although recent calculations elsewhere have tended to assume that the future earnings of educated manpower will increase in relation to increases in income per head, it seems likely, for the reasons given at the end of this article, that in Africa differentials in earnings, at least among persons with higher levels of education, are likely to diminish in the future.

As elsewhere, no satisfactory method was found in the African rate-of-return studies of including external benefits within the calculations, which accordingly usually estimated social returns to be equal to private earnings before tax and private returns to equal private earnings after tax. The effect of this may be either to understate social benefit (the earnings of a poorly paid government doctor in a rural area may have greater social benefit than those of a highly paid physician in urban private practice) or to overstate it. Rado suggests that the private rate of return from acquiring one more level of education than anyone else may stay high long after social benefit has fallen to zero.

As discussed more fully below, the observed salary structure in the modern sector in Africa was highly arbitrary. Only the most convinced neo-classicist could believe that it represented a true measure of social benefit.

Costs

The calculation of costs was generally considered to be a straightforward matter in the rate-of-return studies. But as table IX indicates, the assumptions here (items 8 to 10) may have been no less significant than in the case of the calculation of benefits. All the African rate-of-return studies assumed that marginal costs equalled average costs, that the opportunity cost of students equalled the average salaries of persons in jobs and of similar age and education, and that the present earnings of teachers adequately indicated their own opportunity costs in production. Without going into detail, it can be argued that each of these assumptions led to some overestimate of the marginal costs of education, particularly in a situation of unemployment.

Controls

In addition to the assumptions mentioned above, two other assumptions are implicitly involved in any cost-benefit calculations: an assumption about mortality and/or participation rates in the labour force and an assumption about the extent of unemployment among the educated. As table IX indicates, only the Kenya 1969 and Nigeria 1967 studies explicitly considered these factors. Although unemployment may have been negligible among persons with higher levels of education in the 1960s in Africa, it was by no means negligible among persons at the primary or secondary levels of education. Moreover, there is evidence to suggest that a sizeable proportion of females at all levels of education do not participate in the labour force (or at least in economic activity as conventionally defined). The neglect of mortality and participation rates in the labour force almost certainly decreased the amount of the estimated benefits of education. The effect of neglecting unemployment is more difficult to judge, since this must have reduced the amount of both the estimated costs and benefits of education.

It is, of course, unrealistic to expect reliable assumptions to have been made on all these points, given the enormous difficulty of forecasting five years ahead, let alone for the ten or fifteen years over which rate-of-return calculations remain sensitive. But sensitivity analysis was rarely incorporated in the African rate-of-return calculations, thus making it difficult to judge the extent to which the conclusions would have been altered by changes in the key assumptions.

Results

The results of the rate-of-return calculations are summarised under items 15 and 16 of table IX. In most cases these were given in the form of benefit/cost ratios, though in four of the studies they were shown as internal rates of return, while the Zambian study gave the final discounted value of the stream of expected net benefits.

Considerable variations were found in the benefit/cost ratios between different countries and within countries at different periods. In principle, of course, there is no reason to expect the same or even similar ratios. Circumstances differ. But comparison, for example, of the three studies made of Uganda in 1963, 1967 and 1968 showed remarkable changes in the benefit/cost ratios for each level of education. Obviously proper sensitivity analyses would be required to establish the reasons for this, but the results would seem to be indicative of changes in assumptions and method of calculation rather than of changes in the basic situation.[1]

Most of the studies failed to calculate separately private rates of return and social rates of return. This is unfortunate, since the assumptions underlying private rate-of-return calculations are somewhat weaker than those underlying any social rate-of-return calculation, and also separate treatment would have provided insights into the private demand for education and the effects of education on income distribution. Nevertheless, because of the relatively low income tax in Africa and the extent to which education is generally subsidised, particularly at the secondary and higher levels, one can be confident that the private rates of return were considerably higher than the social rates.

Where private benefit/cost ratios were established, they were, except for Kenya, markedly higher for primary than for secondary or higher education. These results were given considerable emphasis in some early commentaries on the rate-of-return calculations and, if they were certain, they would indeed be significant. Unfortunately, however, they may have been highly biased by the inadequacies of the data on the earnings of persons with and without primary education. The 1967 and 1968 Uganda calculations, for example, were based not on any evidence of actual earnings of primary-school leavers, but on an ad hoc assumption that the earnings of these persons would be 20 per cent higher than average income per head. The 1969 Kenya survey, restricted to urban areas, did at least collect actual data on primary-school leavers' earnings. The Kenya estimates show considerably lower returns to primary education than to secondary or higher education.

There are *a priori* reasons, however, for expecting rate-of-return methodology to produce higher returns to primary education than to secondary or higher levels, particularly in Africa. Pupil/teacher ratios at primary level are often double those at secondary level and four times those in universities. The salaries of primary-school teachers, though still high in relation to income per head, are only a fraction of those of secondary-school or university-level teachers. These two facts explain the very high unit cost or secondary or higher education. On the benefit side, although earnings of primary-school leavers are much lower than those of persons with secondary or higher education, the proportion is

[1] The 1967 and 1968 calculations in Uganda, for example, were based on identically the same earnings data. Although the rank ordering of benefit/cost ratios by different levels of education remained unchanged, there were remarkable differences in the two sets of ratios themselves.

comparable to the differentials in teachers' earnings. Since the methodology generally excludes any future changes in the structure of salaries, differentials in the earnings of school leavers match the differentials in teachers' salaries and higher rates of return follow from the higher pupil/teacher ratios at primary level. To the sceptic, rate-of-return calculations indicate little more than this simple fact.

It is noteworthy that most of the benefit/cost ratios were greater than unity. In principle, this indicates that education is a desirable investment, social or private. Unfortunately, the rates of discount used to calculate these ratios were often well below the social opportunity cost of capital. And even if the calculations had been trustworthy, it is not clear whether education would be a desirable investment in relation to other investment opportunities, given limited resources. Because several of the key assumptions appear to have overstated both benefits and costs (and probably the former rather more than the latter), it would seem that the true benefit/cost ratios may be a good deal lower than those shown. It is thus not certain whether any general reliable conclusions can be drawn—at least regarding the social rates of return.

Concentration on the detailed assumptions runs the risk of overlooking a more fundamental objection. While the present authors frankly admit that they find most of the assumptions involved in rate-of-return calculations far from reasonable—particularly in Africa, where labour markets are full of divisions and imperfections—in their opinion the main weakness of rate-of-return methodology is that it rests essentially on the observed earnings structure in the current situation. In fact, the future involves—or should involve—major structural changes in the pattern of economic growth, especially with respect to employment and income distribution, notably in rural areas. In view of this it is difficult to put much faith in calculations that assume the following:

(1) That an individual's earnings before tax equal his social marginal product (i.e. the value to society of his contribution to the total output of goods and services). Since in most African countries roughly two-thirds of those persons with higher education work for the government or in full-time education (see appendix III), it is difficult to believe that their salaries are indicative of much more than the rules and regulations of the government salary structure. In any case, for most of the occupations concerned it is difficult to identify and quantify the physical results of an individual's work, let alone to put a value on that work. And we have already emphasised that, as regards the lowest end of the income scale, there is virtually no statistical basis for estimating the incomes of the self-employed and the peasant farmers who form the majority of workers with a primary education or less.

(2) That the present structure of earnings will continue unchanged in the future. Even in principle this assumption is unwarranted unless the

different types of manpower are highly interchangeable among occupations or unless only marginal changes occur both in education and in the demand for and supply of educated manpower in the economy. Yet the structure of education in most African countries in the early 1960s was such that changes of a marginal sort would have been totally insufficient.[1] Moreover, even if there had been only marginal changes in education, the whole context of development—independence, growing industrialisation, major alterations in the rural areas, fundamental reforms of education, health and other government services—meant that the structural characteristics determining the demand for and supply of educated manpower in the economy were changing enormously.

(3) That there is no value in localisation except that reflected in paying local personnel lower salaries than expatriates (which would be a negative value if private earnings are assumed to equal social benefits). Yet the political and economic importance of localisation has been considerable and has involved major changes in the basic supply and allocation of high-level manpower with a view to the replacement of expatriates on a priority basis.

(4) That the whole of the differentials in earnings of persons of different levels of education can be attributed to education itself—something that all the African rate-of-return studies assumed. In fact, quantitative studies made in most developed countries (so far none has been undertaken in Africa) suggest that education is accountable for only a certain proportion of these differentials. Although it would be possible to make simple alternative assumptions on the fraction of the differentials to be attributed to education, it seems likely that this fraction may be decreasing in many developing countries. Education appears to be becoming more of a qualifying (ability-identifying and skill-labelling) and selecting process, and less of a training-educating process, at least in terms of relevant skills.

(5) That the existing quality, style and costs of education can be used without modification in calculating the costs and benefits of making changes in education in the future.

For these reasons it seems to us unrealistic to give much credence to the calculated rates of return as indicators of the social benefits of education. Even if we were persuaded of the feasibility and reasonableness of making adjustments to the basic data which would make it possible to apply more convincing assumptions than those outlined above, the calculations would in our view still offer only limited guidance for the formulation of policy. This, briefly, is because they are concerned with

[1] Indeed from 1960 to 1965 data covering from seventeen to thirty-two countries revealed that average increases in enrolments were 6 per cent for primary, 15 per cent for secondary and 20 per cent for higher education. These are hardly marginal changes (Jolly, op. cit., p. 49).

the direction of marginal quantitative change in the existing system, when in our view what is needed is guidance on the direction and size of non-marginal quantitative and qualitative changes in education and the whole wage structure.

Nevertheless, in two respects parts of the rate-of-return approach do have a useful if modest role to play. In the first place calculations of private rates of return do indicate how very high these rates are from secondary and higher education—almost certainly well above what is necessary to induce a sufficient number of persons to seek higher education. Secondly, cost effectiveness techniques can help considerably to minimise the cost of implementing any given educational programme, once its size and character have been determined. The proponents of rate-of-return calculations have rightly stressed that the cost dimension of manpower planning has too often been neglected (though there are exceptions). To reap the full benefit of cost effectiveness analysis, this process should be applied not only to a particular education programme but to alternative ways of offering equivalent education or training. We now turn to one example of this approach.

V. Training

A major deficiency of almost all the African manpower plans was their neglect of training as an alternative to formal education. Where training was expressly taken into account, it was as a supplement to rather than as a substitute for formal education. Yet there is no doubt that a trade-off exists between formal education and training, at least within a certain range.

Using data from the Zambian manpower survey, one of the present authors conducted a detailed investigation of the extent of this trade-off.[1] Diagram 3 summarises some of the results. It shows for one particular occupation (electrical engineers in the mining sector) the various combinations of formal education and training possessed by persons holding the job. Similar contours resulted from calculations for different occupational groups. In each case they were obtained by using standard regression techniques to fit a log or linear function to data on the actual levels of education and training possessed by persons within the occupational group in question.

Diagram 3 also shows the effects of introducing the length of a worker's experience on the job as a further variable. In principle one would have expected that greater experience in any particular occupation

[1] C. L. Colclough: " Manpower planning in developing countries—some problems. An empirical analysis of occupation, education and training with special reference to Zambia ", Ph.D. thesis, University of Cambridge, October 1971.

DIAGRAM 3. ESTIMATED RELATIONSHIP BETWEEN EDUCATION AND TRAINING FOR ELECTRICAL ENGINEERS IN MINING: ZAMBIA, 1965-66

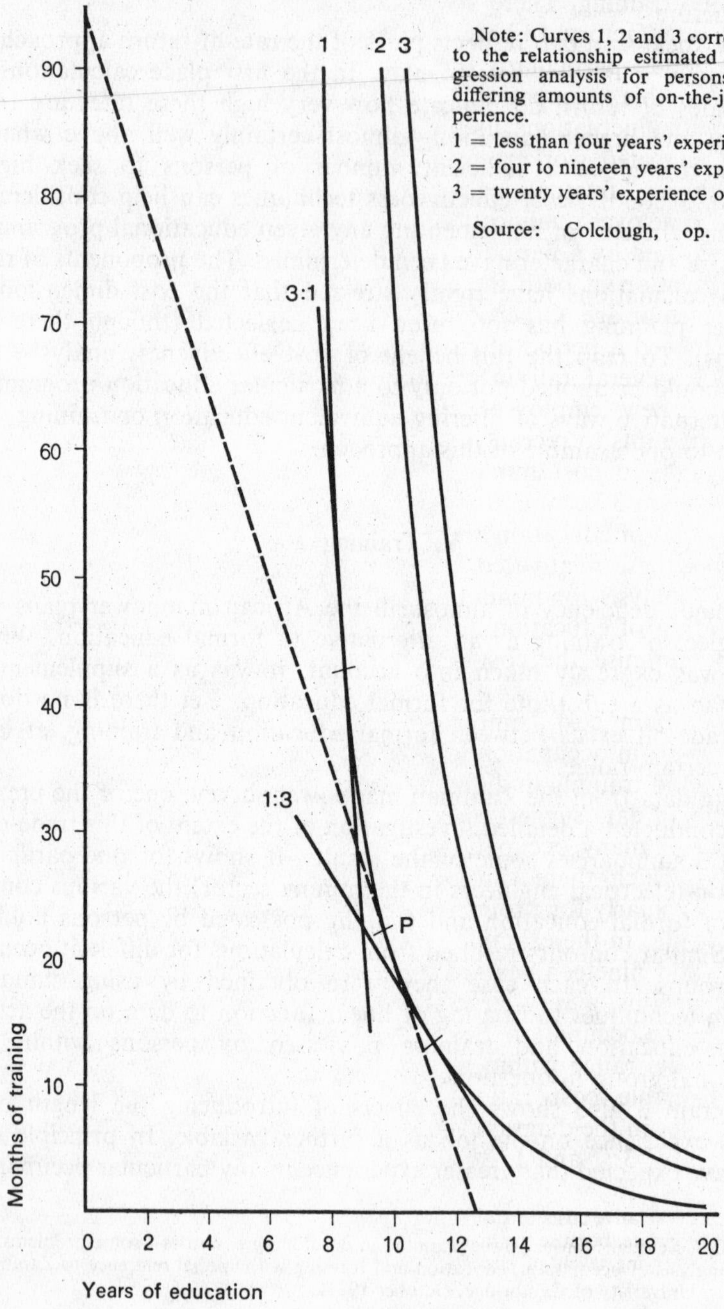

Note: Curves 1, 2 and 3 correspond to the relationship estimated by regression analysis for persons with differing amounts of on-the-job experience.

1 = less than four years' experience
2 = four to nineteen years' experience
3 = twenty years' experience or more

Source: Colclough, op. cit.

means that smaller amounts of both education and training will be needed. In practice, for twenty-seven of the forty occupations studied in Zambia, greater experience was associated with larger amounts of both education and training. There are several possible explanations, though none is fully satisfactory. In part these findings may be due to weaknesses in the basic data—particularly unreliable was the measure of " years of experience in this occupation ". But a more likely explanation is connected with fluctuations in the relative supply of and demand for skilled and educated workers over past years. On certain assumptions " cyclical cobweb " fluctuations could occur in the labour market when a period of relative over-qualification of entrants to a particular occupation would be followed by a period of under-qualification—resulting in some positive correlation of both the education and training of workers with their experience or age. Other Zambian statistics suggested that the early 1960s were indeed a period of rising excess demand for skilled workers, and that the general fall in the amount of education and training possessed by new employees may well have been a symptom of employers' attempts to recruit in an increasingly scarce market.

As a guide to cost minimisation, education-training contours as shown in diagram 3 become useful when combined with information on the relative costs of education and training. The dotted line in diagram 3 indicates how these relative costs might appear. Applying conventional neo-classical analysis for minimum cost production, it will be seen that the combination of education and training shown at point P is the one that would minimise the cost of producing a worker of the type in question.

The minimum cost combination of education and training will naturally vary from occupation to occupation and with the relative costs of education and training in different occupations. Nevertheless, even the limited Zambian data suggest three important characteristics which seem to be typical of many occupations. First, the range of the educational levels within which there can be a trade-off between education and training—particularly for professional and technical occupations—seems to be fairly wide: in the example shown it can be seen that it is between about eight and nineteen years of formal education. At lower levels of education than this, a very large amount of training becomes necessary for entry into the occupation. Secondly, however, the shape of the curves suggests that the range within which there can be an *effective* trade-off with a reasonable cost ratio may be very limited. Thus the two continuous lines in the diagram show that to have cost ratios for training and education of 3: 1 and 1: 3 [1] the range as indicated by the respective

[1] Data on the relative costs of training and education are scanty. They are also, for the most part, inappropriate, because the marginal cost of a given training course will be different for graduates at varying levels of education due, on the one hand, to the importance of

(footnote continued overleaf)

points of tangency is between eight and eleven years of formal education. Too much importance should not, however, be attached to this, since the positions of the estimated curves are subject to a wide margin of error and probably have some downward bias due to the ways in which the variables were measured. Accordingly, the shape of the curves becomes more important than their actual position: in general this example suggests that the optional combinations of education and training in high-level occupations may be fairly insensitive to moderate changes in relative costs. Thirdly, the Zambian data imply that the introduction of the element of experience would not affect the choice between education and training as a basis for preparing new members of the labour force.

Although at this stage the Zambian study must be treated as indicative rather than conclusive, lessons can be drawn from it for manpower planning work elsewhere. At the very least, the collection of data on required and actual levels of training as well as of education, both simply defined, would enable some rough calculations along similar lines to be made in other countries. We would not suggest that, initially, enormous resources should be devoted to this task, but a moderate amount of work might well produce useful conclusions for the formulation of policy.

VI. Conclusions

The effects of manpower planning on policy

In assessing the results of manpower planning in Africa, the first question one wants to ask is: To what extent have these manpower plans affected policy, and have the effects been positive or negative in relation to what would have happened if there had been no plans? Ideally, if one could obtain a fairly precise answer, one would then ask a further question: How do the results of the planning compare with the resources used in undertaking the planning work? In fact, the first question is almost impossible to answer except in terms of general impressions, drawing heavily on a knowledge of the context in which the plans were conceived and of the relationship of the planners to the whole apparatus of government and decision making. The second question involves a degree of rigour which makes it equally difficult to answer except in terms of subjective comment.

---

opportunity cost in the calculation and, on the other, to the link between average salaries and levels of formal education. However, evidence from a recent study of the costs of further education in Great Britain suggests that annual marginal costs per student for higher technical qualifications compared with those per student for degree courses in the same subject vary between about 1 : 3 and 1 : 6, depending on the course and the definitions used in calculating the marginal costs. See C. Selby Smith: " Costs and benefits in further education: some evidence from a pilot study ", in *Economic Journal*, Vol. LXXX, No. 319, Sep. 1970, p. 595. However, at lower levels of formal education capital costs are much less, and the relative cost ratios are likely to be smaller. Thus those shown in diagram 3 are felt to indicate fairly realistic limits to the possible range.

With these general reservations, then, we may draw some conclusions about the influence of manpower planning in Africa in the 1960s, while recognising the necessarily subjective basis of such conclusions. The first point to be made is that many of the weaknesses of the manpower plans are those of economic planning in Africa in general. Since the Second World War, and particularly since independence, there has been a spate of economic plans and most countries have created central planning offices. Nevertheless, the Treasuries remained largely, even if not completely, the focus of economic decision making in the government, and the annual budget continued to be the single most important economic instrument. Only compromise powers were given to the planning offices instead of those that would have been required to make central planning an effective instrument of day-to-day control. Nor were many steps taken to extend the authority of the government over those parts of the economy which were still beyond its control, including the enormous informal sector, both rural and urban. Even with the extension of state enterprise in the modern sector, control has usually been delegated to corporation management with few attempts at centralisation. For these reasons, the general exercise of economic planning was carried out in a framework in which the instruments for effective implementation were not available. In these circumstances macro-economic plans largely remain projections of what the planners expect may happen in the economy at large rather than becoming a programme for implementation.

Given this general situation, it is not surprising that the manpower plans themselves were primarily documents to influence the climate of opinion rather than clear guidelines for action. The extent to which they influenced action appears to have varied considerably from country to country. Where manpower planning was part of the ongoing work of a permanent unit under strong leadership, as in Tanzania, the manpower planning unit appears to have exercised considerable influence on a whole range of policies, particularly in the field of education and localisation. In such a situation the staff of the unit themselves interpreted the relevance of their manpower calculations to whatever element of policy was under discussion and argued that they should be taken into account in specific decisions. Again it is difficult to judge whether in general this was helpful or unhelpful, though at the very least the creation of a greater sense of awareness of the manpower implications of particular policies was no doubt a modest step towards greater rationality. In this connection a much ignored point deserves emphasis, namely that the influence of a manpower planning unit, and of the planning offices themselves, is too often judged primarily by the documents they publish rather than by their ongoing involvement in the formulation and implementation of policy. Anyone with experience in government knows that the impact of a personal statement or brief internal minute at the crucial point of decision is likely to be far greater than that of any general document.

Even judged in terms of this wider role of the manpower planning units, their own technical work, as our earlier analysis of the manpower plans suggests, inadequately served the planners. In the first place their planning techniques were subject to the wide range of technical deficiencies earlier identified—weakness of data, crude assumptions, deficiencies of methodology—many of which could have been avoided with more thought and professional analysis in advance. In the second place the conclusions of this work were not properly focused in terms of the policies to which they were intended to contribute. For example, the manpower plans often assumed that there would be a given rate of localisation instead of exploring the implications of a variety of localisation rates on the calculations. The number of expatriates to be recruited from abroad—or whose services were to be obtained through some form of manpower aid or technical assistance—was scarcely ever calculated in the manpower plan, in spite of this being one of the most important considerations for the formulation of national policy. Similarly, although in numerous countries, after independence, the shortage of civil servants' housing was the major obstacle to the recruitment of additional expatriate manpower, no manpower plan showed any awareness of the importance of housing, let alone made any quantitative calculations as to how to deal with it. This list of shortcomings could be extended. The central point is not that the work on long-run projections was totally useless but that it so often followed a stereotyped pattern, resulting in the production of documents in a conventional form but failing to grapple with a number of policy issues close at hand.

An essential consideration is whether the work on manpower planning has diverted attention from more serious aspects of the problem of human resources development—from what could be done in the short-run, from the qualitative weaknesses of education, from the deficiencies of training, from the costs of education, and from the effects of education on the distribution of income and in creating inequality in general. Here, the argument is not necessarily that the work on quantitative projections was wrong but that, given its inevitable imprecision, the resulting contribution to the improvement of policy was much less than if comparable effort had been expended in other ways. This is a more difficult matter to assess, involving a whole set of speculations about what alternative work could have been done, would have been done, how well, and with what effect on actual decisions. Three points can, however, be made. In the first place we must not ignore the fact that quantitative problems of educational change at the secondary and higher levels were seen as essential problems of educational policy over this period in Africa. The colonial heritage and the challenge of independence accentuated the need to consider the quantitative structure of the educational systems—a need fully reflected in the concern about the matter shown by politicians, civil servants, parents and schoolchildren alike. Although, with hindsight, we may argue that this concern was excessive, it should not be imagined that it was unnecessary or irrelevant.

In the second place the qualitative and even the distribution aspects of education were not neglected by the manpower planners, many of whom argued the need to make education and training relevant to job performance and development far more specifically than was done within the ministries of education. In this respect, though the calculations relating to manpower projects were quantitative, the manpower plans—and the manpower planners themselves as members of the government administration—may have been influential in increasing the general concern for the operational relevance of education in qualitative as well as in quantitative terms.

Nevertheless, it is probably true that preoccupation with the parts of the problem that could readily be quantified often diverted attention and effort from those that could not. Training and informal education, though usually mentioned in passing, were never as fully incorporated into the calculations as were the more easily quantified outputs of the formal educational system. Although a few studies were made of the utilisation of skilled manpower, and of measures to improve skilled manpower efficiency, such studies were rare. Finally, the implications of human resources development for the wage structure, unemployment and income distribution were seldom much explored because of the preoccupation—even the obsession—with the quantitative planning of the supply of and demand for skilled manpower.

Future work

The above criticisms have implications for the balance of future work in this field. Before briefly taking up this point, however, it may be useful to return to the results of the manpower plans in order to indicate how the skilled labour market in Africa and the manpower context are likely to change.

Broadly speaking our evaluation of the projections suggests that most of the African manpower plans overestimated the growth of manpower needs and of employment of educated manpower. In large part this may have been due to over-optimism about the growth of absorptive capacity in the system, though in part it is due also to structural imbalance. Vacancies and expatriates remain, particularly in professional and technical occupations. An obvious need for rural development persists. In spite of pressures to ensure the absorption of the influx of new graduates and school leavers, needs have not automatically been converted into market demand. Perhaps most unfortunate of all, even the skills and training of the manpower that has been educated are often out of balance with the demand that does exist.

In most of the countries, furthermore, the expansion of secondary and higher education has proceeded more rapidly than was estimated to be necessary by the manpower plans. For these reasons, the typical situation in the coming decade, at least in the countries studied, seems likely to be one in which shortages of skilled and educated manpower are first eased and then give way to surpluses at a more rapid rate than was originally envisaged.

What are the likely consequences? At the most general level, one can foresee three stages in the reaction of the labour market to this changing situation. The first will be one in which localisation proceeds more rapidly than was earlier thought possible—though often this will mean that jobs are filled by persons who are educationally qualified but still lacking in experience, particularly broad work experience in more junior posts. The second stage will be reached when the majority of posts have been localised, leaving only a few expatriates with obviously specialised skills. At that stage people with secondary or higher education can continue to be absorbed, but only into jobs formerly filled by persons with a lower level of education. The extent to which educated persons will be taken on in this way depends mainly on how far and how quickly they are prepared to adjust their sights, on the extent to which less qualified persons can be squeezed out (thus providing more employment opportunities for the educated than if they were only to have access to additional posts) and on the extent to which remuneration rates for the educated are adjusted downwards. Whatever the precise degree of adjustment along each of these lines, there seems little doubt that earnings differentials associated with education will decrease, making possible some additional employment, though often at the expense of less qualified persons. Table VII has already indicated the enormous earnings differentials based on education inherited from colonial times, and a narrowing of them seems desirable, both in order to reduce indefensibly large incentives and as a modest step towards decreasing income inequality at least among wage earners.

Nevertheless, it is not clear how far this process can go before it is successfully resisted by those whose earnings are falling. At that point stage three will begin, in which open unemployment of educated manpower emerges in a virulent form. This stage has been reached in many of the developing countries of Asia and Latin America, where unemployment rates among the educated often far exceed those among the uneducated. Even then different outcomes are possible. With a rapid adjustment to the realities of the situation, educated persons may shift into self-employment, urban or rural. If they are successful, they may still turn their education to productive use and unemployment need not be extensive. Or the depressed opportunities deriving from education may have repercussions on the educational system, greatly discouraging the public demand for education and leading to a falling off in enrolment after some time-lag. Alternatively, the frustrations of this whole cycle may interact with other developments and lead to basic changes in the whole structure of production and the organisation of work and government. There is little at this level of generality that analysts can say in advance, beyond indicating that the range of options is large.

In this emerging context, what lessons can be drawn for future work in manpower planning? First, it seems obvious that much greater attention must be paid to the manpower implications of the structural problems that have appeared and are increasingly likely to appear over the next decade. These include, particularly, the tendency for income distribution to become more unequal (in part because of the increasing numbers of educated personnel), the relatively slow growth of wage-earning employment as compared with the rate of growth of the labour force, and the tendency for the rural-urban gap (or gaps) to widen. Manpower planners should consider measures to deal with this whole set of problems, with their direct implications for the quantities, types, location, uses and incomes of skilled and educated workers.

Although in our view long-term manpower projections at the macro level are still of some value for purposes of analysis and development planning within this changing context, only limited insights can be expected from them and the balance of effort should be shifted to micro studies, for instance at the sectoral or occupational level. Detailed studies of clusters of related occupations—for example of medical occupations, of the occupations involved in government administration, of clerical occupations, of the occupations in the building and construction sector (engineers, architects, technicians), etc.—could greatly contribute to an assessment of the adequacy of the training and education of the skilled and educated workers in these occupational groups, of the incentives offered to them and of the institutional arrangements for their employment. Such studies would have to take account of quantity as well as quality, of informal as well as formal education and training, of the efficiency with which the persons concerned are employed, of the adequacy of the labour market in allocating persons between jobs and of the whole range of incentives and institutional arrangements involved in the employment of the skilled and educated manpower in the occupational groups concerned. They should give particular weight to issues of employment and income distribution and to their links with education and relevant skills, especially in rural areas. And finally they should consider what structure of institutions and incentives would help win support for effective change.

Inevitably studies on these lines would be more varied and less uniform than earlier manpower surveys. They would rely more heavily on impressions obtained from interviews than on statistical calculations. They would draw upon the skills of the sociologist and the social psychologist and administrator as much as on those of the economist.

They might well start with problems of job analysis and proceed from there to the question of skills needed, and then to specification of the training required. This does not mean embarking on a perfectionist solution. We fully recognise that the staff available to undertake such studies will continue to be limited. In our view useful studies on these lines could be undertaken and completed in many of the smaller African countries. In other words, they would be well within the resources of many of the manpower planning units and, in all, not much more burdensome than the manpower planning already engaged in. But their results would be likely to be of much greater value for policy and their benefits far greater than the costs.

Appendix I. Bibliography

AFRICAN MANPOWER SURVEYS [1]

Country	Year of publication	Document
Basutoland	1964	Elkan, W.: *Report to the Government of Basutoland on the manpower situation* (Geneva, ILO) (mimeographed document ILO/TAP/Basutoland/R.1).
Cameroon	1962	Casselman, P., Andoff, J., and Fabri, M. M.: *Rapport au Gouvernement de la République fédérale du Cameroun sur une mission inter-organisations d'enquête sur la main-d'œuvre* (Geneva, ILO) (mimeographed document OIT/TAP/Cameroun/R.3).
Egypt	1966	Institute of National Planning: *Manpower planning in the United Arab Republic* (mimeographed).
Ethiopia	1967	Greene, S.: *Report on manpower requirements to fulfil the third Five-year Plan* (mimeographed).
Ghana	1960	Loken, R. D.: *Survey of high-level manpower in Ghana* (Accra, Government Printer).
,,	1963	Idem: *Report of the Subcommittee on Education, Manpower and Employment* [of the National Planning Commission] (mimeographed).
Ivory Coast	1964	Gorecki-Leroy, M.: *Rapport au Gouvernement de la République de la Côte-d'Ivoire sur l'évaluation et la planification de la main-d'œuvre* (Geneva, ILO) (mimeographed document OIT/TAP/Côte d'Ivoire/R.1).
Kenya	1962	Hunter, G.: *High-level manpower in East Africa: a preliminary assessment* (mimeographed).
,,	1965	Davis, C. F.: *High-level manpower requirements and resources in Kenya 1964-70*, publication of the Ministry of Economic Planning and Development (Nairobi, Government Press).
,,	1969	Carr, K.: *Manpower survey and manpower report*, publication of the Ministry of Economic Planning and Development (Nairobi, Government Press).
Malawi	1967	Brown, R.: *Report on the survey of requirements for trained manpower in Malawi* (mimeographed).
Mali	1967	Lê Thành Khôi: *Rapport au Gouvernement de la République du Mali sur l'évaluation et la planification des ressources humaines* (Geneva, ILO) (mimeographed document OIT/TAP/Mali/R.6) (restricted).
Mauritius	1969	King, J.: *Manpower—facts and perspectives* (mimeographed).

[1] Where specified in the document, the manpower surveys have been identified by the main author, even though many of the documents were the work of a team and were issued as government publications.

Country	Year of publication	Document
Nigeria	1960	Harbison, F.: " High-level manpower for Nigeria's future ", in *Investment in education ; the Report of the Commission on Post-School Certificate and Higher Education in Nigeria* (London, St. Clements Press), pp. 50-72.
„	1964	National Manpower Board: *Nigeria's high-level manpower, 1964-70* (Lagos, National Press).
Rhodesia	1964	Taylor, W. L., and Pearson, D. S.: *The requirements and supplies of high-level manpower in Southern Rhodesia, 1961-70*, University College of Rhodesia and Nyasaland, Department of Economics, Occasional Paper No. 3 (Salisbury, Unitas Press).
Senegal	1966	Gorecki-Leroy, M.: *Rapport au Gouvernement de la République du Sénégal sur la méthodologie à appliquer en matière de prévision des besoins et des ressources en main-d'œuvre* (Geneva, ILO) (mimeographed document OIT/TAP/Sénégal/R.7).
Sierra Leone	1964	Brown, R.: *Interim report to the Government of Sierra Leone on the manpower situation* (London, Department of Technical Co-operation) (mimeographed).
Somalia	1965	Nigam, S. B. L.: *The manpower situation in Somalia* (Mogadiscio, Ministry of Health and Labour).
„	1970	Idem: *Report to the Government of the Republic of Somalia on manpower assessment and planning* (Geneva, ILO) (mimeographed document ILO/TAP/Somalia/R.6).
Sudan	1965	Seal, J. B., Jr: *High-level manpower requirements and resources 1968-72* (Khartoum) (mimeographed).
Swaziland	1965	Tottle, A. V.: *Report to the Government of Swaziland on manpower assessment* (Geneva, ILO) (mimeographed document ILO/TAP/Swaziland/R.1).
„	1970	Manpower Planning Unit: *Swaziland's survey of manpower resources and requirements, April 1969-March 1974* (Mbabane) (mimeographed).
Tanzania	1962	Hunter, op. cit.
„	1963	Tobias, G.: *High-level manpower requirements and resources in Tanganyika 1962-67*, Government Paper No. 2 (Dar es Salaam, Government Printer).
„	1965	Thomas, R. L.: *Survey of the high-level manpower requirements and resources for the Five-year Development Plan, 1964-65 to 1968-69* (Dar es Salaam, Government Printer).
„	1969	Government of Tanzania: *Tanzania Second Five-year Plan for Economic and Social Development, 1 July 1969-30 June 1974* (Dar es Salaam, Government Printer), Vol. IV: *Survey of the high- and middle-level manpower requirements and resources.*
Uganda	1959	Thomas, R. L.: *Report on the survey of manpower and training in the Uganda Protectorate, July-October 1959* (Washington, DC, Ford Foundation) (mimeographed).
„	1962	Hunter, op. cit.

Country	Year of publication	Document
Uganda *(cont.)*	1965	Bennett, N. L.: *Uganda manpower projections* (mimeographed).
,,	1968	Ministry of Planning and Economic Development: *High-level manpower survey, 1967, and analyses of requirements, 1967-81* (Entebbe, Government Printer).
Zambia	1964	Taylor, W. L., and Pearson, D. S.: *The requirements and supplies of high-level manpower in Northern Rhodesia, 1961-70*, University College of Rhodesia and Nyasaland, Department of Economics, Occasional Paper No. 2 (Salisbury, Unitas Press).
,,	1966	Office of National Development and Planning: *Manpower report—a report and statistical handbook on manpower, education, training and Zambianization, 1965-66* (Lusaka, Government Printer).
		RATE-OF-RETURN STUDIES
Ghana	1969	Hinchcliffe, J. K.: *Educational planning techniques for developing countries, with special reference to Nigeria and Ghana*, M.Phil. thesis, University of Leicester.
Kenya	1968	Rogers, D. C.: *The returns to investment in higher levels of education in Kenya*, Discussion Paper No. 59, Institute of Development Studies, University College, Nairobi (mimeographed).
,,	1969	Thias, H., and Carnoy, M.: *Cost-benefit analysis in education: a cost study in Kenya* (Washington, DC, IBRD) (mimeographed document EC-173).
Nigeria	1967	Bowles, S.: " The efficient allocation of resources in education ", in *Quarterly Journal of Economics* (Cambridge, Massachusetts), Vol. LXXXI, No. 2, May 1967, pp. 189-219.
,,	1969	Hinchcliffe, op. cit.
Rhodesia	1960	Sampson, W. J.: *The return on investment in primary and secondary education in Central Africa* (mimeographed).
,,	,,	Idem: *The return on investment in post-school certificate education in Rhodesia and Nyasaland* (mimeographed).
Uganda	1963	Ilett, J.: *A cost-benefit evaluation of education to school certificate and graduate levels* (mimeographed).
,,	1967	Smyth, J. A., and Bennett, N. L.: " Rates of return on investment in education: a tool for short-term educational planning illustrated with Ugandan data ", in *The World Year Book of Education, 1967: educational planning* (London, Evans), Ch. 17, pp. 299-322.
,,	1968	Ministry of Planning and Economic Development, op. cit.
Zambia	1966	Baldwin, R. E.: *Economic development and export growth* (University of California, Bureau of Business and Economic Research).

Appendix II. Details of basic statistics of employment of skill in African manpower surveys, according to ye

	Basutoland	Botswana		Cameroon	Egypt	Ethiopia		Ghana		Ivory Coast	Kenya		
	64	67	70	62	66	67	70	60	63	64	62	65	69
Coverage of data on employment of SEMP													
1. Minimum educational level [1]	D	D	C	T	T	D	T	D	T	T	B	D	D
2. Sectors excluded (none (N), agriculture (A), commerce (C))	N	N	N	N	N	A	N	A	N	N	N	A	N
Basic data on SEMP presented in the surveys													
3. Occupations by major ISCO [2] groups	×			× [3]	×	×	×	×	×	× [3]		×	×
4. Occupations by minor ISCO [2] groups for professional, technical and administrative jobs	×					×	×	×				×	×
5. Occupations by minor ISCO [2] groups for all jobs covered	×					×	×	×				×	×
6. Education: actual attainment													×
7. Education: required attainment [4]		(2)	(2)		(2)	(2)	(1)	(2)	(2)	(2)	(2)	(3)	(1)
8. Race	×										×	×	×
9. Nationality		×	×							×			×
10. Sex													×
11. Age				×									×
12. Earnings	×												×
13. Number of economic sectors	3	16		8	18	9	9			8	5		
Cross-tabulations presented in the surveys													
14. Actual education (6) × occupation (3/4/5)													×
15. Required education (7) × occupation (3/4/5)						×		×	×	×		×	×
16. Education (7) × race (8)											×	×	
17. Education (7) × nationality (9)													
18. Education (7) × sex (10)													
19. Education (7) × age (11)													
20. Education (7) × earnings (12)													
21. Education (7) × sector (13)		×			×	×				×	×		
22. Occupation (3/4/5) × race (8) or nationality (9)												×	×
23. Occupation (3/4/5) × sex (10													×
24. Occupation (3/4/5) × earnings (12)	×												×
25. Occupation (3/4/5) × sectors (13)	×			×	×	×	×			×			
26. Sector (13) × actual education (6) × occupation (3/4/5)													
27. Sector (13) × required education (7) × occupation (3/4/5)						×				×			
Vacancies and unemployment													
28. Vacancies × occupation							× [8]	×				×	
29. Unemployment													
Medium-term projections of demand for SEMP (about five years)													
30. Occupation structure	×			×	×	×		×	×	×		×	×
31. Occupation × sector	×				×	×				×			
32. Education structure		×			×	×		×	×	×	×	×	×
33. Education × occupation						×		×	×	×		×	×
34. Education × sector					×	×				×			
35. Education × occupation × sector						×				×			
Long-term projections of demand for SEMP (about ten to fifteen years)													
36. Occupation structure			× [11]		×		×						
37. Occupation × sector					×								
38. Education structure		×			×		×						
39. Education × occupation													
40. Education × sector					×								
41. Education × occupation × sector													

[1] For levels A to D, see table I, note 1; T = all education and skill levels. [2] ILO: *International Standard Classification Occupations* (Geneva, 1959). [3] The occupational groupings used in the manpower plans for the French-speaking African co tries are only roughly equivalent to the ISCO major groups. [4] (1) = employers' requirements; (2) = planners' specificatio (3) = Thomas categories (see R. L. Thomas: *Manpower problems and programmes for solving them: report to the President* Tanganyika] (1963)) applied to occupational distribution. Several surveys under (2) used variants of the Thomas approach; o

nd educated manpower (SEMP) and projections of demand given f publication of the survey *(× = available data)*

	Malawi 67	Mali 67	Mauritania 67	Mauritius 69	Nigeria 60	64	Rhodesia 64	Senegal 66	Sierra Leone 64	Somalia 65	70	Sudan 67	Swaziland 65	70	Tanzania 62	63	65	69	Tunisia 65	Uganda 59	62	65	68	Zambia 64	66
	C	T	T	D	B	B	C˜	T	C	C	T	D	T	D	B	D	D	D	T	D	B	B	D	C	D
	N	N	N	N	N	N	N	N	N	N	N	A	N	N	N	A	A	A	N	A + C	N	N	N	N	N
	×	×[3]	×[3]	×		×		×[3]	×	×	×	×	×	×		×	×	×		×			×		×
	×			×		×			×	×	×	×	×	×		×	×	×		×			×		×
	×			×		×			×	×	×	×	×	×		×	×	×		×			×		×
																									×
		(2)	(2)	(3)	(2)	(1)	(2)	(2)		(2)		(3)		(2)	(2)		(3)	(3)			(2)	(2)	(1)	(2)	(1)
		×					×								×	×	×			×	×	×	×	×	×
	×					×			×	×	×	×	×	×				×	×				×		×
						×													×				×		×
																			×				×[5]		×
											×														×
	8	8	10		10	9	10	8	8	3	9				5				13		5		3	10	10
																									×
		×	×[6]	×		×				×		×		×			×	×					×		×
		×					×	×							×		×				×	×	×	×	×
						×						×		×				×					×		
						×																	×		
																							×[5]		×[7]
																									×[7]
		×			×	×	×	×							×						×		×	×	×
	×	×				×			×	×	×	×	×	×		×	×	×		×			×		×
																							×		×[8]
											×														
	×[9]	×	×			×[9]	×		×[9]	×	×												×[8]		×
																									×
		×				×[9]	×																		×
	×			×		×	×				×	×		×			×	×		×			×		×
										×	×														×
	×	×	×	×		×		×[10]	×	×	×	×		×		×	×	×	×	×			×		×
	×[9]	×	×			×[9]		×[10]	×[9]		×								×				×		×
		×	×[6]	×		×		×[10]		×		×	×	×			×	×	×			×	×		×
				×		×		×[10]		×		×		×			×	×					×		×
		×				×		×[10]					×										×		×
						×		×[10]															×		×
																							×		×
																							×		×
					×		×																×	×	×
																							×		×
					×																		×		×
																							×		×

hose which used it strictly are classified under (3). [5] Only available for top managers, administrators and professional workers. Public sector data only. [7] Actual, not required, education. [8] Available for major ISCO groups only. [9] Available for wo sectors—public and private—only. [10] Annual requirements over five-year period including both requirements for growth nd wastage. [11] For graduate-level manpower only.

Appendix III. Percentage distribution, by sectors, of employed educated manpower

Sectors	Botswana (1967)	Ethiopia (1967)	Ivory Coast (1960)	Kenya (1961)	Malawi (1966)	Nigeria (1963)	Sierra Leone (1964)	Somalia (1968)	Tanzania (1961)	Uganda (1967)	Zambia (1965-66)
Category A [1]											
All education	10.6	17.8	. [2]	15.1	34.6	20.6	17.7	12.1	14.3	38.4	28.2
Public sector	64.5 [3]	44.0	33.0	23.8	28.0	45.2	52.2	66.7	28.8	33.6 [4]	21.1
Private sector											
Mining, manufacturing and public utilities	6.6	12.6	9.6	} 61.1	} 37.4	11.4	} 30.1	6.5	} 56.9	} 28.0	22.2
All other	18.3	25.6	57.4			22.8		14.7			28.5
Total	100.0	100.0	100.0	100.0	100.0	100.0	100.0	100.0	100.0	100.0	100.0
Categories A, B and C [1]											
All education	5.0	12.0	. [2]		31.2	33.6	34.5	13.9		16.9	9.2 [5]
Public sector	64.9	14.2	43.6		43.5	48.2	34.3	57.3		52.3 [4]	17.4 [5]
Private sector											
Mining, manufacturing and public utilities	4.6	34.5	8.3		} 25.3	6.0	} 31.2	13.7		} 30.8	30.8 [5]
All other	25.5	39.3	48.1			12.2		15.1			42.6 [5]
Total	100.0	100.0	100.0		100.0	100.0	100.0	100.0		100.0	100.0

[1] See table I, note 1. [2] No separate data available for education; teachers are probably included in the private sector under " All other ". [3] Including public education. [4] Including public utilities. [5] 1965.

Source: calculated from the manpower surveys.

ILO publications on employment

Agrarian reform and employment

Particular developing regions and countries are examined in this collection of essays, originally published in the *International Labour Review*, in an effort to shed light on the potential of agrarian reform for increasing the volume of productive and remunerative employment.

ISBN 92-2-100083-4

Essays on employment

Contributions on labour force, employment projections, and employment promotion in agriculture, industry, construction and services, covering a wide range of the employment problems characteristic of underdevelopment. Selected from recent issues of the *International Labour Review* and introduced by Professor Walter Galenson, Consultant to the ILO's World Employment Programme.

ISBN 92-2-100065-6

Urban unemployment in developing countries

The pace of urbanisation in the developing countries is now so rapid that the size of the total urban population considerably exceeds that of the active population engaged in manufacturing. This is quite unlike the situation that existed in the countries of continental Europe during the early stages of their own development: in fact, in the developing countries urbanisation is a forerunner of industrialisation and growth rather than their consequence. The result is the extremely high unemployment rates that characterised the towns of the Third World during the 1960s. What are the causes underlying this state of affairs, and what measures may be put forward as a remedy? These are the two major questions that this study attempts to answer.
The author, Paul Bairoch, is Professor of Economics at the Sir George Williams University in Montreal and Assistant Director of Studies at the Ecole Pratique des Hautes Etudes in Paris.

ISBN 92-2-100998-X

Education and the employment problem in developing countries

Are there reasons to think that the quantity and quality of education in a country make a significant impact on the employment problem of developing countries? If so, how can educational systems be reformed so as to maximise the rate of growth of income-earning opportunities? Which policies are actually feasible in the light of different national conditions? It is questions of this kind that are tackled in the present study, a fluently written and highly articulate work by Professor Mark Blaug, of the University of London Institute of Education and the London School of Economics, who is one of the world's leading specialists in the economics of education and in educational planning in general.

ISBN 92-2-101005-8

Mechanisation and employment in agriculture

Will the mechanisation of agriculture in the developing countries lead to more or less productive employment on the land? What policies can be introduced to make agricultural machinery "land augmenting" rather than "labour replacing"? What are the likely linkage effects on employment levels in other sectors? The authors of the six case studies, covering four continents, presented in this collection attempt to answer these questions, which are among the most urgent being posed by development planners, policy makers and aid organisations today. An introduction by Keith Marsden of the ILO puts the agricultural employment problem into the context of over-all development strategy, brings together the common elements in the six case studies and offers some explanations for the divergences in experience and interpretation which are found.

ISBN 92-2-101009-0

Employment in Africa: some critical issues

Written by well-known specialists with wide experience of the African scene, the studies collected in this volume review some of the critical issues of employment as they arise in different countries and propose new approaches for meeting the challenges arising from mounting unemployment and underemployment and from the widening gap between the minority who benefit by economic development and the majority left outside its mainstream.

In their introduction Philip Ndegwa, Permanent Secretary to the Treasury, Ministry of Finance and Planning of Kenya, and John P. Powelson, Professor of Economics in the University of Colorado, and Adviser to the Planning Department of the same ministry, take stock of the findings and suggestions presented, and offer their views concerning diagnosis of the employment problem and approaches to its solution. This collection should lead to a better understanding of some specific characteristics of the employment problem in Africa, and will also be of interest to policy-makers and others concerned with the formulation of development strategies that take employment as an objective in its own right.

Price (Europe only) : 17.50 Swiss francs

ISBN 92-2-101008-2